Matthew Condon is an award-winning author of several novels, works of non-fiction, and is the two-time winner of the Steele Rudd Award for short fiction. His novels include *The Motorcycle Café*, *The Pillow Fight* and *The Trout Opera*. His non-fiction titles include *Brisbane* and, as editor, *Fear, Faith and Hope: Remembering the Long Wet Summer of 2010–2011*. He lives in Brisbane.

THREE
CROOKED
KINGS

MATTHEW CONDON

UQP

First published 2013 by University of Queensland Press
PO Box 6042, St Lucia, Queensland 4067 Australia
Reprinted 2013 (three times), 2014

www.uqp.com.au

Cover design by Design by Committee
Cover photo illustration by Josh Durham
Back cover photo: Brisbane CBD, 1971 © Peter Wilson, courtesy
   of the State Library of Queensland (27530-0001-0002)
Author photo © Russell Shakespeare
Typeset in 11.5/16 pt Bembo by Post Pre-press group, Brisbane
Printed in Australia by McPherson's Printing Group

Quotes from an interview with Raymond Whitrod in 2000 for Film
Australia's Australian Biography Series 8: *Ray Whitrod*, 2001, reprinted
by permission of the National Film and Sound Archive of Australia.

Quotes from *Before I Sleep* by Raymond Whitrod reprinted
by permission of the Raymond Whitrod Estate.

Quotes from *Trial and Error* by Don Lane and *The Sundown Murders* by
Peter James reprinted by permission of the Boolarong Press.

All attempts have been made to contact copyright licensees for
permission to reproduce material. If you believe material for which
you hold rights is reprinted here, please contact the publisher.

National Library of Australia cataloguing-in-publication data
is available at http://catalogue.nla.gov.au/

Three Crooked Kings / Matthew Condon
ISBN: 978 0 7022 3891 8 (pbk)
              978 0 7022 4910 5 (epdf)
              978 0 7022 4911 2 (epub)
              978 0 7022 4912 9 (kindle)

University of Queensland Press uses papers that are natural, renewable and recyclable
products made from wood grown in sustainable forests. The logging and manufacturing
processes conform to the environmental regulations of the country of origin.

*For Katie Kate
and our children,
Finnigan and Bridie Rose*

BY THE TIME HER CHILDREN peered through the bedroom door and discovered her body, she had been dead for several hours.

Her petite corpse, dressed in a summer nightie, was propped up against some pillows in the narrow bed of the spare room. Her hand was raised in a claw. Her face, partially lit by the morning light through frosted louvres, was fixed in a grimace.

The dead woman's small son fled to his father in the back bedroom of the flat in Bonney Avenue, Clayfield, in Brisbane's inner north-east. The eldest daughter, who had also come to the bedroom doorway, stopped and stared in shock, then ran to the phone and called the ambulance.

It was about 8.15 a.m. on Saturday 4 March 1972.

In the bed in that cramped, airless room was the late Shirley Margaret Brifman, thirty-five, former prostitute and brothel madam, and informant and lover to senior corrupt police in Queensland and New South Wales.

The year before, she had blown the whistle on the bent coppers she had been paying off for over a decade, agreeing to a live national television interview and effectively signing her own death warrant.

In less than five weeks she was due to appear as the chief witness against a senior Queensland detective in a perjury case.

She knew it was coming and that she had to die. She knew too much, and had said too much. Brifman had been given an ultimatum by the former cops she'd once called her close friends – either commit suicide, or we'll kill your children.

Brifman had overdosed many times in the past. But against all odds she had continued to survive.

Only hours before her kids found the body in a state of rigor mortis, Brifman received a visitor to the flat in Bonney Avenue. She knew someone was coming to deliver her a cocktail of drugs that would finally do the job properly.

Brifman and the visitor talked quietly in the foyer of the first-floor flat, then she was handed a small amber jar of lethal drugs. The visitor left around midnight.

So Shirley Brifman, crying and shaking with fright, swallowed the contents of the jar, stuffed it under the mattress in the spare room, reclined on a bank of pillows in the dark, and saved her children.

Later that chaotic Saturday, when the police and ambulance officers and coroner's officials had left the scene, the shock of her mother's sudden death finally hit Shirley's eldest daughter.

Mary Anne Brifman, just fifteen years old, issued a scream of grief so loud it disturbed the elderly neighbours in the house out the back.

Shirley Margaret Brifman would be buried in an expensive casket in her home town of Atherton in Far North Queensland. There would be no inquest into her death. Her official 'suicide' file would vanish into police headquarters' archives.

But her death, and her name, would continue to haunt those men who destroyed her.

1940s–1950s

The Probationary

The storm blew in from the west around 6.10 p.m.

It had been a humid Sunday, and the wind and rain roared over the tree fringes of Mount Coot-tha and down into the bowl of the inner-Brisbane suburbs of Bardon, Rosalie and Paddington, strafing the ridges and gullies and the suburbs' timber and corrugated iron houses. Other dangerous cells were ranging across greater Brisbane, throwing lightning to earth.

Trees were felled. Rectangles of roof iron lifted off and sliced through electrical wires. Flower beds were beaten down.

By 6.30 p.m. the storm had passed, and residents of the city's inner west, their evening dinner interrupted, emerged to inspect the damage. It was 16 January 1949.

Up on the neighbouring ridge of Petrie Terrace, 110 young police cadets, in training at the police depot – an imposing brown-brick edifice and its attendant two-storey wooden sleeping dormitory facing the Brisbane River and the wild pubs and bordellos of South Brisbane – had had their tea in the ground floor canteen.

For nine weeks the recruits, young men from all over the state, had lived shoulder to shoulder. Most had little formal education. Some had worked as post office boys, or on the land on the family property, or behind the counter in grocery stores, before entering the machine of Queensland's postwar constabulary.

5

The Americans had left Brisbane a few years earlier, and the town had settled back into its quasi-rural mediocrity. Pike Brothers menswear in Queen Street no longer had a need for its specialist military cutter, and orders for 'Imperial' winter coats dropped to nothing.

In the wake of war, Brisbane was forced to stare, once again, at its own face – plain and unremarkable; a sub-tropical tableau that, for a few years in the 1940s, had doubled in population with the arrival of the US military, and become something resembling glamorous. The city – all ox-blood iron awnings, sandstone banks and the Salvation Army Band playing in King George Square – was inexplicably at the forefront of things that mattered in the world. And it was crawling with US military men in their expensive and beautifully made salmon-hued uniforms. Hollywood no longer belonged on the screens of the Regent and Her Majesty's and the Metro. It was living and breathing on the streets of Brisbane.

Then the chic evaporated, and Brisbane went back to being Brisbane, and in the residue of a city once bristling with wartime strength and force and protection, and missing some of its young women, caught in the slipstream of the Americans' departure, came an inevitable vacuum. The Queensland capital needed to firm up its local police force.

So on that Sunday night, in the aftermath of the storm, the city cleansed and steaming, the police cadets at the depot returned to their quarters – a long, rectangular dormitory crammed with steel cots and lockers.

Some of the men were nervous. From this night on, there would be no more lectures from former school teacher Senior Constable Merv Callaghan. No more marching with old rifles on the parade ground. No more memorising and tests.

For those several weeks they had risen at 6 a.m., made their beds with precision, attended classes on policing and the law, performed physical training exercises, and retired to their cots by 9 p.m.

They were not permitted to socialise, despite the Christmas and New Year season. They could not catch a quick tram into town and buy yuletide gifts for their families, their girlfriends. They had to sit through fifty-two lectures before their training was done.

As the storm headed out into Moreton Bay, the men joked and smoked, or contemplated the view of the parade ground through the lattice on the verandah of the dormitory. They had, the day before, been issued their navy police uniforms: two pairs of trousers, two shirts, four detachable collars, a tunic, a tie, a white helmet and a pair of black boots. Each was also handed a wooden baton and a pair of handcuffs, some so ancient they didn't function.

On that weekend, they made sure their collars were starched at the local cleaners. That Sunday night after tea, a young cadet, Terence (Terry) Murray Lewis, twenty, sat on his bed and buffed his new boots.

Just a few months earlier, he'd been manning a counter at the Main Roads Commission's Liquid Fuel Control Board office at the corner of Adelaide and Turbot streets. And before that he'd worked as a messenger boy for the US army, Small Ships Branch, Water Transport Division, across the river at Bulimba during the war. And prior to that he'd manned another counter, at Pike Brothers menswear. And another, at Greer and Jamieson clothiers, before that.

Lewis had been looking for direction, for some semblance of a career, since he left school at the age of twelve following the separation of his father and mother. By chance, at the Liquid Fuel Control Board, opposite the Roma Street police station, he'd found one.

He'd got to talking with former detectives and constables who worked with him at the Fuel Board, and they suggested he join the police. Young Lewis was a little in awe of one of the men – Walter (Wally) Wright. Walter had been a detective. Another was Stewart (Stewie) Willis, a constable based at Nundah police station who'd retired early due to injury.

'Why don't you go up to the police depot and join?' they suggested.

'They're desperate for keen young men,' they told him. 'If you can breathe in and out, you'll qualify.'

Lewis was tall, over 180 centimetres, and weighed in at 67 kilograms. He was living in Hawthorne with his mother and stepfather, though he would never think of him, let alone refer to him, as his stepfather. Lewis played no sport. He had few, if any, male friends. As a child of the Depression, he was tight with his finances. Recently, though, he'd met a pretty young woman, Hazel Gould, who had come into the Fuel Board for the motor loss assessor she worked for.

He was tired of his living arrangements, and of working on the busy counter. He saw no future for himself. But he did quite literally see the Roma Street police station every day when he came to and left work. And suddenly it made sense. The police force. It was structured, and its administrative demands – record-keeping, diaries, logbooks, charge sheets – would complement his fastidious nature. It was regular pay. It would take him away from counters.

And there was Hazel, sixteen, who would soon become his first ever formal girlfriend, to consider.

So colleagues Wright and Willis took Lewis up past the rail yards to the depot on the Petrie Terrace rise, where he met two sergeants and lecturer Callaghan, and had his medical. He was a little underweight, but they needed new recruits. Although he was twenty, he had the face of a hurt, vulnerable boy. And about him, too, was a vague aura of disappointment. He'd already been out working in the world for eight years, and it seemed to have prematurely wearied him.

He was estranged from his father, who was still living in Ipswich after his wife abandoned him. Lewis's mother – originally from Brisbane and a part of the large Hanlon family, prominent in the city's horse training and racing circles – never took to Ipswich. It was devoid of glamour. It was too far from the charmed racing suburbs of Ascot and Hamilton and, specifically, the Doomben and Eagle Farm racecourses.

Lewis, then ten years old, came home from school one day to find his mother and only sister, two years younger, had simply disappeared. He waited alone until his father came home from work at the Ipswich Railway Workshops.

The boy was offered no explanation as to the absence of his mother and sister. It left him feeling bemused. Rejected. 'I realised it would have been her fault, not his,' Lewis reflects on the separation and subsequent divorce. 'I can't even remember her [ever] kissing me, actually. I can't remember it.' A year later he, too, made the decision to leave his father behind, and joined his mother in Brisbane, where he was relegated to a cot bed on the side verandah in Hawthorne.

Lewis had a confused concept of family, until the police took him in. He entered the police depot as a probationary constable on 8 November 1948.

The staff at the Fuel Board farewelled him with the gifts of a travelling bag and a wallet.

Those weeks of training and cramming and neatly making his bed at the police depot eventually paid off. On 7 January 1949, he sat his probationary examination in law and police duties. (Define 'offence'. Define 'assault'. Define 'arrest'.) Lewis secured fifty-seven and a half marks out of eighty. He came third in his class.

On the night of the storm, at lights out, Lewis knew that when he woke the following day he would be stepping into a new life. On a Monday morning in mid-January, he and his fellow recruits would be formally sworn in as officers of the Queensland police force and issued their official officer numbers, fitted on their epaulettes.

His ambitions at that moment may have extended no further than to one day work in plain clothes – like former Detective Walter Wright from the Fuel Board – down at the Criminal Investigation Branch (CIB) headquarters in a cluster of old church outbuildings at the corner of Elizabeth and George streets, the city.

There, bracketed by the state's grandiose Treasury and Executive buildings, once stood the Cathedral of St John, demolished in 1904. The cathedral's outbuildings, a rectory and church institute built in the 1890s, were soon seconded by the CIB, and detectives for decades had toiled away in their brick and VJ-boarded warrens, cold in winter and sweltering in summer. In this one-time holy place, with its narrow arched windows and arched doorways, came and went the city's underclass: prostitutes and their bludgers, petty thieves and the occasional cross-dresser, murderers and vagrants. Any notion of sacred soil was scotched in 1930 when a new by-law decreed that no public meetings or preaching be held in the vicinity of the Executive Gardens – fashioned on the grounds of the former cathedral and abutting CIB headquarters – without written permission.

Lewis, if he'd been allowed to leave the police depot that stormy Sunday night, might have strolled down to CIB headquarters and come across Anthony (Tony) Murphy, twenty-one, a tough and ambitious officer from Brisbane's working-class Yeerongpilly.

Murphy also left school early and worked as a telegram boy in the post office at Amberley RAAF base, eight kilometres south-west of Ipswich. In the early 1940s 'Amberley Field' was a hive of activity – constructing and repairing aircraft, training, hosting US troops. And the post office was authorised to issue money orders and old age and invalid pensions and handled personal mail that went out all over the world.

In one instance, the alert Murphy noticed that money was missing from a particular envelope and he established that a work colleague was forging his signature. The police were called in. It was a turning point in Murphy's life.

Shortly after, Murphy stopped off at a barber shop for a trim one afternoon and he noticed in the newspaper an advertisement for police cadets. He decided to join up. It was 1944. By 1949, after a stint in the Photographic Section, Murphy was already a rising star in the force.

Lewis might also have encountered the locally famous Sub-inspector Francis (Frank) Bischof, forty-four, a huge, imposing figure both in the corridors and hutches of CIB headquarters and among his men.

At 188 centimetres and 102 kilograms, Bischof had been a part of the CIB since 1933 and had a habit of positioning himself at the forefront of the city's major criminal investigations. Wherever there was murder and death, there was Bischof.

Born on the family dairy farm at Gowrie Junction outside Toowoomba, up on the range 127 kilometres west of Brisbane, the 'Big Fella', a Mason, was working on a fatal house fire and the mystery of a corpse found on Stradbroke Island as Lewis prepared for his induction up at the police depot.

Another former Toowoomba boy, Glendon (Glen) Patrick Hallahan, also the son of a dairyman, was at that moment working as an aircraft apprentice at Wagga Wagga RAAF base, 452 kilometres south-west of Sydney.

Within two years he would abandon the apprenticeship, return to Queensland due to a family tragedy, and take up odd jobs before joining the police force and becoming one of the state's most celebrated detectives alongside Bischof, Murphy, and Lewis.

Down in Adelaide, thirty-three-year-old police detective Raymond (Ray) Wells Whitrod was having a busy Christmas and New Year. Whitrod had been a South Australian detective before the war, and after serving as a navigator in the RAAF in Europe and North Africa, he returned to police duties in Adelaide.

As new recruit Lewis was performing drills on the Petrie Terrace parade ground, Whitrod was involved in high-speed police car chases across the City of Churches, and investigating the drowning suicide of a young Australian digger who had left a note, his great coat, and shoes at the end of Henley Jetty.

And up in Atherton, on the elevated tableland inland from Cairns in Far North Queensland, a young, petite, athletic brunette called

Shirley Emerson was celebrating her thirteenth birthday. She loved ball games and fashion. She was a Girl Guide. She was one of thirteen Emerson children.

But for all her external vivacity and obsession with clothes, she struggled through an impoverished and itinerant childhood. Her father was an alcoholic and several of her older brothers could look forward to run-ins with the law. And her mother, the child of a relatively well-to-do family from the coast south of Brisbane, would look at her lot in Far North Queensland, and her pitiful husband, and wonder where she took a wrong turn.

Shirley Emerson's life would intersect spectacularly with those of Bischof and Murphy, with Hallahan and Lewis and Whitrod. But not yet. In January 1949, she was just a child enjoying a Christmas holiday, a girl on the brink of adolescence, during which she would become Atherton's belle of the ball, its princess, chased by suitors and sartorially imitated by her female peers. All that beauty, before she ran away to nearby Cairns and made a singular decision that would determine her destiny and tragically shorten her life.

And just a month after Lewis started his police training in late 1948, the first-term Country Party state member for Nanango – Kingaroy peanut farmer Johannes Bjelke-Petersen – refused a parliamentary salary rise and to join the parliamentary pension scheme. He said the pension, in particular, 'savours too much of feathering one's own nest'. 'I would not touch it with the proverbial forty-foot pole,' Bjelke-Petersen reportedly said.

Back at the police depot on Petrie Terrace, Terry Lewis, son of a railway storeman, rose by 6 a.m. on Monday 17 January, and dutifully made his bed. He had breakfast in the canteen then dressed in his constable's uniform.

Later that morning, the new recruits entered the lecture room of the police depot and were asked to take the oath by Chief Inspector John Smith. (Even the cadets had heard the rumour that Smith had changed his name by deed poll from 'Schmidt' after the war.) The men were told that each and every one of them had an opportunity to rise to the top of the Queensland police force. There was no casual banter or congratulation. With that, the chief inspector left.

'Get down to Roma Street,' they were ordered.

The new constables proceeded outside to Petrie Terrace. Across the pubs and shopfronts, residents of Rosalie and Bardon and Paddington were cleaning up after the storm, gathering broken branches, inspecting damaged roofs and attempting, in vain, to right fallen flowers.

Lewis – daunted, conspicuous in his new uniform (the trousers were a little baggy, the jacket too tight) in the punishing humidity – and his colleagues hopped a city-bound tram – no fare, police officers travelled for free – and went directly to Roma Street police station, in view of Lewis's old counter at the Liquid Fuel Control Board, and reported for duty.

Within moments, Constable T.M. Lewis (No. 3773 on his uniform; No. 4677 when mentioned in any correspondence) was walking down Albert Street and into the crosshatched streets and noon shadows of Brisbane city's heart. He was officially on duty.

At some point in the next few months, he secured an old and unused 362-page leather-bound government minutes book and began a diary of personal arrests.

On page one he wrote a brief summary of his antecedents, schooling, and employment history. On page two he glued in his typed farewell card from the Liquid Fuel Control Board. On page three he affixed his final examination paper from the police depot.

And on page four he recorded the details of an early arrest, William Joseph Thornhill, twenty-one years of age: 'That on the 11th day of June 1949, at Brisbane, in a Public Place, namely the Hong Kong Café in Queen Street, he did behave in a disorderly manner.'

Terence Murray Lewis was on his way.

Constable Lewis on the Beat

In his first few weeks as a constable, Lewis was based out of the old two-storey Roma Street police station. The basement housed the Brisbane Police District, the next floor the Traffic Branch, and the top floor the Licensing Branch (including a 'wet bar' – beer only).

Roma Street was dubbed 'The Order of St Francis', for its heavy representation of Roman Catholics. Similarly, the Woolloongabba CIB was called 'The Vatican'.

Lewis was quickly seconded to traffic and performed point duty on several of the city's major intersections. He oscillated between the 7 a.m. to 3 p.m. and 3 p.m. to 11 p.m. shifts.

With the majority of business concentrated in the city grid, commanded down its centre by Queen Street, Lewis was keeping order in a hive of trams, cars, lorries in and out of the Roma Street markets, and pedestrians. Brisbane's population was around 442,000.

On point duty, Lewis worked alone. And despite the mundaneness of the task, he managed to collar a few drunks and vagrants whose faces would become familiar to him over the years. There was Bill Millwood, forty, who behaved in an indecent manner in Albert Street. And Ed Ebzery, forty-four, who in Queen Street called Lewis a 'fucking choco cunt'.

All the while, he was getting to know and understand the rhythm of the city and its people. He became acquainted with members of the legal fraternity and journalists, with shopkeepers and business operators. He began to understand who drank where, the patterns of vagrancy and begging alms, the different complexions of the city during the day and at night.

Not far away, up at the police depot, a former London police officer – Jack Reginald Herbert, twenty-four – was jumping through the same training hoops as Lewis had only months before, eating in the same canteen and bunking down in the evening in the latticed dormitory on Petrie Terrace.

Herbert had drifted to Australia after the war, keen for sunshine and adventure, and had kicked around Victoria and hitchhiked to Toowoomba with a mate before deciding to join the police in Brisbane.

He was a restless man, always on the lookout for a better deal. 'Until now I had been a young bloke in a hurry to be somewhere else,' he reflected in his memoir. 'But I knew that sooner or later I would need a place to settle down. I never imagined that place would be Brisbane but at the same time I knew I hadn't been happy anywhere else.'

In December 1949, he spotted a young redhead across the dance floor at the famed Cloudland Ballroom in Bowen Hills. Her name was Peggy, and she was a typist at the Immigration Department offices in the city. It was Peggy who gave the restless Herbert a reason to stay in Brisbane.

By mid-1950 Lewis found himself behind the handlebars of a police motorcycle. Here, he encountered some action.

His first mention in the press as a policeman came after a wild, sixty-miles-per-hour chase on 25 August. At about 7.40 p.m., Lewis and another motorcycle cop noticed three youths travelling in a utility truck along Main Street, Kangaroo Point. The vehicle did not have its headlights on.

They stopped the driver – Norman Gleeson, twenty, a seaman – who said the truck lights had fused and he had left his driver's licence at home. Also in the truck were John Croke, seventeen, and Alexander Philp, twenty, both labourers. Lewis said they'd follow Gleeson home to check his licence.

The truck drove off at twenty-five miles per hour but soon hit forty and the chase was on. Gleeson sped through stop signs, crossed to the opposite side of the road on numerous occasions, swept in front of trams and narrowly missed a group of pedestrians in Fortitude Valley.

Lewis repeatedly drew alongside the vehicle and shouted to the driver to stop, but Gleeson attempted to run him off the road. Croke then hurled three milk bottles at their pursuers and one shattered on impact. The youths were ultimately apprehended after several hair-raising miles through the suburbs of Spring Hill, Morningside and Woolloongabba.

The chase was news: THREE YOUTHS FINED AFTER WILD JOY RIDE. After nineteen months in the job, Constable T.M. Lewis had made the newspapers.

He also received, as a result of that job, his first official favourable citation from the chief inspector: dated 25 September 1950, Lewis and Duncanson 'of the Traffic Branch, Brisbane, are commended for the good work performed by them in these cases. Have this memorandum noted by the Police concerned, and returned.' It was signed 'J. Smith'.

Over the next two months Lewis continued to pursue more drunk drivers across the city before noticing gazetted vacancies in the CIB.

The recruitment drive was part of a major restructure of the CIB, courtesy of a six-month European study tour of police methods – particularly those of Scotland Yard – taken the previous year by Brisbane CIB chief Tom Harrold and Sub-inspector Frank Bischof. The new crime-busting techniques were to be implemented by early 1951.

Down at CIB headquarters they were putting the finishing touches to a new 'information room', where detectives and radio operators would control the movements of squad cars across Brisbane. As part of the fresh plans, the public would be able to phone the CIB – at no cost – and report suspected crimes or suspicious individuals. The plan was based on Scotland Yard's revolutionary 999 system.

In addition, the Survey Branch of the Lands Department was preparing the most comprehensive map of Brisbane and its suburbs – from highway to back alley – ever attempted. It would be installed in the information room and affixed with variously coloured small flags apportioned to different types of offences.

As the *Courier-Mail* reported, 'The information officer will then be able to tell at a glance where more concentrated police effort is required and will switch cars from quiet areas to the one needing attention.'

It was the type of exacting detail that would have excited Lewis. He had, to that point, been a diligent officer. He kept his police diaries up to date, continued recording arrests in his own personal logbook, which had reached fourteen pages, and he'd been commended by the upper hierarchy.

He was only twenty-two in November 1950, when he went to work with the big boys in the old church buildings at the corner of Elizabeth and George streets. He would leave the stiff-collared uniform behind and replace it with a jacket and tie.

And Lewis would no longer work alone, but be partnered on jobs – theft, robbery, assault, prostitution, even murder – with fellow CIB officers. One of the first of those partners would be Tony Murphy.

Hallahan Comes Home

As Lewis was chasing hoodlums across Brisbane on his police motorcycle, Glendon Patrick Hallahan's dream of a future in the RAAF evaporated when his father fell gravely ill back in Toowoomba. Hallahan returned home from the air force base in Wagga Wagga to help out with the family ice and milk run, but the business soon foundered.

The tall, dapper Hallahan was just eighteen years old and even then was showing a restless nature, constantly on the alert for greener grass. He would chase it for the rest of his life.

After the family business was sold, he took work as a labourer with the Forestry Department and was based in Cooran, a small, pretty village nestled in a valley between Noosa and Gympie.

Cooran had the ubiquitous railway hotel, a school of arts, a king street. In the 1920s its bananas were proudly displayed at the Brisbane exhibition every August.

The town also had a plethora of saw mills, a toy factory, a joinery, and a thriving dairy industry. By the time Hallahan arrived, the town sported its very own branch of the Queensland Band of Hope Young People's Temperance Union.

Hallahan, as with Lewis and Murphy, hopped from job to job looking for a purpose. Unlike the early work of those men, however, he immersed himself in physical labour. He would soon leave Cooran and try his hand at cutting sugarcane up the Queensland coast.

It was unusual, given his intelligence, and his aborted bid for a RAAF apprenticeship. There was plenty of employment for canecutters after the Second World War, but it was serious, back-breaking labour, working in gangs for more than forty hours a week with a seventy-centimetre wood-handled cane knife.

Around 1950, farmers began burning their sugarcane crops prior to harvest to expunge them of vermin and rubbish, but the stalks were sticky with sugar syrup and the cutters would finish the day covered in soot.

At some moment, bearing down on a clutch of five-metre cane stalks with his machete, brushing away bees attracted to the sugar, a career in the police force entered Hallahan's mind.

Sub-inspector Bischof Investigates a Gross Fraud

Labor Premier Edward (Ned) Hanlon secured another term after the 1950 state election thanks to his pre-installed gerrymander, an act that would similarly advantage the Country Party if and when it ever took power after seemingly endless years of Labor domination.

But the purse-lipped, autocratic Hanlon, his health in the early stages of decline, came under ferocious attack from members of the Opposition, in particular the eloquent businessman and leader of the Liberal Party, Thomas Hiley, over an apparent irregularity in election ballot papers at a polling booth in the riverside suburb of Bulimba, just east of town.

As the political furore was building in the final weeks of 1950, Lewis was ensconced in the CIB and assisting in his first big arrest as the new boy in the branch.

The defendant, apart from committing dozens of break and enters, had stolen 174 pounds from the trustees of the Hibernian Australasian Catholic Benefit Society, Southern Queensland District. He was prosecuted and jailed.

Among the officers on the case were Detective Senior Constable A.B. (Abe) Duncan, Detective Sergeant W. Beer, Police Constable T.M. (Terry) Lewis, and Police Constable A. (Tony) Murphy. All officers received for their work a letter of appreciation from Inspector Jim Donovan, a Catholic.

Before Christmas, Lewis would nab some car thieves, nick two men who had stolen eight tons of firewood, and arrest a Moorooka house-maid for stabbing a man with a butcher's knife after a party fuelled by cheap wine.

Lewis loved the CIB work, relished being around tough senior police like Bischof, Norm Bauer, Don (Buck) Buchanan, and Syd Currey. He worked obsessively, putting in long hours. He was by no means physically imposing with his thin frame and his narrow, sloped shoulders, but he discovered a talent for observation – vehicle plates, items of clothing, faces – and was in thrall of the architecture of hier-archy. Throughout his career he would always refer to senior officers by their rank, friends or otherwise.

From the outset he was perceived by many in the branch as akin to the kid who always came top of the class but desired to hang around the tough guys. By association, that gruff and powerful exterior might rub off on him. Some instantly assessed Lewis as 'weak as piss'. He was the runner, the messenger boy, the fresh recruit who dashed out at lunchtime for pies for the senior men.

The rumour in the branch at the time was that the only reason the powerful, punting-addicted Bischof had any interest at all in the young constable was that Lewis was connected, via his mother, to the Hanlon family – rich, as it was, with horse trainers, jockeys, and aficionados of the track.

In January 1951, Bischof – always available for investigations with a political connection – was put in charge of the Bulimba poll fraud case. Following the 1950 state election, the Liberal Party candidate for Bulimba had asked for a recount and the issue was investigated by the acting chief justice, who concluded in a 10,000-word report that corrupt practices in relation to the vote had taken place. Eleven fake ballot papers were discovered.

Over the next two months the government and police were criticised for the tardiness of Bischof's investigation, then, on the morning of 9 March, Queensland's chief electoral officer, long-time public servant Bernard McGuire, was arrested at his home in Kedron Park and charged with having forged a ballot paper.

McGuire would face three trials over the fraud, with each jury disagreeing and a nolle prosequi entered. He took some long service leave in the aftermath of the drama.

What the Bulimba case ignited, however, was an enduring enmity between Liberal leader Hiley and the police force, in particular Frank Bischof.

In parliament in March, Hiley baited Bischof, hinting that the inspector had ignored evidence of a ballot paper fraud in another electorate. Then, on the evening of 4 April 1951, at a function in support of a Liberal by-election candidate, Hiley unleashed an extraordinary attack on the police and the government.

In a forty-five-minute tirade, he declared that Labor had protected major SP bookmakers from police action. He added that the government was misusing the police force and telling them how to conduct political investigations. He further alleged that one of the state's biggest SP bookies was a member of the Police Boys' Welfare Club and a personal friend of Premier Hanlon.

'Every politician knows that the handling of SP in this state has become a highly political racket,' Hiley reportedly said.

He continued his attack the following week, naming an Ipswich SP bookie – the brother of a state Labor member of parliament – who had been 'protected'. The police force, Hiley said, wanted to do its job but had to 'close its eyes' when an issue involved politics. He said some SP bookies were 'the Royal favourites' and enjoyed protection.

'One of the operators in Ipswich is a J. Marsden,' Hiley said. 'When I noticed that Marsden was untouched though every other operator in Ipswich was put through the hoops, I wrote to the Police Commissioner. Shortly afterwards Marsden for the first time was convicted.'

Hiley was hinting at the existence of a so-called Premier's Fund – a slush fund used to finance favoured candidates in state elections. The word was that the money – cash only – was provided by SP bookies, collected by the private secretaries of ministers of the day, and delivered in black bags to the premier's office.

After his twin-forked verbal spray, Hiley was naturally criticised by the government, but a slow fuse that would burn across decades had been lit, and Hiley and Bischof would memorably collide again in the future.

The Clever Mr Whitrod

Back from the war, where, during his two tours of duty as a RAAF navigator, he specialised in coastal surveillance, Raymond Wells Whitrod returned to the Adelaide CIB. He was war weary.

Whitrod's two small sons barely recognised their father, and he had difficulty adjusting back to civilian life. In the CIB, he recognised some old faces and saw many more new ones.

Then, out of the blue, he received a phone call from a well-known Adelaide lawyer named Bernard Tuck. Whitrod recalled the conversation in an interview:

> [Tuck] said, 'I don't suppose you know what I want to talk to you about'. And I said, 'Yes, I do . . . You'll be looking for some good field investigators . . . I'm one of the best.' And he said, 'How did you know that I'd be looking for field investigators?' I said, 'Well, Mr Tuck, you were a very prominent lawyer in Adelaide. You suddenly disappeared . . . You closed down your law firm. Nobody knows where you've gone to.' I said, 'It coincides with the creation of the security service [in 1949].' I said, '. . . Blind Freddy would have worked out where you were . . .' He said, 'Well nobody else has worked that out.'

By coincidence, too, the first director-general of the Australian Security Intelligence Organisation (ASIO) was Geoffrey Reed, a South Australian Supreme Court justice. As a detective, Whitrod had, on many occasions, given evidence in various cases before Justice Reed.

Whitrod was hired by ASIO. He was excited. It was, he thought, work of national importance. The family moved to Sydney and Whitrod began duties in ASIO headquarters – a one-time four-storey brothel known as Agincourt. It was one of the last great harbourside mansions left standing in Wylde Street, Potts Point, after the resumption of land and construction of a nearby graving dock. Whitrod thought it was a perfect home for ASIO – built of sandstone and flanked on three sides by the naval dockyard.

He was put in charge of a small team of investigators, some returned veterans and former police like himself – the best of the state forces – and his brief was to locate the organiser of a wartime Russian spy ring based in Australia. The counter-espionage team was named B2. Whitrod's men were keen, enthusiastic, and patriotic in the aftermath of victory in Europe. In a pre–Cold War environment, they rightly assessed that Australia's next enemy would be the Soviet Union.

B2 worked with a British MI5 liaison officer and they charted a dozen or so members of the supposed spy ring, shadowing local members of the Communist Party (controversially banned by Prime Minister Robert Menzies in October 1950) and its leadership tier. Whitrod used his own family car for these subterfuge missions.

One of the team's primary targets was journalist Fedor Nosov, the Sydney-based correspondent for Soviet news agency TASS. He had a flat in Kings Cross and came under intense surveillance. Whitrod even arranged a crude bug to be installed in the flat, without the permission of the director-general. A team member and his wife rented the apartment above Nossov and had drilled a hole down through the floorboards and into Nossov's plaster ceiling to secure the listening device. At one point, in a comedy of errors, Whitrod had to get the caretaker to open Nossov's flat to clean the plaster crumbs off the carpet.

The brief was not met – years later it was proved that Nossov was indeed a Soviet spy – but the experience was Whitrod's first in a managerial capacity. He liked being in charge and absorbed the lessons it taught him.

Despite failing to expose the spy ring, Whitrod's work was noticed by his superiors, and he was transferred to Melbourne.

Debutante

Lewis and Murphy were working together in the CIB; Hallahan was about to enter the police depot on Petrie Terrace for police training, physically hardened from a season cutting cane; and up in the little town of Atherton, Far North Queensland, young Shirley Emerson was about to make her debut in the region's hectic ball season.

She was one of thirteen children, had many friends and loved to socialise. While her brothers – timber workers and labourers – were in and out of court on minor charges of theft and public drunkenness, Shirley left behind her squalid life, if only for a few hours, dancing at balls and functions across the tableland and as far away as Cairns.

The Emersons were prone to accidents. Shirley's tumble from a bicycle earned a line in the local newspaper. In 1940, a brother, Vic, lacerated his foot with a saw and was treated in hospital.

The eldest Emerson child, Horace, twenty-five, was seriously injured after being crushed by a log at Danbulla, north-east of Atherton, and spent nine months in the local hospital. However, one leg healed shorter than the other and Horace was soon back in hospital, this time in Brisbane, for corrective surgery. He died following the operation, and his case was subject to a government inquiry. It was a big working-class family, well versed in hard luck and misfortune.

Shirley, however, maintained a sunny outlook: 'I was so active. I was never at home,' she would later describe her youth in a newspaper report. 'I would travel sixty or seventy miles a night to a dance and I would go dancing six nights a week. My girlhood was one of the happiest imaginable. I wish I could have it all over again. I wouldn't change it – or only a few things.'

What would become, with time, one of the highlights of her life was the military debutante ball in Atherton on Thursday 3 July 1952.

On that night little Shirley led the debutantes, partnered by a Private Bourke. According to the *Cairns Post*, she wore 'an exquisite frock of *broderie anglais* over ice-white satin. The fitted bodice had puffed sleeves and a portrait neckline with a wide shawl collar and her skirt featured voluminous fullness. Short mittens of matching material with a deep frill at the wrist had the edge of the frill cut to show the broderie pattern. She wore a cape of fur fabric.'

Later in life she would tell a newspaper reporter, 'The military ball at Atherton was the one I remember best. I was the littlest deb there and I was chosen Queen of the Debs and Belle of the Ball.

'I was so scared I couldn't believe it when the brigadier who received the debs congratulated me. Life is what you make it. You can have plenty of happy moments, and you can have bad ones too.'

The Ascent of Detective Lewis

It was a quiet Sunday night on 23 March 1952, when Detective Lewis, now stationed at the Woolloongabba CIB, and Detective Merv 'Hoppy' Hopgood made a routine patrol of the back streets of South Brisbane.

In less than four weeks Lewis would marry his one and only sweetheart, Hazel Gould. She had secured a job as an usherette at the Tivoli Theatre, opposite the Brisbane City Hall, with its pitched roof and broad balcony facing Albert Street, when Lewis was training at the police depot, and then she was poached by the Metro, further down Albert, as Lewis was doing traffic point duty through the CBD. The Metro reputedly had the prettiest usherettes in the city, and the most fetching uniforms.

Their courtship, since meeting at the Fuel Board, had not been the stuff of high romance. They went to the cinema. If his Traffic Branch shift allowed it, he met her after her own shift at the Tivoli or Metro, accompanied her to the ferry near Petrie Bight, travelled with her the short trip across the Brisbane River to Kangaroo Point, where she lived, and walked her to her door.

It was Hazel who was keen to marry. Lewis, though exasperated he had attracted the attention of such a pretty young woman, was completely consumed by his police work and the prospects of promotion. If it had been up to him, he would have waited a couple of years for the greater financial security that promotion would have brought them.

They married on Saturday 19 April, at the St Peter and Paul Catholic Church in Bulimba (Lewis had spent 1939 – his final year of schooling – at St Peter and Paul School). His father did not attend the ceremony.

The couple then held their reception at the popular Eton Private Hotel – hot and cold water in every room, elevator, roof garden – on the corner of Wharf and Adelaide streets. The Lewises stayed the night at the Eton then honeymooned at Coolangatta on the South Coast – a trip organised by Lewis's more worldly partner, Hoppy Hopgood.

On patrol that Sunday, however, having had a pie at Barnes Auto Co. (the 'We Never Sleep' twenty-four-hour garage) at the corner of Queen Street and North Quay, Lewis may have been fantasising about his nuptials as he and Hopgood headed over the Victoria Bridge and turned into Cordelia Street, South Brisbane.

They were met by a woman's high-pitched scream. They noticed a man fleeing into Merivale Street and made chase. Hopgood overtook the man, who stopped, raised his hands, and said, 'Don't shoot. I stop.' He then said, 'I just kill my girl. I stab her.' He was Josef Dvorac, thirty-two, labourer.

Back in Cordelia Street, Lewis attended to Pompea Lengo, twenty, stabbed in the back, and her father, Sergio, also stabbed in the back and lower leg after a struggle with Dvorac. Although an ambulance was on its way, a passing taxi was hailed and Pompea was rushed to the Mater hospital, an action that probably saved her life.

Pompea, a factory worker, had, as it turned out, rejected Dvorac's proposal of marriage and he had threatened to kill the entire Lengo family. He later confirmed to police: 'She my girl friend and she no marry me, so I kill her and go to South America. She promised to marry me and then she say she no want, so I kill her.' When told that Pompea was gravely ill in hospital, he replied: 'I don't care. It all finished with now. I die soon.'

Dvorac was sentenced to seven years' hard labour. In December 1955 he would be found hanging by his belt from his cell bars in Boggo Road gaol.

It was Lewis's last major job before his wedding. On the big day, he wore a dark suit and tie, and the couple was photographed, for a local newspaper, standing in front of a two-tier wedding cake. In the picture he is beaming – unusual for the young man – and a weight appears to have been lifted from him.

After the honeymoon the couple rented a small room in Abingdon Street, Woolloongabba. The house was owned by two spinsters who had a habit of entering tenants' rooms to check on electricity use. Lewis fetched wood for the chip heater so his bride could enjoy a warm bath. The room, too, was close to Lewis's work.

He was back at his desk by late May, apprehending purse snatchers, burglars and Australian army deserters.

Detective Tony Murphy, married the year before to Maureen, was already an unofficial apprentice to Detective Inspector Bischof. Murphy looked up to him and the Big Fella kept an eye on his protégé, encouraging him, pushing him onto cases that should have been the province of more senior detectives. As with Lewis, Bischof became a father figure.

Murphy, a keen rower and cyclist in his youth, was physically imposing and was fearless in calling a spade a spade. He was the spoilt youngest child of six boys to elderly parents, and from the outset he understood that whatever he wanted was his. Robin Gibson, who would later become one of Queensland's most famous architects and design the Queensland Art Gallery, was a boyhood friend of Murphy. He recalled that after a game of summer street cricket with Murphy, Gibson's bat went missing and was never seen again. He laughingly remembers that Murphy probably nicked it.

Meanwhile, over at Roma Street police station, the newly inducted Constable Glen Hallahan was serving his apprenticeship at the Traffic Branch, just as Lewis had done before him. Hallahan, as exemplified by his days working the timber forests north of Brisbane, and cane cutting up and down the coast, preferred his own company.

Hallahan was sworn in on 18 February 1952. He probably didn't have the time or the inclination to notice, let alone befriend, a new cadet by the name of Donald Lane, from Warwick, who had joined exactly a week earlier. Lane, sixteen, was so appalled at the behaviour of some of his fellow cadets in the dormitory at night that his father rushed down from Warwick and installed the teenage boy in the Church of England–administered St Oswald's Hostel at North Quay. It housed fifty country boys who were either studying at university or embarking on a professional life in the big smoke. Only a handful, Lane included, were not educated in private schools, and he felt conspicuous.

As for Hallahan, he exuded a preternatural confidence, had a taste for the latest fashionable clothing and wore palmfuls of cologne – his distinctive scent led workmates to jokingly question his sexuality. He was a strapping young man, but friends and acquaintances remember that he spoke so softly you had to draw yourself close to even hear him. In the city bars of the day where police gathered after work – the Treasury, the Belfast, the National, the Grosvenor – Hallahan stood out. He was the only man not wearing a hat.

Miss Shanks

On Saturday 20 September 1952, Brisbane woke to a local murder so shocking that it was later viewed as a sociological turning point for the city and its inhabitants. The victim was Betty Thompson Shanks, twenty, a Commonwealth Government public servant.

At 9.35 p.m. the day before, Shanks had disembarked from her tram at the Grange Terminus in the city's north-west and was heading to her home in Montpelier Street, having attended a late lecture in the CBD. As she passed the corner of Thomas and Carberry streets – just a few blocks north of Montpelier – she was surprised by her attacker, thrown into a nearby yard, then sexually assaulted, bashed and kicked in the head before being strangled.

Despite several nearby residents hearing her moaning, nobody investigated. Her body was found the next morning by an off-duty policeman – who lived next door to the scene of the murder – fetching his morning newspaper.

It was an epochal killing for Brisbane. A young woman is snatched, brutalised, molested, and murdered within sight of her suburban home. Attendances at theatres like the Metro plummeted immediately following Shanks's death. The city restaurant trade slowed. People stayed at home and, for the first time for many, locked their doors. Over at the Cloudland Ballroom in Bowen Hills, five hundred women were given a self-defence class by the Brisbane Judo Club. The only men present were the instructors, and the women pledged not to reveal what they had learned.

Dozens of police, including the bulk of the CIB, converged on the suburb of Grange and the scene of the crime.

Lewis was on duty that Saturday morning at 6 a.m. His shift was due to finish at 2 p.m. His police diary entry for Saturday 20 September 1952 read: 'In Car 18 to 1 Dean Street, Toowong and conveyed Dr. O'Reilly [deputy director of the Laboratory of Microbiology and Pathology in Brisbane] to Thomas Street, Wilston where Betty Thomson [sic] Shanks had been murdered during night. Returned Dr. O'Reilly to the morgue.

'To CIB and drove men to scene of the crime and handed car to Det. Snr. Sgt. Bauer. Then with P.C. Constable C.J. McDonald and interviewed all the residents of Grange Road re a possible suspect. To

Wilston Police Station at 1:00pm. Then to Evelyn Street and inter-viewed all residents. To Station. Then with Det. Const. Hopgood, P.C. Consts. Skanlon and Harvey in Car 22 on patrol of Grange and Wilston areas until 11:pm. To Station and then to C.I. Branch. Off duty at 12:m.night.'

Bischof was repeatedly photographed by the press, addressing senior field investigators at the crime scene in his pale dustcoat and expensive tie, or raking out a drain looking for clues.

The murder investigation on that Saturday morning quietly revealed the distinctive cliques within the Queensland police. The CIB was the glamour squad. It possessed a sense of entitlement in small-town Brisbane. CIB detectives galloped in en masse and took over investiga-tions, and their standard-bearer was Frank Bischof.

Edwin (Ted) Chandler, of the Fortitude Valley police precinct, was the first non-commissioned officer on the Shanks scene that day. It was correct police procedure, as he understood it, for the first officer on the scene of a killing to take possession, per se, of the body and any personal effects.

Then Detective Sub-inspector Jack Buggy from the CIB turned up.

'You can knock off duty now, there's no need for you to work on,' Buggy told Chandler.

'I was the first police officer on the scene here, so it's incumbent on me to take charge of this body, have it transported to the city morgue and take possession of the dead woman's belongings,' Chandler replied.

Buggy said: 'I am taking charge here, and I am telling you to return to the office and cease duty – there is no need for you to perform any overtime.'

Chandler knew that the Brisbane CIB chief, Inspector Jim Donovan, was on his way and held off to seek his opinion. Donovan told him to continue with his duties. 'I am in charge of the CIB, not Mr Buggy,' Donovan told him. 'I will tell you when to knock off duty.'

The retort from Donovan, a Catholic, may have exposed his enmity towards Bischof, a Mason, and his acolytes. There was no love lost between the men.

Decades later in a memoir, Chandler recalled that 'the CIB arrived at the scene, obviously expecting a quick kill and they rode roughshod over those who were painstakingly checking on available clues at the scene. If ever a murderer was protected, this was one.'

After an eighteen-hour shift, Lewis had a day off on the Sunday following the murder. On the Monday he patrolled the streets of Wilston, Newmarket, Windsor and Herston in Car 27 with Detective Sergeant Wex. It was to be his last Shanks-related duty. On the Tuesday he arrested Leslie Michael Wells for stealing '3 gents athletic singlets, 1 two piece pyjama suit and one gents shirt', the property of the Mater hospital.

Just six days after the Shanks death, there was debate in the press about offering a reward to help catch the killer. Premier Vince Gair, who had replaced Ned Hanlon earlier in the year following Hanlon's death in office on 15 January, said the matter of a reward was up to the police commissioner. By 30 September an official one-thousand-pound reward was posted for the crime, which was already predicted to go down in history as one of the state's unsolved mysteries.

Ladies Lounging in Cane Grass Chairs

On 22 April 1953, seven months after the Shanks horror, the *Courier-Mail* published a special investigation into vice, SP betting, and prostitution in Brisbane.

The paper had recently treated its readers to a racy exposé on Brisbane's 'sly-grog' dens. Now it was tearing back the 'vice-curtain' and presenting 'a sordid picture of gambling, drink and sex'. And it held no punches in what it thought of the Queensland government's responsibility for the city's new-found loucheness: 'It is obvious that police condoning of vice in Brisbane is based on Government policy,' the report said. 'Court prosecutions prove that the Licensing Branch vice-squad is doing its job – as far as Government policy allows.'

Brisbane, since Shanks's death, had finally become a city big enough for its seamy underworld to be worth investigating by the press.

The report underlined the government's so-called obsession with gambling, by citing the findings of the previous year's SP Betting Royal Commission and its conclusion that millions of pounds were being funnelled through off-the-course bookmakers. In the aftermath of the commission and its revelations, Premier Gair's government proposed that some of its recommendations – maintaining SP bookmaking as an offence but permitting lawful business with customers who lived beyond the reach of actual race meetings – be put to a referendum. The idea was met with widespread ridicule.

The newspaper investigation also dared to venture into the state of the city's prostitution rackets.

'The final link in Brisbane's vice-chain are the four officially rec-ognised brothels,' it went on. 'They are in Margaret Street, City; Albert Street, City; Montague Road, West End [Killarney brothel, actually in Lanfear Street, off Montague]; and Ernest Street, South Brisbane. The oldest established of these dens [Albert Street] has a palm-decorated entrance around which the prostitutes lounge in cane grass chairs – leading from a city pavement.

'Their human frailty might not be of their own making. Perhaps they cannot always be blamed.

'Here may be a girl who has been abandoned by the father of her baby – maybe a divorcee whose home has been broken, or it may be the good-time girl – or a hardened get-rich-quick type, snapping her fingers at the world and its morals.

'Here is a school of embittered women.

'Their only protectors now are the police. And that protection is absolute.'

The journalist added that the selection, or 'sanction', of girls enter-ing the 'houses' was a virtual 'police dictatorship', as the brothels were a font of information on criminal activity. 'What they talk about in the hire-girl's sordid surroundings might become "police business".' Girls who did not cooperate with police did not remain in the 'profession' for long. Taxi drivers were also a vital link in this police 'spy-ring', the article said.

'To justify their attitude police claim there would be a lot more sex offences if hire-girl establishments were banned. They regard them as a necessary evil.'

The article – which had more than a hint of unnamed police cooperation about it – ended with a prophecy: 'The truth about [vice-dens] does not make a pretty story. It is told here so that the people of Brisbane and Queensland can ask: Is it an inevitable part of a city of half-a-million?'

Two days after the *Courier-Mail* exposé, there was a flurry of pros-titute arrests.

Detective Lewis recorded his movements in his police diary: 'At office at 6.40am. On duty with Det Hopgood. Then to 74 Dornoch Terrace, and interviewed prostitute Vera Jackson and [taxi] driver Michael Maloyba. With Det Chalmers to Barnes Auto and located Annie Ellen May Harris (19) and later arrested her on charge [insuf-ficient lawful means] . . . then arrested Gloria Millicent Redpath (18) [insufficient lawful means] . . . to court where Harris and Redpath appeared before Mr Burchill C.S.M. Both pleaded guilty. Each con-victed and sentenced to one month imp.

'To office and all of Consorting Squad interviewed by Inspector Bischof.

'Off duty 3:50pm.'

As is the way of newspapers, the *Courier-Mail* triumphantly claimed partial responsibility for the arrests: 'The first teenage girl vagrants arrested since the *Courier-Mail* vice disclosures on Wednesday were sent to gaol yesterday. They were arrested after complaints of girls' conduct at night in North Quay.'

Harris was homeless and possessed nothing but a port full of dirty clothes. And Redpath slept in parks and on railway stations. She had sixpence in her possession when she was arrested.

By the following week the great exposé of Brisbane's vice scene had gone dry, as had the police's public crackdown on the city's 'school of embittered women'. When the publicity ceased, so did official police attention towards prostitutes.

It underlined a curious exchange at a Police Appeals Board hearing a few years earlier, where Detective Senior Constable Abe Duncan – who would investigate the Betty Shanks killing, and twenty years later conduct lengthy interviews on police corruption with Shirley Brifman, nee Emerson – was seeking promotion.

During the appeal debate, Inspector Jim Donovan said that as an officer he would investigate housebreaking charges ahead of bigamy charges.

The chairman of the board asked in response: 'Are you saying you regard material crimes as more important than those against the moral order?'

It was precisely what the inspector was saying.

The South Brisbane Scrapper

Just before 10 a.m. on Monday 28 September 1953, hundreds of mourners began filing into the quietly eerie Byzantine-influenced St Andrew's Presbyterian Church at the corner of Ann and Creek streets in the city.

Brisbane was burying another Queensland premier, this time William Forgan Smith, who had died of a sudden heart attack in Sydney while on business for the Sugar Board.

The *Courier-Mail* reported that 'many high and humble people' rubbed shoulders at the service; the minister presiding said that 'truly a prince among men has fallen'.

Among the many dignitaries in the church that day was Inspector Frank Bischof of the CIB. It was a surprise to many that Bischof was still serving in the city.

Just a few months earlier, with the Shanks murder still unsolved, the government announced that Bischof, 'one of the state's top detectives', had been appointed to take control of the Toowoomba police district. This was Bischof's home turf. He had specifically applied for the position.

Then three weeks later the transfer mysteriously fell through. According to the government, Police Commissioner John Smith recommended that the Big Fella remain in Brisbane, and Bischof cited 'domestic reasons' for staying put.

Also in the church that day was lawyer and Brisbane Vice-mayor Colin Bennett. Bennett was short, wiry, handy with his fists and the father of seven children. Born in Townsville in 1919, he went to school in Ayr in north Queensland, then Nudgee College in Brisbane before gaining a Bachelor of Laws degree from the University of Queensland. Bennett was a law clerk and maths master at the elite Brisbane Grammar School before entering private practice in 1948. He was elected a Brisbane City Council alderman the following year. A Catholic, he had a deep social conscience and feared nobody when he sensed injustice, particularly towards the city's underclass.

Professionally, Bennett was in a curious position. He worked in the early- to mid-1950s as vice-mayor and simultaneously conducted a successful career as a criminal lawyer. In court, he would often defend the impoverished and the down-at-heel, then act on behalf of senior police during promotion appeals. He mixed equally with Brisbane's elite and its most despised. And by representing prostitutes, thieves and vagrants, he began to amass a street-level appreciation of crime and corruption throughout the city.

After the funeral service for Forgan Smith, the mourners joined a mile-long cortege, headed by mounted police, through the streets of the city. Both Bennett and Bischof were part of that cortege. In a few short years they would become bitter adversaries, and the epicentre of their conflict would be a pretty young debutante from the Atherton Tableland.

Her Majesty Comes to Visit

Three weeks before the Forgan Smith funeral, Inspector Bischof again had his photograph in the *Courier-Mail*, this time sitting around a table of the state's police top tier discussing plans for the royal tour in March 1954.

Bischof is a study of concentration next to Inspector Donovan, Chief Inspector Harrold, Deputy Police Commissioner Glynn and Police Commissioner Smith. 'A police official said last night that subjects included security, traffic control, and the movement of police to centres which would be visited by the Queen,' the paper reported.

In late 1951 Bischof had been named as one of two Queensland police officers to help guard the royals during their Australian tour the following year, unexpectedly cancelled after the death of King George VI on 6 February 1952.

Now Bischof was back in the thick of royal fever. On the exact day the picture of Queensland's elite police was published, the Attorney-General's Department in Canberra informed Ray Whitrod that his appointment as director of the Commonwealth Investigation Service had been 'confirmed by the Governor-General in Council'.

The new head of ASIO encouraged Whitrod to apply for the position and revitalise the ailing service – essentially the Commonwealth police force – which was formed in 1917 at the request of Prime Minister Billy Hughes. An egg had been thrown at Hughes during a public rally over conscription in the Queensland town of Warwick, and he didn't trust the Queensland government or its police force to thoroughly prosecute. So he formed the national squad.

The force's counter-intelligence duties were handed over when ASIO formed. It also lost the bulk of its quality investigators to the new body. By the time Whitrod took over, it was run-down and had a poorly defined charter.

Whitrod strongly believed the royal tour of 1954 would go a long way to re-establishing the credentials of the Commonwealth Investigation Service. He would officially become chief Commonwealth security officer for the tour.

As chief, he was required in advance to visit every state to coordinate security arrangements. 'The states resisted this encroachment on their traditional responsibilities,' Whitrod would later record in his memoir, 'and it took some delicate balancing over a number of royal tours for me to be accepted as the principal adviser. I took a fair battering from the state officers in the meantime, for police are touchy about trespassers in their patch.'

It was Whitrod's first clash with the Queensland police.

Queen Elizabeth and Prince Philip arrived in Sydney on 3 February 1954. They hit Brisbane on 9 March and commenced a nine-day tour of the capital and regional areas.

The visit precipitated the greatest singular concentration and organisation of police officers in the state's history. In early February, Chief Inspector Harrold travelled to Sydney to study crowd and traffic arrangements on the ground. In Brisbane, police expected 500,000 citizens to line the royal route from the airport at Eagle Farm to Government House in Paddington, in the city's inner north-west.

In late February, Police Commissioner Smith announced that 805 uniformed police and 156 plain-clothes detectives would be mobilised for the royal tour, and that men would be brought in from Ipswich and distant Charleville and Roma to satisfy the demands of security and crowd control.

Premier Vince Gair anointed himself the state royal tour minister.

Meanwhile, Ray Whitrod was getting close to the royal couple.

'I accepted personal responsibility for the safety of the royals and went everywhere with them,' he recalled in his memoir. 'The prince discovered that I shared his interest in wading birds, and whenever an opportunity presented itself, he would get me to drive him to some isolated spot to photograph Australian migratory waders.'

Between official engagements, Whitrod escorted Prince Philip in his second-hand Holden to various bird-watching spots around Canberra, and even took him 'mist netting' at Lake George, north of the city. Mist netting involved setting up almost invisible nets before dawn, trapping birds as they foraged for dawn food, and tagging them. 'He enjoyed that very much,' Whitrod later recalled.

When the Queen finally arrived in Brisbane, Detective Lewis was rostered on for duty at 3 p.m. but came in to the office an hour and a half early. His role that day was police driver.

'On duty with Det. Gorman. Then in Car 19 conveyed Dets. Balderson and Fox to the Exhibition Ground [where the royals were to be formally displayed to the Brisbane public] and drove men from there to Govt. House.' Similarly, he wrote the following day: 'Then in Car 30 to Govt. House and obtained meal for Dets. Currey and Cole.'

The grand royal ball was held at Brisbane City Hall on the evening of 10 March. The royals were driven from Government House around 9 p.m. and dazzled the local residents of Rosalie who had lined Fernberg Road for a glimpse of the Queen and her tiara. They arrived at 9.15 p.m. to be greeted by 1,150 guests and eight koalas, a wildlife treat for the special visitors.

It had been speculated months before that Brisbane Vice-mayor Colin Bennett would be the first to dance with Her Majesty. Mayor Roberts couldn't muster a dance move to save himself. The Queen only stayed at the ball for one hour and seven minutes and was returned to Government House, but that didn't stop the press declaring it 'the most spectacular and successful ball in Brisbane's history'.

During the remainder of the tour, Lewis arrested a serious jewel thief but spent much of his time 'attending files' or 'on reserve'. He was present on the corner of Albert and Turbot streets as the royals' procession passed through the city on 17 March.

It is not known if Whitrod, as royal security chief, ever encountered the likes of Bischof, Hallahan and Murphy during his stay in Brisbane. He had no contact with Lewis. He would accompany the royals on to Perth, and, at a farewell function on the royal yacht, *Britannia*, Prince Philip would present Whitrod with his book, *Birds of the Antarctic*. It was inscribed, 'To Ray Whitrod with many thanks. P.P.'

A month and a half later, an insignificant, three-line personal classified advertisement appeared in the Saturday edition of the *Cairns Post*. It simply read: 'COLIN EMERSON is urgently required to communicate with his sister, Shirley Emerson, of Atherton.'

Shirley had disappeared.

Family Men

Lewis's first child, also Terence Murray, was born on 20 January 1953, virtually nine months to the day after his marriage to Hazel.

Soon after, they bought a block of land at 45 Albert Street, Holland Park, in the city's south-east, for three hundred pounds, and had the Queensland Housing Commission construct a small, box-like timber and fibro-roofed dwelling, identical to others being built up and down the unpaved street. Lewis actually gives two versions of how the young couple raised the money for their first block of land: on one hand he says 'we saved every bloody penny we could and I got every bit of overtime I possibly could . . . and over time we racked up 300 pound';

and on the other hand he says they were given the 300 pounds by guests at their wedding.

The ambitious Detective Lewis, after an emotionally difficult childhood – who could he trust, with a mother who abandoned him and a meek father who quietly accepted the sudden departure of his wife and remained indifferent to the impact of their divorce on his children? – came uncomfortably to his own family life.

He says he found it difficult to express love towards other human beings, even his wife and children. Deeds, he believed, were more important than words. He proved his worth by *doing*.

By the time the Lewis family moved into Albert Street, he had well and truly set his priorities. Work came first. Family came second.

They had little furniture – a bedroom suite, a refrigerator, and a cot for baby Terence. They had no phone and no car. Hazel washed clothes and nappies in a downstairs copper, and the toilet was at the bottom of the yard.

Lewis worked obsessively at the CIB, often getting caught on jobs for twenty-four hours straight. There was no way he could communicate to Hazel that he wouldn't be home for dinner. He'd grab a bite at Barnes Auto Co., or pick up a quick bottle of milk from the Paul's milk factory down on the bend of the river in South Brisbane, within sight of Killarney brothel.

Across town Tony Murphy was faced with the same predicament – long hours at the office and small children at home.

Missing from the household for days at a stretch, he would tell his wife, Maureen, that if he was going to get ahead in the force, he'd have to make these contacts.

He never performed tasks like bathing or feeding the children, and was often impatient with them. He was mixing with dangerous criminals, with murderers, and had little time for domestic minutiae. As they grew older they feared him. 'He only had to breathe,' says wife Maureen, 'and they knew they had to behave.

'He was very cranky a lot of the time. He never laid a hand on the children. He just had to raise his voice and they'd all behave. Tony didn't discuss a lot of things, even with me. And the cases he was on. He never came home and discussed them.'

One night, unusually, he quietly hugged and kissed his children at bedtime and told Maureen he was off to do 'a hard job'. She thought there was a chance he might not come home.

He was at CIB headquarters when Maureen was about to give birth to one of their children, and he told her to catch a taxi and he'd meet her at the hospital. In the maternity ward, with the baby born, Murphy rehearsed his evidence for an impending trial.

Murphy would do anything to get 'a kill'. He had extremely reliable 'dogs', or informants, and criminals, too, began to fear being taken up the stairs at CIB headquarters. A flogging at the hands of senior detectives was not just a possibility but almost a certainty.

Former detective Ron Edington recalls Murphy in action: 'He'd get someone up there and say – "Who's going to tell the first lie? You or me?" He'd ask a prisoner to sit down then pull the chair out from under him. Most of his violence was done verbally.'

By the mid-1950s Lewis and Murphy could see that Bischof was heading for the police commissionership, and they were his chosen boys. This, in turn, created resentment among some members of the CIB, and pro- and anti-Bischof camps began to form. Rumours of corruption started to circulate.

Charles Fenwick Corner had started his career as a constable in Mount Isa in the late 1930s and in 1952 was transferred to the Brisbane CIB.

One day Bischof instructed Corner and two other detectives to go with him to the Athenian Club in Charlotte Street in the CBD, where, once inside the club, Bischof indicated elderly men playing dominoes and cards. He then accused the owner of the club, Jack Smith, of keeping a disorderly house.

Corner knew Smith and noticed that he came to the counter at CIB headquarters later that day and asked for Bischof. Smith later confided in Corner that Bischof had demanded payment from him. Corner had also heard whispers of Bischof receiving payments – collected by members of the CIB – from prostitutes working the city's four tolerated brothels.

Edington, who would go on to run the powerful Police Union, rightly observed that regular graft was absorbed from the brothels. 'If a madam wanted to employ a new girl,' he recalls, 'she would check with the officer in charge of Consorting, who would check out her record and lay down the law. She would have to have a house name, be registered on police books, wasn't allowed to drink at work, and had to be medically checked each week.'

Lewis's police diaries for the mid-1950s record two parallel narratives – constant vigilance over the tolerated brothels, and immediate intolerance of prostitutes and their 'bludgers' working outside the agreed houses.

Known prostitutes working the tolerated brothels were constantly visited by police or asked to come to CIB headquarters. New girls were interrogated and their antecedents scrutinised. The home addresses of prostitutes were regularly monitored and updated. Girls found operating out of private flats or premises not sanctioned by police were drummed out of the business and their bludgers arrested for living off the means of prostitution, or were escorted to the New South Wales border. Disputes between clients and the tolerated brothels were regularly resolved by police without charges laid.

Years before Bischof was promoted to CIB chief in 1955, and ultimately the commissionership, he showed an extraordinary interest in the machinations of the city brothels.

Lewis noted in his police diary:

Tuesday, May 11, 1954: To Albert Street and Nott Street brothels and advised Marcia Graham and Bale Amiott to call at CIB tomorrow and saw 3 new girls at Nott Street.

Saturday, May 15, 1954: Interviewed Merle Joan Fenwick an inmate of Nott Street brothel. She admitted only being 19 years of age, and she was advised to return to her parents at Southport.

Monday, May 24, 1954: In car 12 to 284 Hamilton Road, Chermside, re: prostitute Joyce Brownjohn, but she is not residing there. To 23 Armagh Street, Clayfield, re: prostitute Lorna Rose Evans, but her husband, Joseph Chamberlain Evans, admitted he was living with her but would not permit us to enter house.

Tuesday, May 25, 1954: To Albert Street and Margaret Street brothels and checked all inmates.

Friday, May 28, 1954: Interviewed Joyce Brownjohn at office re: her changing from Nott Street to Killarney brothel.

Monday, July 5, 1954: In Car 12 to all brothels and private homes and advised all owners and keepers to see Insp. Bischof at 11am tomorrow.

Wednesday, March 16, 1955: To National Hotel Lounge and there saw Margaret L.N. Clark and Pauline B. Honke. Questioned them at Office and both admitted not having any employment other than prostitutes in brothels for past 12 months. Inspector Lloyd instructed that they not be charged with vagrancy.

Wednesday, July 13, 1955: Interviewed Shirley Yvonne Cruise who wanted to enter a brothel. To gardens and located Adolf Beck. To office where he was questioned. They were then both interviewed by Insp. Bischof. To Roma St. Station and collected all their luggage. To Interstate Station and they both left on 11:48am train, car 13, seats 35 & 36.

The unwritten rule with the brothels was containment and control, and it had been so for decades.

Killarney and Nott Street brothels had been attracting the services of soldiers and graziers and cattlemen in town on business since the First World War.

On 2 September 1914, the *Brisbane Courier* reported the 'sudden death' of William Robertson of Mount Helmet Station at Springsure, 765 kilometres north-west of Brisbane, in a house in Nott Street. In 1941, two soldiers were imprisoned for three months after they smashed their way into 'a house in Lanfear Street', chased 'the inmates into the street and chopped up the furniture' with axes. And on 15 October 1952, the Divorce Court heard of the sad and sorry case of the Terliers. Mrs Janet Dickson Terlier was granted a decree nisi for divorce from her husband, Leslie, the former manager of the stock and property department of a pastoral company. The court was told that on 23 August 1952, at Nott Street, South Brisbane, Terlier 'misconducted himself with a woman unknown to Mrs Terlier'.

But how to explain Bischof's obsession with these houses?

And why did the brothels get almost constant attention from the CIB and its Consorting Squad and not so from the Licensing Branch? Consorting may well have come across local and interstate villains via the girls, and may have tapped into important information about the city's criminal milieu, but why attend to them with such monotonous regularity? Weren't they the province of Licensing?

There was no hiding the resentment between the two departments. Consorting saw Licensing as a bunch of boozers and bludgers, and Licensing dismissed the CIB as a stable of show ponies.

Killarney and Nott Street brothels were briefly targeted by Licensing – not Consorting – in June 1954. Acting on complaints that Killarney was being used as a 'house of ill-fame', Licensing staked out the properties on the evening of 23 June and observed that '11 men were seen to enter, and 10 leave'. They carried out further observations on the following two nights.

Joyce Gibson, thirty-two, single, was charged with having kept Killarney for the purposes of prostitution and fined fifteen pounds.

Over at nearby Nott Street, Vera Jackson was charged with managing a house for the purposes of prostitution. That both madams were charged at the same time would be an extraordinary coincidence if this wasn't a desultory, prearranged raid.

Self-confessed bagman, perjurer and former Licensing Branch officer Jack Herbert recalled in his memoir: 'Every two or three months we used to raid the brothels and take the girls to court.

'Ron Donovan insisted on us doing it correctly, sitting off the premises for a couple of days, writing down who went in and out. It was a pretty monotonous job and none of us took it very seriously.

'I remember once sitting outside Nott Street for three days with [self-confessed corrupt officer] Graeme Parker. At least that's what we were supposed to be doing.

'In fact we sat in the pub up the road [most likely the Coronation Hotel in Montague Road] and just wrote in our notebooks. "Two in, one out, ten o'clock." Eventually we went in and booked the girls.

'The rumour around the Licensing Branch was that [our] raids were ordered by . . . Bischof.'

Lewis remembers that the personal lives of the prostitutes were kept under unusually intimate scrutiny: outside the brothels, the girls weren't permitted by police to 'have a husband or a fellow living with them' as they were 'usually a criminal'.

He also recalls that the CIB had a 'special register' for prostitutes working in the city. It contained their real names and personal particulars and was constantly updated. In short, it was a brothel staff list. The 'register' was kept private from the prying eyes of other squads, particularly Licensing.

Despite Lewis's almost frenetic visits to the city's brothels, hotels, bars, and wine saloons, and being at the beck and call of Bischof, he was still a minor player within the CIB.

Then a case came along that ignited his friendship with the powerful Detective Tony Murphy.

Watching Amelia Street

On Thursday 6 October 1955, Lewis was in the office by 8.20 a.m. and straight into Car 27 with Detective Murphy. They drove past the old police depot and down Caxton Street to Lang Park.

The park, later to become famous as a sporting venue, was the former home of the Paddington cemetery and for years had hosted sporting events and been used by the children of the crowded, inner-west working-class suburbs of Petrie Terrace, Paddington and Red Hill. During the Second World War, army huts and other war buildings had been built in some parts of the park. After the war, the buildings were used as temporary housing camps and rented out by the Queensland Housing Commission.

Debate on the use of Lang Park swirled around for years. Meanwhile, the camps, and their tenants, remained. The entire park was held under trust by the Brisbane City Council from the state government.

The council beseeched the government to have the lease surrendered so it could develop a major sporting facility, but negotiations languished, and the park and its camps became squalid. Local citizens, too, felt free to dump their household rubbish there, including bathtubs and dunny soil.

On that Thursday morning, Murphy and Lewis made their way to Hut 4B where they interviewed a Mrs Elliott and her sixteen-year-old daughter, Shirley Ann Elliott.

Shirley had a story to tell. Seven weeks earlier, she had gone to a house in Albion, in the city's inner north, and secured an abortion. Murphy had somehow come across information of Shirley's clandestine operation and had already interviewed her in secret down at CIB headquarters. She had been uncooperative.

Now it was time to bring Lewis on board to see if he could coax any information from the young woman, and to inform her mother what had been going on.

It was a smart move by Murphy. Lewis's demeanour was largely placid and kindly. He was impeccably mannered and judicious in his choice of words. Unlike Murphy, who would fire off exactly what he thought at any given moment.

And in a sectarian police force, the topic of abortion had to be delicately handled. Some agreed with the practice, some didn't. It was the same in parliament. Murphy had to work out who he could trust with the case. He punted on Lewis, and sought senior counsel from Abe Duncan.

On that Thursday afternoon, Shirley Elliott and her mother accompanied Lewis and Murphy to CIB headquarters and the girl made a formal statement about the abortion. The gentle persuasion of Lewis had worked.

The next morning detectives launched a full investigation. Lewis went to the Main Roads Commission and checked on the registration of cars owned by several suspects. Surveillance began on two primary houses – one in Prospect Street, Fortitude Valley, and another in Amelia Street, Albion. It was at the latter that Shirley claimed she procured her abortion at the end of winter.

Later on the same day, police began discreet observation of the two houses. Using binoculars, they kept up twenty-four-hour vigils on Prospect Street from a classroom of a nearby state school, and on Amelia Street, from a local sawmill.

After several weeks of careful scrutiny the twelve-man team simultaneously raided the houses on the morning of Saturday 26 November.

Entering Amelia Street with a warrant, a sledgehammer, and axes, Murphy and his team, including Lewis, encountered Violet Myrtle Coman, forty-five, a nurse also known as 'Sister Byrne', who screamed and began sobbing. 'Calm yourself, Sister. It is no use getting upset,' Murphy told her.

'Don't hit me, don't hit me . . . I've heard about what you do to people,' she replied.

Murphy also heard George Frederick Richards, forty-four, a postal employee, shout: 'Look out, police. Look out, police.' Also arrested were Richards's wife, Rebecca Theresa, fifty-five, and George Robert Jones, fifty, a house painter. Jones supposedly said to Lewis: 'We have been caught cold. I won't give you any trouble.'

Police found four young women in the back bedrooms of the house, and they were each rushed to the Brisbane General hospital by ambulance. The government medical officer attended the women in hospital and would later reveal in court: 'In my opinion, what happened to the women was brought about by certain interference . . . When I saw the women, there was no immediate danger of their losing their lives.'

A gynaecologist performed 'certain operations' on the girls, and foetuses were presented as evidence in the trial of the four defendants.

All were found guilty and sent to Boggo Road gaol for between two to three years.

In sentencing, the judge said: 'All of you indulged in this practice for the purpose of making money. It is incidental that you managed to assist other people . . . The amounts you charged – 125 pounds and 135 pounds – appear to be in the nature of abortion.'

Lewis remembers that the investigation, prior to the raids, was kept largely secret from Bischof until the last moment, given the disparate views on abortion held within the force. However, Lewis's diaries reveal that on the first day of the investigation Mrs Elliott and her daughter were interviewed by Inspector Bischof at CIB headquarters. He was also regularly updated on the progress of the case, was telephoned on the evening before the raid, and was consulted about witnesses for the prosecution prior to the matter going to court.

There may have been a reason he wanted to be kept au fait with all the details of the great abortion raid, beyond being the man in charge of the CIB.

In 1952 Detective Ron Edington bumped into an old school classmate in the CBD. She was upset, telling Edington, 'Mum got me aborted when I was eighteen', and that the abortionist was now black-mailing her.

'What do you mean he's blackmailing you?' Edington asked.

'He's making me meet anyone who's going to be aborted, to stay with them, comfort them until they pass the foetus,' she admitted.

'You're an accessory,' Edington said. 'You'll go down the chute. Can you help me catch him?'

'You've got no chance of catching him.'

'Why not?'

'Because Frank Bischof, the commissioner, and Nobby Clark, the inspector in the Valley, they visit his premises at 28 Ivory Street, Fortitude Valley, regularly on the pretext of looking for missing girls.'

Edington said: 'The next time you get someone there, give me a ring.'

The friend contacted him shortly after; she was at Ivory Street, assisting a girl who was unsuccessfully trying to abort.

Edington secured a search warrant, but by the time they got to the house they were met by Sub-inspector R.T. (Bob) Nesbitt and Senior Sergeant Tom Donovan.

'They accompanied us, trying to curtail my activity,' Edington recalls. 'We got in there and there was the girl and she was nearly dead . . . She had septicaemia. So I got the government medical officer to come down and he put her into hospital and saved her life.'

Edington arrested the abortionist – James Henry Manuel, fifty-five, labourer – and was offered a bribe.

'He told me Bischof used to get money in a boot polish tin. That was the money the abortionist gave to Frank Bischof when he used to come. He showed me the tin and I said you can shove that tin up your arse, mate. You're going in.'

Manuel was convicted and sentenced to seven years' hard labour.

During his trial, Manuel claimed that four hundred pounds found in 'a boot polishing outfit tin' at Ivory Street was winnings from the races.

Ada and Gunner

On Thursday 3 February 1955, Lewis was rostered on at 3 p.m. but, as usual, he was at CIB headquarters an hour and a half early. He spent the extra time attending to files and writing up his police diary. He was on duty with Hoppy Hopgood and Buck Buchanan.

Patrolling Brisbane's south side, Lewis arrested a man for being drunk in Russell Street, had his evening meal at CIB headquarters from 6.40 p.m. to 7 p.m., then cruised the Fortitude Valley wine saloons looking for trouble.

In a place called Johnstone's, the officers came across Robert James Mutton carrying a loaded .32 pistol in his pocket. The firearm was licensed but Buchanan 'retained' it.

Then, later in the evening, they were called to a curious job. They drove to 40 Clarke Street, Hendra, a small postwar bungalow with a curved corner verandah in the shadow of Doomben racecourse, where they interviewed Alfio Vito Cavallaro.

Cavallaro alleged that he had been assaulted and robbed. Under further questioning, he said the attack came after he had been entertained by a prostitute called Anne Bahnemann. He said he had been in bed with Bahnemann when two men entered the bedroom and stole their clothing.

Lewis and team then proceeded to Kent Street, New Farm, where they interviewed an Ada Louise Bahnemann. She admitted she'd been in bed with Cavallaro and directed them to a house one street over, where they found her husband of just seven months, Gunther 'Gunner' Bahnemann.

Bahnemann, thirty-three, had an extremely colourful history. He had been a hero in the panzer division of the German army during the Second World War and fought with Rommel's Afrika Korps in the Western Desert. When in 1941 he heard a rumour that his father, a postmaster, had been executed by the Gestapo as a traitor, he deserted to British forces in Libya. He arrived in Australia on 14 December that year as a prisoner of war and was transferred to a camp at Murchison, near Shepparton in Victoria. Along with other German POWs, he was held in the Dhurringile mansion near Murchison until he was released 'under supervision' into the community in late 1946.

In a report on Bahnemann compiled in 1947 by Commonwealth Investigation Service Director Longfield Lloyd, the former German war hero was described as having 'a very unsavoury history', indicating he was 'totally unscrupulous and not to be trusted'.

Bahnemann later settled in Fourth Avenue, Mount Isa, with his first wife, Vera, and became something of an eccentric local identity. Claiming he was a master mariner, he built a boat in the mining town and intended to use it for crocodile hunting in the waters of northern Australia and Papua New Guinea.

In 1953 Vera fled to Cloncurry after a fight with Bahnemann. He telephoned her and said he was on his way to shoot her dead. Police managed to intercept him at the Cloncurry railway station, where they alleged he was carrying a rifle and explosives.

In a pique of jealousy and rage, Bahnemann wrote to Customs in Cairns warning that his wife may attempt to flee to Papua New Guinea under a false name and passport.

'I notified Immigration Dept. Brisbane, of false statements made in her British Passport,' he wrote. 'My wife is easily identified owing to extreme blond hair, near white, small slim and thirty of age, and well versed in life aboard ships. Kindly notify me should she try to obtain a clearance for territory outside of Australia.'

His divorce to Vera was formalised in June 1954, and he married Ada Louise Ruby the following month in Brisbane.

Three weeks after being interviewed by Lewis, Hopgood, and Buchanan over the Cavallaro incident at Hendra, the Vacuum Oil Company made a formal application for an employee, Gunther Bahnemann, to enter Papua New Guinea. 'With regard to transport,' their covering letter stated, 'we wish to advise that he is being booked on the earliest available Qantas Aircraft departing Brisbane.'

In the application, Bahnemann gave his home address as 'care of' Mrs Ruby, Whites Road, Lota.

The application was refused. In private correspondence within the Department of Territories in Canberra, Bahnemann was not to be given the entrance permit 'under any circumstances'.

Did Bahnemann attempt to flee Brisbane after coming to the attention of police?

According to a Queensland police report compiled on Bahnemann, he had supposedly forced his wife into prostitution and she resisted. After several violent clashes with Bahnemann, Ada entered a 'house of ill-fame' in South Brisbane, funding him and his quixotic seafaring adventures. Police suspected Bahnemann was living off the immoral earnings of his wife, but they didn't have enough evidence to prosecute.

Then, on Thursday 3 May 1956, Lewis recorded in his police diary that he went to 'Nott Street brothel' and 'saw Ada Louise Bahnemann', also known as Vengert, nee Ruby.

Soon, Ada would go to work at nearby Killarney brothel, next to the old Foggitt Jones fish cannery in Lanfear Street. Soon, she would be plying her trade alongside a young girl called Shirley Brifman from Far North Queensland.

The Time of the Mason

The mid-1950s was an excellent time to be a Catholic in Brisbane. The ruling Labor Party was brimming with them, as was the police force and its so-called Green Mafia. Both subsets had had an unusually good, and long, run.

Premier Gair was demonstrably proud of his Catholic faith. At a massive family rosary crusade in the spring of 1953, Gair addressed the 85,000-strong crowd gathered at the exhibition grounds in Bowen Hills. 'The greater the number of families that engage in family prayer,' he told them, 'the more multitudinous becomes the innovation of God's help in the community.'

In late 1954 he was accused by the Queensland Teachers' Union of being more interested in Catholic schools than in the state education system. He labelled the accusation 'in defiance of all logic, reason and justice'.

Addressing past students of his old school, St Joseph's Christian Brothers' College in Rockhampton, the same year, he warned of the need for a 'realistic' approach to the menace of communism.

The *Rockhampton Bulletin* reported the speech he made at a communion breakfast celebrating the school's jubilee: 'Most of you stand charged and found guilty of apathy and lethargy for many years when you succumbed to the belief that communism was an innocuous thing confined to Russia.

'You have seen the progress made by communism in our country. I know you are more conscious of it now, but some twenty years ago, when someone tried to organise a front, what was the attitude adopted?

'I appeal to you to be unselfish in this work. If you are not prepared to inconvenience yourself for this country and for the future of your children and generations to come, I say, God help Australia.'

By 1955, the Labor Party would split in Victoria over the matter of communist domination of the unions, the issue brought on by challenges from the Catholic 'Movement' – Catholic agitators who formed anti-communist factions and tried to seize control of the unions themselves.

This destabilising phenomenon would ultimately make its way to Queensland. Meanwhile, Labor's central executive in Queensland had grown concerned at the gulf between the party's philosophical imperative as an organisation for the working class, and Premier Gair's parliamentary party and the extent to which he was implementing, or not, the party's broader objectives. Who made the important decisions – the executive, or the premier?

In 1957, an industrial dispute in Queensland over increasing workers' annual leave led to the party's implosion – the Great Labor Split – and in April, Premier Gair was summoned to a central executive hearing, where he was expelled from the Labor Party for not accepting the party's rules.

Premier Gair responded by gathering his supporters and forming the Queensland Labor Party. He continued to govern as head of a minority government but an election was called after the premier and his party were defeated on a supply bill.

After a quarter of a century in the cold, a coalition of Country Party and Liberal Party members won office, and 'Honest' Frank Nicklin became premier. Having spent a seemingly interminable sixteen years as leader of the Opposition, the old hand cautiously steered his party members through the opening months of the new government.

If it hadn't been for the Labor split, Francis Bischof, too, may not have been elevated to police commissioner. Now, with Labor gone and the Catholics on thin ice, it was the time of the Mason.

When Nicklin came to power, Tom Harrold had been police commissioner for less than a year and was coming up to retirement age. More than two hundred applications were received for the position. One was from Bischof, another from the more experienced Jim Donovan.

Former Liberal Party leader Thomas Hiley, who had had some public run-ins with Bischof and the police in the early 1950s, was appointed treasurer and was part of the Cabinet discussions to choose a new police commissioner.

He recalled that prior to the new appointment he had become aware – through the complaints of constituents against individual police – of what he called 'the cult of the solid police'.

Being 'solid', as Hiley understood it, was when an officer would do anything for another officer, 'including lying in evidence, seeing and hearing nothing if a detained person was threatened or bashed by a fellow officer, giving false evidence to support an alleged confession'. This outlook, Hiley rightly concluded, became potentially more hazardous when it involved commissioned officers.

As a member of the selection committee for the next police commissioner, Hiley wanted to test the 'solid' cult with his applicants.

'I can recall that Jim Donovan and Frank Bischof were the leading applicants for the job,' Hiley later told the Fitzgerald Inquiry in the late 1980s. 'When we interviewed Donovan he advocated no change in the status quo. He had no new ideas.

'Bischof provided a complete contrast. He was confident, personally impressive, and he presented ideas for police development and practice. He refused to support the concept of the solid policeman.

'I can recall Bischof saying that his duty to the state outweighed his duty to any fellow officer.'

Hiley, however, had been offered hearsay about Bischof being corrupt. Bischof loved the racetrack. He had developed a peculiarly intimate relationship with Brisbane prostitutes and their madams. No wrongdoing, though, could be substantiated.

According to Ron Edington, two policemen in the know about Bischof tried to block any chance he had at being appointed police commissioner.

'There were two fellows, one named Charlie Corner, who went down to Parliament House and signed statutory declarations saying that Bischof was corrupt and shouldn't be appointed,' Edington recalls. 'Charlie was a fanatical kind of bloke and everything he said was true but he was such an eccentric.'

Hiley later said he made an off-the-cuff comment to another member of the selection committee: Bischof should either be anointed police commissioner, or kicked off the force.

Bischof was formally sworn in as police commissioner on 30 January 1958.

His appointment saw him pictured on the front page of the

Courier-Mail the next day, beaming alongside his wife – unnamed in the report – and their golden cocker spaniel, Sunny.

Readers were informed that Mrs Bischof was a woman 'of quiet dignity' who was locally renowned for her sponge cakes. She enjoyed hosting luncheons and cocktail parties in their Ashgrove home (Frank had a penchant for bow ties), and tending their cacti garden. Frank was responsible for planting the annuals. Lewis says he rarely met Mrs Bischof. 'I'd drive him home sometimes or pick him up but I barely saw her. I can't remember ever seeing her at any functions.'

Inside the newspaper that day, a staff reporter wrote how Bischof had 'moved fast yesterday' into the new job. At 1 p.m. he had been called to a ministerial conference in the Treasury building on George Street and told of his new position. He left the conference room at 2 p.m. and fifteen minutes later was installed behind the police commissioner's desk at the police depot, Petrie Terrace.

Lewis remembers that the comical story of Bischof racing from the CBD to Petrie Terrace and into his new office did the rounds at the time. 'He got there as quick as he could,' he says, 'before anyone could take the position away from him.'

What several of Bischof's colleagues knew, but his wife and the general public certainly didn't, was that Bischof had, a year prior to his big promotion, begun an affair with a Brisbane woman, Mary Margaret Fels, then in her late thirties.

Fels lived with her husband, balding farmer Alfonso, and their six children on a small property on Underwood Road at Eight Mile Plains, in the city's south-east.

An attractive honey blonde, Fels was having minor trouble with one of her sons and Bischof, always obliging to wayward teenagers, stepped in to counsel the boy.

The kindly Bischof opened the door of his office – before and after becoming police commissioner – to the city's wayward youth every Saturday, and the press made much of his dedication to the children of

Brisbane. But Saturday was also race day, and underling police officers on duty could barely concentrate with Bischof's radio blaring with all the news from the track. Did he really care so much for troubled kids, or did Saturday in the office give him an opportunity to keep his eye on corrupt payments being collected from SP bookmakers on the busiest race day of the week?

The affair with Fels began almost immediately, and the pair had sex at the Fels family farm and at a house in Fortitude Valley. The rumour around the police force was that Bischof was even bold enough to take Fels away on vacations to the South Coast.

It was dangerous territory for a new police commissioner in a small town like Brisbane.

'They said [Fels] wasn't a bad-looking mother – the story then around the ridges was that he was rather attracted to her,' says Lewis. 'I never saw Bischof with his wife at any function probably because she was very deaf . . . This other lady, we were told, was rather presentable. I suppose he thought he better hop in for his chop.'

Still, as the Big Fella celebrated his new position, a spectacular murder case was playing itself out in far-off Mount Isa. Glen Hallahan, in charge of the local CIB, had just collared a brutal killer in a case that would become known as the Sundown Murders.

It would, overnight, make Hallahan the most famous young detective in Queensland.

The Curious Corruption Incubator of Mount Isa

James Michael Jorgensen, thirty-five, itinerant barman, sometime station hand, drinker and renowned pub brawler, was buried at the Mount Isa Sunset Lawn Cemetery on 14 March 1956, in grave number 805.

The tale of Jorgensen's death, largely forgotten now, is a small window into not only how tough the frontier mining town of Mount Isa was in the 1950s, but also its police. There, in the far north-west of the state, were smelters and sprawling corner pubs, miners' dormitories and unpaved, treeless streets of wooden cottages. It was a place of heavy drinking and heavy gambling. It was populated with a high degree of misfits and eccentrics.

One of them, a German army deserter by the name of Gunther Bahnemann, bemused locals for years while he constructed a large motor boat in his yard.

Local Dick Bentley remembers Bahnemann coming to the house and regaling him and his family with tall tales of his military experiences, of engineering and captaining vessels off the north Queensland coast.

'He always wanted sour milk, and he ate raw mince,' Bentley, who was a boy at the time, says. 'We once went up to Thursday Island on an old 112-foot Fairmile wooden boat – they were used in the war – skippered by Bahnemann. He had about twenty South Sea Islanders on board and they'd hunt for trochus, spear turtles and Torres Strait pigeons.

'I had some spears I'd brought back from New Guinea and he asked me if he could have them to decorate his new boat. I liked Gunther immensely. He was a great storyteller. I never had a bad opinion of him.'

Dick's mother, Clare, loved a flutter, particularly with the local SP bookmakers, and held regular poker nights at the house. Her other preoccupation was gossip.

She certainly knew of Mount Isa's outstanding young detective, Glen Hallahan, and kept notes on the progress of his career. 'She thought he was a rogue,' says Dick, 'a pretty crooked policeman. As for Hallahan and Bahnemann, there is absolutely no doubt they knew each other in Mount Isa. They were well known to each other.'

The death of James Jorgensen in early 1956, while shocking, would not have seemed out of place in a town like Mount Isa. Here, the plain-clothes officers wore full suits and felt hats even at the height of summer. When they walked the main streets of town, pedestrians stepped off the footpaths to let them pass.

As for Jorgensen, he had a history of alcohol abuse and violence, and was well known to proprietors and patrons of the town's three major hotels – the Mount Isa, the Boyd and the Argent. On 7 February 1956, he was drinking with a friend who was arrested for being drunk and disorderly. Jorgensen was also threatened with arrest and he questioned police: 'What for?' He said he'd done nothing wrong.

He was then punched by the arresting officers – Constables Paul McArthur and Eric Murray – and transferred to cells at the Mount Isa police station. He was charged with inciting a prisoner, his friend, to resist arrest.

A coronial inquest into Jorgensen's death revealed that once the prisoner was in his cell, McArthur, twenty-one, and Murray, twenty-four, entered. 'I told Jorgensen to take off his shoes, but he didn't,' McArthur told the inquest. 'Murray said: "You heard what he said," but still Jorgensen didn't take off his shoes. Murray then cuffed him over both ears and hit him in front of the neck with the back of his right forearm.'

Jorgensen alleged in a statement that a police officer had driven two hard punches into his stomach.

That night, Jorgensen suffered acute pain and an ambulance transferred him to the local hospital. After several operations, he died of severe internal injuries. Constables McArthur and Murray were later charged with unlawful killing and suspended.

Seven months after the incident, the two young officers were discharged. The judge ruled that the case against them was based solely on circumstantial evidence.

This was Detective Glen 'Silent' Hallahan's small world. As CIB chief, his work rate was prodigious. The police district encompassing Mount Isa was based out of Cloncurry and run by District Inspector Norwin 'Norm' Bauer. Whenever the Circuit Court came to town, Hallahan travelled down from Mount Isa for trials.

Young Constable Don Lane – the sensitive recruit from Warwick who preferred a hostel over the police dormitory – had been posted to Cloncurry in 1957 and remembered the impact of the glamorous detective from Mount Isa.

'I got to know him as well as anyone could,' Lane recalled in his memoir, 'largely because of the fact that he was a notorious loner.

'Hallahan would invariably have 80 per cent of the cases going to trial before the Circuit Court . . . and was highly regarded for his police work by both his colleagues and the legal profession.'

Here, Hallahan would have begun his professional friendship with Bauer, a farm boy, horse breaker, and hunter from the hills around tiny Swanfels, east of Warwick.

Bauer, in the great tradition of future senior Queensland police, left school aged thirteen and worked as a bullock driver transporting timber. He proved an adept horse rider and regularly competed as a teenager at country carnivals and shows. He joined the force at twenty-four and was seconded to the Brisbane Mounted Police, later working as a trooper in the St George police district, quelling sheep thefts and assisting in law and order during the famous shearers' strike in 1931.

He was brought to Brisbane in 1932 and worked out of Roma Street police station as a bicycle night patrol officer, then served at Bulimba and Southport police stations before joining the CIB in 1936.

He spent more than seventeen years in the Southport CIB and then Brisbane, where he developed a loyal friendship with Bischof.

In 1956, the year Jorgensen died after being assaulted in the Mount Isa police cells, Bauer was appointed Cloncurry district inspector. He was, by that time, heavily involved in Masonry, and would ultimately become grand master of the United Grand Lodge of Queensland. He also penned short stories for *True Detective*.

Constable Don Lane had an unexpected run-in with Bauer not long after he started work in Cloncurry, courtesy of a new arrival, reputable investigator and incorruptible officer Don Becker. Becker had landed in the Wild West in pursuit of a quick promotion. The police gulags hadn't always existed for the purposes of punishment or misdemeanours.

In his memoir, Lane recalled that Becker, on his first weekend in the country town, had wandered the main streets and become suspicious of two premises, both run by Joe and Bob Bakhash, well-known businessmen and proprietors of a jewellery store, a tobacconist, and a billiard hall.

Lane told Becker that the two premises were renowned SP betting shops, but police had been instructed to ignore them. Becker didn't. He approached the shop and interrogated one of the Bakhash brothers, securing several ledgers and placing them under lock and key at the police station. Becker advised that he would be taking out summonses in relation to the SP bookmaking.

Bauer, on learning of the news, was furious, and demanded to know the whereabouts of the ledgers. Lane recalled: 'Before I could answer him, Sergeant Becker appeared from around the building and confronted Bauer. A violent row took place, in which Inspector Bauer made it plain to Becker that the SP shops were to be left alone. Becker stood his ground and proceeded with the summonses.'

Lane said that he and Becker were offered bribes for the safe return of the ledgers, but the court case went ahead.

On Tuesday 21 January 1958, just over a week before Bischof was crowned Queensland police commissioner in Brisbane, the industrious Detective Hallahan was on duty in Miles Street, Mount Isa, with his partner, Detective Bob Pfingst, when he noticed a black DeSoto.

The day before, police nationwide were told to be on the lookout for a similar car towing a caravan, and that it may be linked to a triple homicide committed in early December near Sundown Station, south of Kulgera, across the Northern Territory–South Australia border.

The dead were Thyra Bowman, in her early forties – wife of Peter Bowman, manager of Glen Helen Station, two hundred kilometres from Alice Springs – their daughter Wendy, fourteen, and visiting family friend Thomas Whelan, twenty-six. All three – along with Wendy's two dogs – were driving to Adelaide to see friends and family. Peter Bowman and their other daughter, Marian, flew to Adelaide and were waiting for their arrival.

When they hadn't turned up by 8 December, Peter contacted roadhouses on the vehicle's planned road route, then alerted police. The story of the missing car and its occupants was reported in the Adelaide press two days later. Witnesses claimed the car was last sighted at a petrol station in Kulgera.

The police and the flying doctor service turned up nothing, so the RAAF was called in. Then, on Friday 13 December, the captain of an air force Lincoln was banking his aircraft just over the South Australian border when he spotted the car hidden in scrub off the dirt highway.

The case immediately became known as the Sundown Murders.

Thomas Whelan had been shot four times, once in the back of the head. Thyra Bowman had been bludgeoned and received one bullet to the head. Wendy had been similarly bashed, and had a bullet wound to the temple. The two dogs had also been shot to death.

Over the next month witnesses emerged, telling police they had either seen or personally spoken to the driver of a black DeSoto towing a cream-coloured caravan in the vicinity of and around the time of the murders. The man was travelling with his wife and three-year-old son. One witness reported the man had introduced himself as Bailey and said that he and his family were travelling to Mount Isa. The witness had spotted a rifle on the front seat of the DeSoto.

Armed with this information, police sent out a national notification for the vehicle and van, and the next day it came into the sights of Glen Hallahan.

He and his partner kept the car under observation until they saw a small-framed man approach the vehicle at about 6.20 p.m. Both officers approached the DeSoto.

'I'm Detective Hallahan and this is Detective Pfingst,' Hallahan said. 'What is your name?'

'Ray Carter,' the man replied. He later claimed to be Ray Bailey, having used a pseudonym for 'tax purposes'. He had been working as a carpenter on the new Mount Isa hospital since before Christmas.

Hallahan accompanied Bailey, twenty-six, to the police station, and on inspecting the vehicle allegedly found a .32 calibre revolver and leather holster concealed in the front seat. Hallahan, Pfingst and other police then went with Bailey to a camping reserve outside town to check out the suspect's pale blue and grey caravan.

There they talked with Bailey's wife, Patricia. Hallahan discovered .22 calibre rifle bullets in the van. The Baileys and police then returned to the station with the caravan in tow.

At 9.30 p.m., Bailey, a carpenter of no fixed address, was charged with possessing an unlicensed firearm and with obtaining a car under false pretences.

Incredibly, the arrest was the page-one lead in the *Courier-Mail* the next morning. Either District Inspector Bauer or the increasingly publicity-conscious Detective Hallahan, or someone else, phoned the newspaper offices in Brisbane or sat down with a stringer in Mount Isa itself and provided lengthy and exacting details of the dramatic arrest and formal charges in time to make deadline.

The story involved some creative licence – times wrong, incorrect details of who was where and when – but it was a huge coup for the Queensland police, potentially capturing a triple murderer after a nationwide alert.

All this action, just as Cabinet in Brisbane was debating who would be the next police commissioner.

The next day, the *Courier-Mail* followed the drama, saying an arrest for the triple murder was imminent. Bauer had secured an eight-day remand on Bailey so he could be interrogated by Adelaide police.

Two days later, a photograph of the diminutive Raymond John

Bailey, charged with murder, graced the front page of the *Courier-Mail*. He was pictured with Pfingst on his left and Hallahan on his right. In the photograph the officers are staring at the camera with half-smiles on their faces. Hallahan, in dark suit, tie, and hat, is holding some paperwork in his right hand.

After his court hearing, Bailey asked for a Church of England clergyman. Patricia Bailey collapsed on the verandah of the police station and was carried into the recreation room, where she recovered. She collapsed again some time later, and was 'given an injection by a doctor'.

She and her son, Michael, lived in the caravan on the grounds of the police station while Bailey was on remand nearby.

At Bailey's trial in May 1958, Hallahan claimed he knew nothing of the connection between Bailey and the Sundown Murders when he apprehended him in Miles Street. He just knew about a suspect car. He stated he wasn't aware of the Bailey–Sundown link until the next day, when the *Courier-Mail* splashed the story on page one.

If he knew nothing, who gave the newspaper the information of the arrest? And if Bauer leaked it, why wouldn't he confide in his star Mount Isa detective on such a crucial matter?

Why, too, was Bailey placed on an eight-day remand, sought by Bauer, over insignificant firearm and vehicle offences?

Hallahan also told the trial he began interviewing Bailey in the presence of Bauer – who 'happened to be passing through Mount Isa on another matter' – from 10 a.m. on Wednesday 22 January. Detectives Moran and Hopkins from Adelaide were due in Mount Isa at about 3.30 p.m. that day. By the time they arrived, Hallahan and Bauer had secured a confession.

Bailey would reveal at his trial that on the night before his interrogation by Hallahan and Bauer he was locked in a padded cell and 'woken every half hour by a torch being flashed in the trap and if I did not move they came in and woke me'.

'During the next morning, I could hear my wife crying downstairs. I told them where I had been and what I had been doing, but they just kept on questioning me and didn't seem to believe me. By midday I was in such a state I didn't know what I was saying.

'I also asked to see a lawyer but Hallahan said I was not allowed to speak to anybody . . . even my wife . . . my wife was about six weeks' pregnant and she had a miscarriage while she was at Mount Isa.'

Hallahan would tell the court that Bailey had confessed to his own father-in-law that he had committed the murders. Bailey said this was untrue. Hallahan said he had no notes recording the confession.

As Hallahan gave evidence, Bailey reacted from the dock: 'He's telling lies. Tell the truth, that's all I want.' He cried as he remonstrated.

Despite Bailey's claims of innocence, legal doubt lingering over his alleged confession, and allegations in court that police mistreated Patricia Bailey in order to get to her husband, he was found guilty of the murders and sentenced to death. A subsequent appeal was heard and dismissed.

Bailey was hanged on the morning of 17 June 1958, the last man to suffer such a fate in South Australia.

Author Peter James, who analyses the trial evidence in his book *The Sundown Murders*, concludes: 'If it is only a partly accurate record of Bailey's time in the Mount Isa watchhouse, it could represent the first occasion that brainwashing techniques were successfully used in the state of Queensland to get a murder confession.'

A few weeks later, the new Queensland police commissioner, Frank Bischof, arrived in Mount Isa as part of his statewide campaign to familiarise himself with the troops.

Bischof clearly had his eye on Hallahan, the stellar detective who had arrested a potential triple murderer. Hallahan, he must have realised, was a 'solid' policeman, the type that Minister Thomas Hiley warned of. He was a 'worker' and he got his 'kills'.

Unsurprisingly, Hallahan was transferred to the Brisbane CIB the following month. (He would be replaced at the Mount Isa CIB by Don Lane.) So too was Bauer, Bischof's Mason mate. Bauer would take charge of the Licensing Branch, and would soon be overseeing a young officer by the name of Jack Herbert.

Hallahan and Bauer. The young detective and his Cloncurry district superior. Hallahan and Bauer. The two men alone in that interview room at the Mount Isa CIB when Bailey made his confession to multiple murders. Hallahan and Bauer, shifted together back to Brisbane, each knowing what went on in that stifling room and the role each played in prising the confession from Bailey.

Did Bischof transfer them together because of their exceptional work on the Sundown Murders? Or was it safer for the new police commissioner to keep them in the same orbit if, indeed, they had concocted a false confession from Bailey?

Says Lewis: 'Bauer possibly corroborated [Hallahan] on some of the [Sundown Murders case] things. He and Bauer were always close. They were mates. It's not something they'd talk about.'

Was Bailey framed by Bauer and Hallahan?

'The two of them would have done it,' Lewis says.

In *The Sundown Murders*, Peter James surmised that Bauer's potential involvement in a conspiracy that led to the hanging of an innocent man would have made him vulnerable now Hallahan 'had the wood on the top Mason in the state'.

'If this outline of the situation is even partially correct,' James wrote, 'then it is not difficult to see how it would be impossible for Inspector Bauer ever to discipline Detective Hallahan again.'

At the end of 1958, just as Hallahan was settling in to the big smoke, Lewis was partnered with Murphy for several weeks leading up to Christmas.

They may have discussed the police interchange program – a system that saw Queensland police serve for a period of weeks in Sydney, and vice versa, to gain experience in interstate police practice and to meet up-and-coming young detectives.

Lewis's last interchange had been earlier in the year. He caught the train from Brisbane to Sydney on Saturday 22 March, arriving the next day. According to his police diary, on Monday he reported for duty at the Sydney CIB and was partnered with 'Dets. Curtis (South Aust.) and [Eric] Pratt (Vict.)', who was his roommate for the next four weeks and would become a lifelong friend.

It was through the interchange program that Murphy and Lewis would meet the biggest southern coppers of their day.

'That's when I probably met fellows like Fred Krahe and [Ray 'Gunner'] Kelly,' says Lewis. 'They were leading young detectives, they were workers.'

While in Sydney, Lewis was caught up in the investigation of a horrendous murder. In the early hours of Friday 11 April 1958, labourer John (Jack) Smith, drunk, broke into the dormitories of the Methodist Ladies College, Burwood, and abducted at knifepoint fourteen-year-old schoolgirl Margaret Thomas.

He took her to Queen Elizabeth Park in the neighbouring suburb of Concord, where he raped and stabbed her to death. An autopsy would reveal fifteen puncture wounds.

Within hours, following a tip-off from a taxi driver, Smith was arrested and taken to Burwood police station. That morning, Lewis viewed the suspect then acted on a hunch – the murder bore similarities to that of Betty Shanks years earlier in Brisbane, and a savage attack on another Brisbane woman, Beverley Mackenzie, in early 1957.

While Lewis investigated Smith's background, another Queensland detective from Brisbane CIB flew to Sydney to assist. Together they interviewed Smith, who initially admitted to break and enters in the Brisbane suburbs of Inala and Ascot, then to the rape and attempted murder of Mackenzie.

It was a fruitful month-long secondment to Sydney for Lewis.

Back in Brisbane on Friday 5 December, Lewis and Murphy were working the 7 a.m. to 3 p.m. shift, questioning petty thieves and suspected prostitutes across the city when, having returned to CIB headquarters, they bumped into Inspector Voigt.

Lewis noted in his police diary: 'Saw Insp. Voigt re: Albert St brothel and he stated that Mr Bischof had instructed that we were not to tell any inmates to leave brothels and were not to arrest any inmates unless they were committing a Crime, such as stealing. We are not to charge any with vagrancy or to arrest any keepers. Off duty at 4pm.'

On Tuesday 16 December at exactly 3 p.m., Lewis recorded for the first time working with 'Det. Hallahan'.

Three days later, early on that Friday morning, he was on duty with both Hallahan and Murphy in Car 12. It was an eventful day. He registered several arrests: drunk in Musgrave Park; insufficient lawful means; break and enter.

In Car 12, on a Brisbane summer morning in 1958, the future Rat Pack had come together.

Shirley's New Life

In 1954, Colin Emerson of Atherton may have been searching for the whereabouts of his young sister Shirley through the classified advertisements of the *Cairns Post*, but if he'd wandered into the Court House Hotel on Abbott Street, not far from the police station in downtown Cairns, he would have found her pulling beers behind the bar.

Shirley had left her family behind in Atherton sometime early in the year, determined to set out on her own. She had a much older sister, Marge Chapple, living in Cairns, but sought from her no help with money or accommodation.

The Court House Hotel had once been salubrious. In 1939, following a renovation, it exemplified the modernisation of Cairns. The front of the building had been rebuilt and a new accommodation wing and staff quarters had been added. A private bar, described as 'continental' in atmosphere by the local press, consisted of jade green and cream tiling and an end wall filled with refrigerated cabinets with plate glass mirrors and shelves.

By the 1950s it had become rundown and its lower status matched its clientele. In March 1950, a Polish immigrant named Szama (Sonny) Brifman arrived in Sydney on board the passenger ship SS *Otranto* after a five-week voyage from Europe. He made his way up to Cairns and by 1954 was the licensee of the Court House Hotel, alongside his wife.

'Meet Mine Host and Hostess,' he advertised in the *Cairns Post*, 'in the friendly atmosphere of this modern and up-to-date Bar and Lounge. Enjoy Your Drinks to Peter Ward's Bright, Sparkling Music.'

According to Shirley's family, Brifman's adventure as a hotel proprietor was funded by his then wife, who died in 1955. They believed Shirley, after starting work as a barmaid under Brifman's charge, was living in staff quarters at the hotel.

Very soon, though, she had moved in with Brifman himself. Back in Atherton, Shirley's parents disapproved of the coupling. Brifman was twenty years older than Shirley, of ordinary appearance, and seemed to enjoy 'living off women'. Whereas Shirley was young, outgoing, attractive, and just starting to live her life.

But there was a problem. The naive Shirley Emerson had fallen pregnant to Brifman. In July 1956, Shirley – four months into the pregnancy – made an extraordinary 5000-pound claim against Brifman in the Townsville Supreme Court for alleged 'breach of promise to marry'.

She gave birth to her first child, Mary Anne, in December, and by June the following year, Shirley and Sonny were finally married at the Cairns courthouse and held a reception in the Court House Hotel, attended by her sister Marge Chapple and Marge's children.

Shirley Emerson was now Shirley Brifman. And if she had a flaw, according to relatives, it was her taste for the good life. Once she'd savoured it, she refused to let it go. The family rumour was that Shirley had begun a career in prostitution from out of her husband's hotel before, if not shortly after, their marriage.

By early 1958, the Brifmans were heading for the bright lights of Brisbane, where Shirley could make more money.

Within weeks of hitting the city and starting work at Killarney brothel alongside Ada Bahnemann near the fish cannery on the south side of the river, Brifman made a firm and fast friend in the local CIB. His name was Tony Murphy.

Murphy, in turn, introduced her to Glen Hallahan when he arrived from Mount Isa in the aftermath of the Sundown Murders case.

She also became acquainted with Terry Lewis: 'I've got no idea where I met her,' he says. 'I might have met her in the Grand Central and Murphy would have introduced me to her.'

Brifman and her husband and child were living in Belmont, a bushy, semi-rural suburb twelve kilometres south-east of the CBD, when she met Hallahan. He was living in inner-city New Farm. Both had strong personalities and an eye on the main game.

Hallahan quickly confided in her.

'Glen hit the pot over the Sundown murder,' she later recalled in a police interview. 'It was pot. I had seen the pot. I used to cop it night after night. Hallahan said that the real killer was free. It did really play on his mind and I thought he was going to go off his head over it.

'At that stage I would say he was not crooked but after that he went bad. I never saw anything eat a man inside like that did.

'All he used to talk about was this murder. He said: "The man walks free. We know who he is." He said: "I will never be able to live with myself again. He should never have been hung for it."'

Brifman would also soon meet the police commissioner. Author Peter James once interviewed Bischof's former driver, Earl 'Slim' Somerville: 'He told me he used to drive Bischof around to all the brothels once a week. The madams and the girls would all be standing to attention when he arrived, and handed over the money.'

Brifman's working name was Marge Chapple, taken from her sister.

As far as her family knew, in Brisbane she had launched a new and promising career – as a receptionist.

Rats, Bodgies, and Drinks at the National

Members of Brisbane's CIB noticed a change in Detective Lewis by the late 1950s, when he started regularly partnering with Murphy and Hallahan.

Up until then, Lewis was considered a smart operator but not a hard-nosed police officer. It was a combination of his demeanour, his sloped shoulders, his slight lisp. There was the rumour, too, that he had only been granted the favour of Police Commissioner Bischof because of his family connections to the Brisbane racing scene via his mother and the Hanlons. For whatever reasons, he was seen as a weak officer, not handy with his fists, not easily driven to the sort of snap violence and brute force that had served many of his colleagues so well.

But when he teamed with Hallahan and Murphy, they noted a different Lewis. He drew off the substantial physical presence of both men. He enjoyed their power. While remaining largely in their shadow, his association with the two possibly fulfilled something lacking in his character. Conversely, being a component of the trio gave him a form of proxy protection both within the force and on the street. It was now Murphy, Hallahan, *and* Lewis.

'In those days, meeting Lewis was about as exciting as watching grass grow,' former *Telegraph* police reporter Ken 'Digger' Blanch recalls. 'He was a pleasant young fellow, and said to be good at his job, but I can't remember him making any important pinches.

'He always seemed to us to be one of the quiet coppers. He

wasn't flamboyant. But for some reason Bischof teamed him up with Hallahan.

'You have to remember that the Consorting Squad in those days was extremely powerful. The consorting laws gave them enormous power. If you were eligible for the Consorting Squad's attention, there was no invitation to come and have a talk at the CIB. The invitation was to get in the fucking car.'

It was around this time, too, with the teaming of Lewis, Murphy and Hallahan, that the tag 'Rat Pack' – Bischof's favoured trio – first began to emerge.

'There was [a Rat Pack], without a doubt,' Lewis says, 'but I could never understand why I was included in that. I was supposed to give it an air of respectability? I don't know . . . It wasn't until later years it got a sinister connotation.

'I never knew Bischof as a grafter, a crook, a pants man. I knew him as a drinker and a racing man.'

Lewis's police diaries reveal, too, that when he was partnered with Hallahan he repeatedly confronted a different range of offences, and a largely different criminal milieu from his days with, for instance, Abe Duncan and Hoppy Hopgood.

Forget drunks and vagrants, with Hallahan he was now in the thick of rapists, robbers, and interstate criminals. He was also dropping in late at night on the city's many dozens of bars and pubs. The regular visits to the city's brothels continued apace.

A typical police diary entry in early 1959 reads: 'On duty with Det. Hallahan. On foot patrol of Arcadia; Globe; Carlton; Australian; British Empire; Her Majesty's; Grand Central; Embassy; Ulster; Exchange; Victory; Royal; Gresham; Albert; Windsor and Lennons Hotels.' Or: 'On duty with Det. Hallahan. To Margaret Street brothel re: inmates. To Grand Hotel. To Killarney brothel re: inmates.'

Former detective Ron Edington recalls the CIB in the late 1950s: 'It wasn't like going to work, it was like going to a party every day.

You'd go to hotel after hotel and drink. You knew the men who ran the hotels and the waiters.'

Police Commissioner Bischof's favourite watering hole was the National Hotel, owned and run by the well-known Roberts brothers – John Robert (Jack), William Rollinson (Rolly) and Maxwell James (Max). Perched on a corner tongue where Queen and Adelaide streets intersect at Petrie Bight, within view of Customs House, the National was built in the 1880s with two storeys, later expanded to four, and had the prerequisite wrap-around verandahs and cast-iron lace. Upper-level bedrooms in the Victorian Gothic pile had splendid views of the river and Kangaroo Point well into the twentieth century.

But by the time the Roberts brothers took over the hotel in 1958, the establishment was run-down and losing money. Jack was the business brain of the trio. Rolly had been running the Treasury in George Street, opposite CIB headquarters, since 1957. Max was to revitalise the National.

'Bischof was friends with Rolly Roberts,' Lewis recalls. 'They had the National Hotel down the Bight. Rolly had the Treasury and he was a lovely man, very personable and a lovely chap. Jack was a real businessman but nice enough. He was very, very much about business. And Max was the man about town.

'From the Branch, naturally, if we're going to have a beer, we'd go to the Treasury. Rolly then moved down to the National with Max and we would certainly go down there and have a drink with him. Bischof would go there and have lunch with him from time to time.'

Max, the more gregarious of the brothers, lived in the hotel from the time they took over and quickly turned around the hotel's fortunes, reconstructing the internals, installing spaces for a cabaret lounge, snack bar, a more formal dining room, private bars and a 'Steak House'. With the transformation complete, the hotel became hugely popular. By 1963, twenty to twenty-five thousand people were passing through the place per week; the tills were so full of money they had to be emptied on the hour.

On a morning in March 1959 – a Sunday – National Hotel night porter David Young took a phone call at reception from someone who asked to speak to 'Maxie'. He put the call through to Max Roberts, who told Young shortly after that a 'friend' was coming in to pick up some beer – clearly a breach of the *Liquor Act*.

The 'friend' was a police officer, who paid for and left with the beer. He shortly returned with several other detectives. Max Roberts came downstairs and the police informed him and Young that they were to be charged with illegally selling alcohol on a Sunday.

Roberts denied any knowledge of the phone request and the sale of the beer, leaving Young saddled with the blame. Young, in turn, later saw State Licensing Inspector Norm Bauer about the incident. The charges were ultimately dropped, and the word filtered back to Young that the officers involved in the raid were rapped over the knuckles for 'daring' to even attempt prosecution against the National.

Meanwhile, the hotel developed a reputation as the one favoured by the most powerful police in town, and soon assorted police-related functions were regularly held there and visiting interstate officers were booked in to enjoy the hospitality of the Roberts brothers and their old family friend Frank Bischof.

It was stronger than rumour that a call-girl service was operating out of the National. Male visitors would be approached by a girl who asked: 'Do you want a match?' If a man wanted a call girl, he'd reply: 'Oh yeah, well, I'll have to go up to my room.' He would then repair to his room, where a girl would soon call on him. She'd say: 'Here's your towel.' If he wasn't pleased with the look of the girl, he asked for another towel.

Out on the streets, the Rat Pack found a new target – rock'n'roll music. The North American phenomenon had made its way to Brisbane, and Bischof was not a fan of its 'demoralising influence'.

In July 1957 he acted to halt a prospective six-day rock'n'roll marathon to be held at the Caledonian Hall in Elizabeth Street. He informed the event promoter 'of the actions he would instruct detectives to take if and when such contests commenced here'. The contest was cancelled.

The 'actions' of Bischof's detectives became clearer by 1959, as the popularity of rock'n'roll continued unabated and a sub-culture – the bodgies and widgies – developed out of the craze. In their pegged pants and petticoats, they were a phenomenon in the wake of James Dean and maligned as louts, as rockers thumbing their noses at decent values.

And who else would Bischof call upon to enforce his own values in conservative Brisbane but his trusted boys – Murphy, Hallahan, and Lewis?

In his book, *It's Only Rock'n'Roll But I Like It*, Geoffrey Walden records musicians and ordinary Brisbane citizens encountering what colloquially became known as Bischof's 'Bodgie Squad' during the late 1950s.

Brian Gagen of the band The Planets recalls: 'There were a couple of rogues involved in that . . . Hallahan and Murphy, they were involved in the Bodgie Squad. Didn't they have a good time beating people up. They just thought that anyone in rock'n'roll just needed a clip in the ear and they proceeded to give it to them.'

Others had memories of young males being taken down to CIB headquarters, where their dark shirts were replaced with 'Woolworths-type white shirt and suitable tie'.

Walden writes: 'The dark shirt was returned to the owner wrapped with advice: "That's how you come to town, you wear a white shirt and tie, you don't come here wearing a black shirt, you look like a criminal, that's it. Get rid of that haircut, get rid of those clothes, this is how you should be dressed."'

A conservative but expensive dresser, Police Commissioner Bischof was making sure his idea of sartorial decency was forcibly impressed on the next generation of Brisbanites.

A Night to Die

Detective Lewis, on duty with Hallahan, claims he was sitting at his desk at CIB headquarters in the early hours of Saturday 8 August 1959, typing briefs, when he received an unexpected phone call from Killarney brothel prostitute Ada Bahnemann.

He wrote in his police diary: 'Ada Louise Bahnemann then telephoned re: her husband threatening her with a rifle.'

Something was wrong between Ada and husband Gunther – the eccentric former German war hero and boat builder – and it had been brewing for some time.

In February of that year, Lewis recorded in his police diary that he 'saw Ada Louise Bahnemann re her husband's conduct'. Then three months later, while on duty with Hallahan on the night of 25 May, he 'saw' her again, presumably at either the Killarney or Nott Street brothels as both officers were on patrol in South Brisbane.

On that Saturday morning in August, however, Ada told Lewis that Gunther was threatening to shoot her with a .303 at their home at 217 Whites Road, Lota, in bayside Brisbane.

Lewis then telephoned Wynnum police station and instructed Constables John Morris and Jim Shearer to head out to Lota and exercise 'caution'. Lewis and Hallahan, both armed with pistols, then hopped into a squad car and drove to the Bahnemann home.

They arrived at 2.16 a.m. and approached the fibro bungalow – a former army hut – which was set back from the street on a deep block. Ada was at the front door. She warned them that Gunther was in the bedroom with the loaded rifle and had already threatened to shoot the two Wynnum constables. Through the front door Lewis could see his two colleagues in the house.

They found Bahnemann in the bedroom, sitting on the double bed, wearing a pair of green pyjamas. He was holding the rifle with both hands and had his right index finger on the trigger.

According to later statements by Lewis and Hallahan, as Lewis entered the room Bahnemann supposedly said, 'Don't try any tricks, Mr Lewis, and stay where you are, and don't try to draw your gun. This gun is loaded and if you move any closer I'll blow your guts out. I am not joking.'

Bahnemann cocked the rifle and Lewis noticed the gunman had blood on his pyjama jacket and bottom lip.

Lewis then said, 'Gunther, your wife telephoned me and said that you were threatening to kill her, and she asked us to come here and talk with you.'

Bahnemann issued a short laugh. 'Talk,' he said, 'you'll have to do a lot of talking to save her. I am going to kill her tonight and then die myself. Don't you agree, Mr Lewis, that she should die?'

'Why do you want to kill her?' Lewis asked.

'She is of no further use to me. I've killed before and another one, especially her, would be easy.'

Bahnemann then swung the rifle in Hallahan's direction.

'Mister, whatever you said your name was, if you try another smart trick, you're dead. Don't move any closer. I'm not joking. I'll die tonight, but I will not die alone.'

'Gunther,' Lewis said. 'Don't do anything silly with that rifle. You will only make more trouble for yourself.'

Bahnemann then launched into an uncharacteristically formal spiel, taking into account he was drugged, drunk, and surrounded by four armed police officers.

'Mr Lewis, I have taken some tablets and I'm going to die and I will take someone along with me. You know all about me. I was an *ober-leutnant* in the panzer division with Rommel's Afrika Korps. I fought the Australians at Tobruk and killed my share. Killing means nothing to me and I'll kill again tonight.'

Bahnemann then turned the rifle once more towards Lewis. Hallahan pounced. Lewis claimed that in a nanosecond Bahnemann swung the rifle towards Hallahan and fired. The bullet passed through Hallahan's left trouser leg without striking him.

In his statement later, Lewis said: 'I heard a deafening report and I saw the rifle in the accused's hand jump in an upward direction. I then jumped over the end of the bed and onto the accused.

'The accused struggled violently and several times he called out, "I'll kill you all."

'The accused said to Hallahan, "You are lucky, you should have died. You were lucky that time. I'm sorry that I missed you. I'm a German soldier and a man with a loaded rifle should be shot."'

Lewis handcuffed Bahnemann and proclaimed, 'You are under arrest for attempted murder.'

'Mr Lewis,' said the gunman, 'I'm going to die, I don't care anymore. I would not care if it was murder, but I would like to say this, I'm not finished yet, I'll kill her.' Then, pointing to Hallahan, he added: 'I'm not finished with you yet, I missed that time, but I'll get you before I'm finished.'

Bahnemann was then conveyed to the Brisbane city watchhouse.

In contrast to his police diary entries and police statement regarding the Bahnemann incident, Lewis says that he and Hallahan, though they never worked together for long, happened to be on duty that night when 'a call came in over the radio' to say a man was threatening his wife with a gun.

'Anybody could go . . . So we were near the city somewhere so we knew the area. So we went down to Whites Road, I think it was at Lota . . . and there Bahnemann . . . He married this piece, but she was on the game. And apparently he didn't object to that.

'She must have somehow got in touch with police and two uniform men came along to the house and he held them up with the gun . . . [She] must have phoned and said that he held up the two uniform police and that's when we got there and I had never struck him before. I don't think Hallahan had as far as I'm aware.'

In fact, Lewis recorded in his own police diaries that he interviewed Bahnemann in February 1955 over the Alfio Vito Cavallaro incident at Hendra, and his wife in 1956 at Nott Street brothel. With his innumerable visits to Brisbane's brothels over almost a decade, and especially Killarney and Nott Street in the late 1950s, it is incomprehensible that Lewis didn't have intimate knowledge of Ada and her family situation. She was one of a coterie of local prostitutes, along with Shirley Brifman, who were protected from prosecution by Bischof and his trusted boys – Lewis, Murphy, and Hallahan.

And if Lewis, as he says, had 'never struck' Ada's husband before, why, in the statements of Lewis, Hallahan, Morris, and Shearer for the prosecution in Bahnemann's trial, did the accused refer to Lewis as 'Mr Lewis' if they hadn't been introduced prior to that night?

Hallahan's statement differs from Lewis's account. As Hallahan entered the bedroom at Whites Road, he supposedly said: 'I'm Detective Hallahan from the Consorting Squad, what's all the trouble about?'

'Who came with you?' Bahnemann asked.

'Detective Lewis, you know him,' said Hallahan.

Lewis says he didn't think Hallahan had come across Bahnemann before that night in 1959. But what of Bahnemann's extensive periods of living in Mount Isa, and claims from locals that the two most certainly knew each other? Did Bahnemann have something on Hallahan from their Mount Isa days?

Or were Lewis and Hallahan simply protecting an asset – one of Killarney's untouchable prostitutes?

Both Lewis and Hallahan went to great pains in their statements to point out that Hallahan and Bahnemann were not acquainted. 'Mister, whatever you said your name was,' Lewis recalled Bahnemann saying to Hallahan. Hallahan's statement reads: 'Mr. Whatever you said your name was.'

The four original draft police statements also bear some curious features. Lewis's was typed on a different typewriter from those of Hallahan, Morris, and Shearer, who, it seems, all used the same machine. Their statements carry an identical typeface, though a line at the top of each reveals the statements were made in different locations – CIB, Wynnum police station and Woolloongabba police station.

In addition, the statements of Hallahan and Shearer carry amendments in Lewis's own distinctive handwriting.

To confuse things further, Lewis recorded the following in some jottings he made after the incident: 'On Tuesday about 4.30pm in Day Room, Wynnum Police Stn. And Glen typed both statements.'

Police later interviewed Ada, who said she had ceased working as a prostitute on 28 February 1959, but returned to a house of ill-fame shortly after, under pressure from her husband. She said he 'wanted money to complete the building of a new boat' and had threatened her with violence if she did not get back on the game.

She said that on the night of the attempted murder of Hallahan, Bahnemann had again attempted to force her back into prostitution and an argument developed, leading to his threat to kill her.

In his account of the interview with Ada, Lewis curiously wrote: 'She further informed us that her husband had "a set" on Detectives for stopping her at earning money from prostitution.' This would appear to provide a flimsy motive for Bahnemann's attack on Hallahan.

There was a further glaring anomaly in the story, courtesy of Constable Morris's official statement. He said he was on duty in Wynnum when, at 1.15 a.m., he received a phone call from Lewis, who told him that Ada Bahnemann had phoned a few minutes earlier and had informed Lewis that Bahnemann was threatening to kill her with a .303 rifle.

But before Lewis and Hallahan arrived – Morris standing in the bedroom with the agitated Gunther Bahnemann – the crazed gunman made a special request.

'I would like to talk to Mr [Buck] Buchanan or some Vice squad detectives,' Bahnemann said to Morris.

'We will go and try to get them for you.'

Morris said he then left the room and communicated with the CIB 'per medium of the police wireless' and advised the branch that Bahnemann wanted to speak with Buchanan.

But why would Morris leave the scene, and his junior partner staring down the barrel of Bahnemann's loaded rifle, if he knew that Lewis and Hallahan were on the way? He could have asked for more backup from local police stations but instead simply passed on Bahnemann's peculiar request.

At his trial the following month, Bahnemann pleaded not guilty and claimed he'd been verballed. The jury found otherwise, and he was sentenced to seven years' hard labour.

Bahnemann claimed at the trial, and for decades later, that he became suicidal that night because he'd learned that his wife had been working as a prostitute. That's patently untrue, if Lewis's diaries and his record of contact with the Bahnemanns over the previous few years are to be believed.

But did his arrest go according to the accounts of the police present on the night?

At his sentencing in the Supreme Court of Queensland on 20 October 1959, the judge said: 'Well, giving full weight to your condition of mind, I must also give full weight to the evidence, as it appears the jury accepted the evidence, and it is my duty to prevent you and others – who may be like-minded – from attempting to kill policemen, who, in the execution of their duty, are called upon to protect the lives of the citizens of this state.

'I may say now the actions of the policemen concerned in this episode exhibited a very high degree of courage and devotion to duty. It seems to me, in particular, Hallahan, who attempted to disarm you by jumping upon you at point-blank range when you had a loaded .303

rifle in your hands menacing the four policemen who were present, had an almost miraculous escape from your murderous intentions.'

Ada never visited Bahnemann in Boggo Road gaol. She quickly sold the house in Whites Road and moved to New South Wales.

Almost thirty years after the incident, Bahnemann said in a newspaper interview that he had been verballed by Hallahan and Lewis.

'I was mentally deranged . . . a very angry man,' he recalled. 'I took a whole lot of my wife's tablets. I was going to commit suicide. I was on the bed. I had a .303 rifle. I had it lying on top of me with one hand on it. It had one bloody bullet in it. If the tablets didn't work I was going to stick it in my mouth and pull the trigger and go out of this world that way.

'My wife came home and she called the local police. They behaved decently . . . I don't know how Hallahan and Lewis got into the act at 2.30 in the morning. My wife could have phoned them.

'They came in fast. Hallahan grabbed at the rifle. My arms were powerless. I was so stiff from the tablets I couldn't raise my arms.

'Hallahan twisted it and he had his finger around the trigger and it went off. It hit the wall low down.

'I made no threats. If I wanted to kill someone in that small room I couldn't have missed.'

Bahnemann said he believed the police had refused to allow Ada to attend his trial or give evidence, and that she relocated to Sydney at their instigation.

As for the two Wynnum constables, Morris and Shearer, their memories of the incident also throw up anomalies.

More than half a century later, Morris is still reluctant to discuss that night. 'I'm not a person that discusses it with too many people,' he says. 'Well, I don't discuss it because people ask and I'm not prepared to tell them . . . We did our job that particular night and we just became involved in that particular incident. It wasn't our choice; that was a part of our deal, that's a part of being a police officer.'

Jim Shearer says it was not Lewis who first took the call about the unfolding drama that evening: 'I was of the opinion that Johnny Morris took the phone call and I'm of the opinion it came from her [Ada]. And she was ringing from a phone box up the road.'

Both men went to the house and met with Ada. They encouraged her to stay away from the scene while they entered the house and confronted Bahnemann in the small bedroom.

Shearer adds that Bahnemann 'said he wanted to talk to Hallahan and Lewis and so Johnny Morris left – he was the bravest one, he was the smart one, he left and he went out and called out over the car radio to Hallahan and Lewis – and we didn't even know whether they were working or not, but anyway they were'.

As for Bahnemann deliberately trying to murder Hallahan as the heroic detectives attempted to disarm the gunman, Shearer says: 'Yeah, well, you know, we sort of had some doubts. Johnny and I talked about it naturally afterwards, and whether he was actually trying to shoot us or . . . whether it just accidentally discharged.

'A far as a medal went, yeah, I felt Lewis should get one but it was a bit of a toss-up who would get the top one and who would get the bottom one, and I think they just wrote a better story than we did . . . They sort of embellished their part a bit, where we were just the boys in blue in the background.'

Police Commissioner Bischof gave all four police officers commendations, and it was recommended that Lewis and Hallahan be put up for the police force's highest honour – the George Medal for Bravery.

Miss Hamilton Has Had Enough

Hallahan and Lewis were the toast of the town after the Bahnemann conviction.

In the CIB, rumours began circulating that the pair had 'planted' the rifle on the former German war veteran and engineered their own heroics. But other police believed the conjecture was yet again the work of the branch's entrenched 'corridor assassins', intent on upholding the age-old sectarian rifts within the police force and using any circumstance to undermine Police Commissioner Bischof.

Bischof himself took a week's leave in early October. It wasn't by choice. Bischof never took holidays, especially now that he had the top job and with his deputy – the Catholic Jim Donovan, passed over for Bischof's position – breathing down his neck. The police commissioner was ordered to have a break.

As he had before, he spent his vacation at hotelier Rolly Roberts's holiday house on the Gold Coast. He often took his lover Mary Fels, and another rumour riffled through the CIB that a photograph of Bischof and Fels sunning themselves on the beach was in existence. Catholic spies within the force had been diligently documenting Bischof's every move, waiting to entrap him.

While Bischof was out of town, and with Donovan as acting police commissioner, the city's heroes, Hallahan and Lewis, took a small matter of business into their own hands. They went to pay a visit to Miss Leigh Hamilton.

Hamilton, then in her late twenties, had emigrated to Australia from Germany in the early 1950s and ended up in Brisbane a few years later. The brunette worked as a prostitute in the city's tolerated brothels but was deemed a 'troublemaker' by the other girls and by 1959 was working out of her apartment in Ashgrove, in the city's inner west, as a solo operative. She used contacts within Brisbane's taxi fleet to help drum up business.

In Bischof's absence, Hallahan and Lewis visited Hamilton and told her that protection money had now doubled, and they would be around to collect on the next Saturday. Lewis says that Hallahan, who invariably liked to work alone and often disappeared on police partners, went in to see Hamilton that day while Lewis stayed outside the

MISS HAMILTON HAS HAD ENOUGH

property. He says he wasn't aware of what was said between Hallahan and Hamilton during that meeting.

Incensed, Hamilton made a personal complaint to Acting Police Commissioner Donovan. Here, at last, was an opportunity to entrap Bischof's bagmen and potentially bring down the police commissioner himself.

Donovan instructed two inspectors to hide in Hamilton's apartment on the day of the pick-up and catch Hallahan and Lewis in the act.

That Saturday, Hallahan and Lewis were on the 3 p.m. to 11 p.m. shift. They had arranged to meet Hamilton at her home at 3.30 p.m. By chance, Murphy was on duty at CIB headquarters that day when he received a call from another prostitute, tipping him off about the Hamilton sting.

When Hallahan and Lewis arrived for duty, Murphy took them aside and warned them of the trap. The two men had to think quickly – clearly Jim Donovan was onto them, and this had the potential to develop into a major incident. After the Bahnemann success just weeks earlier, the city's heroes now faced exposure as Bischof's collect boys.

With Norm Bauer, now head of the Brisbane CIB, also on leave, Hallahan and Lewis went in to see the acting CIB chief, Bill Cronau – the legendary detective known to all police as 'Uncle Bill' – and tried to pre-empt the fallout.

They spun a story that they had been contacted by a prostitute by the name of Leigh Hamilton, who had made a complaint about a German taxi driver extorting money from her. Could Hallahan and Lewis go out and hide in her apartment and capture the rogue trying to extort from her?

Cronau exploded: 'You've been tipped off. Get out of my office, you bastards.'

Jim Donovan wasn't so dismissive. He instantly demoted the two officers and told them to report for plain-clothes duties on Monday morning at Roma Street police station. Their glittering careers seemed over in an instant.

Lewis's police diary number 896, beginning in February 1959, abruptly ends with a short entry for Saturday 3 October. He clocked on at CIB headquarters at 9.30 a.m. that day, attended to files, wrote up his police diary, went to Doomben racecourse with Hoppy Hopgood, then finished work at 6 p.m. The remaining sixty-three pages of the diary are blank. 'The diary was confiscated,' Lewis says.

Hallahan and Lewis telephoned fellow officer Ron Edington, who in the recent past had had a number of legal confrontations within the force.

'We met at the Highway Hotel at Rocklea,' Edington remembers. 'They gave me the whole story about Leigh Hamilton and Donovan standing them down. They were terrified about what was going to happen. This was it. Donovan was going to expose Bischof and prove he was using men like Hallahan and Lewis – the Rat Pack – to pick up money for him.'

Word got through to Bischof and he rushed back from the coast to Donovan's office up at the old police depot on Petrie Terrace. He immediately terminated the transfers on the proviso that Hallahan and Lewis would not work in the Vice Squad.

Reporter Ken Blanch, who used to pop in to CIB headquarters at least three times a day – the *Telegraph* offices were a short walk away, in Elizabeth Street – remembers entering the old church building shortly after this incident and seeing Lewis at the top of the stairs.

'What are you doing here?' Blanch asked. 'I thought you were on your holidays?'

'Cronau tried to set me and Hallahan up,' Lewis replied.

That was not the end of the drama. Bischof could see a sectarian stand-off looming, or worse, the entire fiasco finding its way to government ears. It could hit the press, and be the end of his commissionership.

He proceeded to invent a fantastic story to cover up the ructions on the ground in the police force, and Hallahan and Lewis's exposure as his bagmen.

Thomas Hiley, the state treasurer of the day and no fan of Bischof, recalled the extraordinary fallout from the incident.

'One day [Liberal Party leader] Ken Morris came in . . . with a Minute to Cabinet – no warning about it – that we close all the brothels. And I remember as well as can be Premier Frank Nicklin looked a bit surprised.'

When questioned by his colleagues about the recommendation, Morris said Bischof was angry with the brothels because they were not passing inside information on the movement of local or interstate criminals back to police. He said they weren't keeping 'their part of the bargain', so the brothels would be padlocked.

Hiley protested that the action would drive prostitutes onto the streets and into hotels and bars in the city.

'Oh well,' Morris replied. 'This is Bischof's recommendation and I'm submitting it.'

The premier was concerned about it. According to Hiley, the then Liberal member for Toowong, Attorney-General and Minister for Justice Alan Munro issued a warning: 'If we refuse . . . and it comes out that after getting a recommendation from the Commissioner of Police that brothels be closed, and this Cabinet intervened to keep them open, we would have some awkward explaining to do.'

Cabinet agreed to the recommendation.

Bischof's smokescreen had worked seamlessly, and he immediately ordered Bauer and others to go around to all the brothels and put brass padlocks on the doors.

Shirley Brifman was working at Killarney brothel when the order came down. She recalled in a police interview years later: 'The collect boys were Lewis, Murphy, and Hallahan. That went to Bischof. How much they got and how much Bischof got I do not know. They were his trusted boys.

'Once he went on holidays and they decided that the fees would go up and collect a bit more for themselves. Bischof came back. He could not charge them. The only thing he could do was to close [the brothels] and shut his mouth.'

The day after the controversial lock-up, a small story featured in a local newspaper: 'Police have taken action on certain houses in Brisbane . . . Last night their doors were shut and fastened with big brass padlocks. It is the first "serious" shut-down since the houses began operating before the First World War.'

The *Sunday Truth* went even further on 18 October: 'Two detectives were taken off the Consorting Squad of the Brisbane Criminal Investigation Branch, and transferred to other duties, this week.

'This was a prelude to further overhaul of the Squad which is now planned, and other action to be taken by the Police Commissioner, Mr Bischof.

'Another result of the moves was that the Government decided to direct the Commissioner to clamp down on certain serious vice activities in the city. As a result, a number of houses regarded as undesirable resorts were closed down during the week, without notice.'

While politically ingenious at the time, Bischof's successful protection of two of his 'trusted boys' and his own personal kickback scam would have huge ramifications for him, the Rat Pack and the force in the near future.

Almost two years later, to the day, the body of prostitute Leigh Hamilton was discovered in a house in Hawthorne, in the city's east. She lived alone and had been dead, apparently from an overdose of sleeping tablets, for about three weeks.

The *Sunday Truth* reported: 'Miss Hamilton, one of the city's most notorious good-time twilight girls a few years ago, hated policemen so much that she was prepared deliberately to trump up charges against them.

'Leigh Hamilton is believed by many to be the woman responsible for the closing of Brisbane's houses of ill-fame in 1959. It has been claimed that because of her vicious under-cover attacks on police that the word finally went out to close the houses.'

In the end, the press asserted – and the public was given to believe – that the brothels were shut down because of the vicious rantings of an alcoholic drug addict and prostitute with a loathing for the law and the men who enforced it.

And Leigh Hamilton – in death – had unwittingly garnered the honour of being the first of several prostitutes to die of a drug overdose after crossing paths with Glendon Patrick Hallahan.

Another Good Day at the Races

When Jack Herbert first reported for duty at the Licensing Branch, on 21 May 1959, on level one of the dour old police depot on Petrie Terrace, he was immediately struck by one thing: these detectives didn't dress like any others he had worked with in Queensland.

Herbert recalled in his memoir: 'Their clothing and cars and what-have-you were much better than what I had been used to and I was older than most of them. That was one inkling I had that there must have been, as I put it, a quid around . . .'

It was whispered, too, that one officer – Senior Sergeant Harry Falcongreen – was taking money for protecting SP bookmakers. Herbert decided to test the rumour.

'I went with Harry Falcongreen one Saturday morning and asked him for a loan of the police motorbike – permission to go to the garage to receive it,' Herbert said. 'He asked me – why did I require the motorbike? – and I falsely stated to him that I was going to follow a bookmaker and obtain the address where he was going to and then I was going to raid the place. It seemed to give him some concern and I also mentioned that to a number of men in the office.'

As he made his way towards the garage at the back of the police depot, fellow officer Doug Chapman tugged at Herbert's coat and asked where he was off to. He explained his plan to nab an SP bookmaker.

Chapman asked him to forget the job and to join him at the Prince Consort Hotel in Fortitude Valley for a drink after 5 p.m. It was just weeks before Christmas, 1959.

When Herbert arrived at the bar he saw Chapman and several other members of the branch.

'After a few beers I was told that from now on I'd be receiving twenty pounds a month as my share of the protection money coming from various SP bookmakers. They called it the Joke.'

Herbert was advised which officers in the branch he could talk to about the Joke. They included two sergeants and an officer called Graeme Parker.

'Bob Johnson was the main organiser of the system and we became quite friendly,' Herbert recalled. 'He had a list of [phone] numbers of all protected SP bookmakers. These numbers were supplied to him by various members of the Licensing Branch.

'On Saturday [race day] morning every person that was working that day would receive a phone call from Bob Johnson in the morning before he proceeded to work and would read out a list of numbers. Those numbers were taken with you to work and that was your list for the day should any numbers come up.'

In the event of any raids, Johnson was to be called in advance and he in turn would contact the bookmakers. When Johnson went on leave, he handed Herbert the operation of the Joke. Herbert was fastidious with most things, and the same applied to his organisation of the Joke.

When cars went out on Licensing Branch jobs, it was always arranged to have at least one member of the Joke in each vehicle so that all possible eventualities were covered.

At least half of the twenty-two-man branch was in on the corruption scam.

'At first Peggy [Herbert's wife] didn't know where the money came from,' Herbert recalled. 'I used to tell her I'd had a good day at the races, although she knew I wasn't a gambler. It didn't take her long to cotton onto what we were up to . . . After that it became a favourite saying of ours. Whenever I handed Peggy some money I'd say, "Another good day at the races."'

Lewis says that at some point in the 1950s he was invited to join the Licensing Branch by Sub-inspector Bob Nesbitt but immediately declined.

'I didn't like the work they did,' he says. 'And the fact that they called themselves detectives. I didn't think they were detectives' arseholes, any of them. And I didn't like the idea of going around and pinching SP bookies because in those days most of them were hardworking, decent people. They were either a butcher or a hairdresser or someone working in a pub.'

Lewis says the Licensing boys 'did nothing' on prostitution.

'But we used to do it in the bloody Consorting Squad because nobody else was doing it. Their job was to go around and check; they'd go around I suppose and say good day and get a quid from them if they could.'

It was clear to Lewis that there was money going around. The Licensing Branch men, for one, had a better cut of dress than the rest of the force.

'They'd roll up to court,' he says, 'having pinched SP bookies by arrangement, there was no doubt about that. And they'd go before the court and when they arrested people they'd take possession of their documents and it was renowned – I don't know if it was provable or not – that after the offender went before the court and was fined the cursory amount of licensing tax, that for a certain amount of money they'd get their records back.'

Nevertheless, Herbert had launched his alternative career as 'the Bagman'. Lewis and Hallahan had escaped demotion over the Leigh Hamilton incident and owed Murphy for their careers. It was fortunate in many ways for Lewis. He was, by now, the father of three children – Terence, seven, Tony, four, and Lanna, eighteen months.

Bischof, in seeking the closing of the Brisbane brothels, had on one hand diverted attention from his corrupt practices and those of a select group of Queensland police officers. On the other, he had sent the city's prostitutes into the CBD and suburbs, where they would compete for business, uncontrolled and unchecked.

Shirley Brifman soon began making her way from South Brisbane across the Victoria Bridge and into the lounges of the Grand Central Hotel and the National Hotel, looking for work.

Gunther Bahnemann sat in Boggo Road gaol, contemplating his seven-year sentence for attempting to murder Hallahan.

Ray Whitrod, director of the Commonwealth Investigation Service, was busily attempting to realise a truly cohesive federal police force. He had already set up a training school in the old quarantine barracks at North Head in Sydney, and through 1959 he held national training workshops for staff from all over Australia.

Whitrod was also knee-deep in writing and rewriting draft legislation for the establishment of a national policing body. It was increasingly what he loved about the job – the organisational side of policing, the lobbying, the translation of big ideas on paper to functioning bodies on the ground. He revelled in the intellectual rigour of the profession.

Premier Frank Nicklin was beginning to think about the state election the following year. His coalition government had benefitted from the Great Labor Split of 1957, but had they done enough to convince Queenslanders they were worthy of being returned to power? The feisty member for South Brisbane, Vince Gair, would be running again as leader of the Queensland Labor Party. Still smarting over the split, he had never stopped attacking his former colleagues in the Australian

Labor Party, giving Nicklin and his Country and Liberal members a relatively easy run.

Meanwhile, Police Commissioner Frank Bischof, childless, was named Queensland's first ever Father of the Year and presented, by the premier, with a silver tray. At the age of fifty-three and over one hundred kilograms, Bischof humbly accepted the honour and declared that – as police commissioner – it was part of his duty to look after the welfare of everyone else's children.

He was applauded for his weekly 'Saturday morning child clinic', as he described it. 'My wife and I have never had the luck to have our own children,' he reportedly said. 'But at least I intend to do my best for other people's kids.'

Lewis ended the decade with a flurry of arrests for obscene language, car theft and aggravated assault. After the Leigh Hamilton incident in October 1959, he was never again partnered with Hallahan.

Big Frank Bischof had other plans for officer number 3773/4677.

The Little Boy Lost from Paradise Street

Just before 5 p.m. on Sunday 27 December 1959, Colin Bennett, his wife, Eileen, and their eight children arrived at the Davies Park public swimming pool not far from their home in Paradise Street, Highgate Hill, for a quick dip.

It was a happy time for the family. Six days earlier, Alderman Bennett, lawyer for the down-at-heel, and the Brisbane City Council's Labor Party leader, had been preselected for the seat of South Brisbane in the forthcoming state election. One of his opponents would be the former premier, Vince Gair.

Bennett was relishing the challenge. And those close to him knew that he would be a formidable presence on George Street if he were elected.

In recent years, as he continued his pro bono work for the city's vulnerable, he had heard dozens of interesting stories of the city's underworld, and steadily a picture had emerged from the puzzle. He was told of protection money demands on prostitutes and SP bookmakers. He was informed of widespread police verballing. He was compiling a substantial dossier on corrupt police, politicians, public servants and even the city's powerbrokers from these anecdotes coming off the streets – the earliest blueprint of a system that had aligned in the innocent 1950s, and would galvanise and deepen in the 1960s.

In state parliament, Bennett could finally take what he had learned and start holding certain people to account.

It was still hot that Sunday at the pool, despite the lateness in the day. Pool lessee Bill Fleming – an old friend of Colin Bennett's from his days as a student at Nudgee College – had started draining the pool and most of the crowds had left, but it was still half full when the Bennett children took to the water.

The pool, perched on the bank of the river at the end of Jane Street, used regular city water but, without chlorine added, had to be drained three times a week. Fleming simply released it directly into the Brisbane River. It took hours to completely empty the pool.

'We often went down to the pool when it was emptying to do some swimming training,' remembers Mary Bennett. She was fourteen years old that summer. 'Little Colin had also just started to learn to swim. I was the eldest child and I didn't want to go down to the pool that day, but I was a worry wart, I'd always be running around and counting the children.'

On arrival, Eileen Bennett quickly went to say hello to Mrs Fleming in the caretakers' house adjacent to the pool. Colin Bennett, meanwhile, thought his five-year-old, Colin junior, was with his mother.

Within minutes, another swimmer yelled out: 'There's a kid on the bottom of the pool!' Colin junior was pulled from the water.

'The moment I heard that, I just knew it was Colin,' Mary says.

There was immediate panic. Bill Fleming raced to the boy's aid. He had recently learned the new technique of cardiopulmonary resuscitation and pushed water out of the child's lungs. Just a few months earlier Fleming had saved another boy in similar circumstances by using the life saving method. He applied mouth-to-mouth to Colin until the ambulance arrived.

The other Bennett children were herded towards the kiosk, where, still wet from the pool, they kneeled around a wooden table, beneath the advertisements for Golden Top pies, and recited decades of the rosary.

Mary hurried into the kiosk and tried to phone the family's parish priest at the small wooden St Francis of Assisi Church up on Dornoch Terrace, not far from Paradise Street.

'It was one of those old-fashioned dial-up phones, and I was shaking so badly I couldn't get my fingers in the holes,' Mary recalls. 'I was told that Monsignor Keating was having a rest and couldn't be disturbed.

'Then I rang Father Thompson down at St Mary's. I wanted Colin to receive the last rites. I was worried that because he had not yet had his first communion he didn't need to get the last sacraments.

'Father Thompson said I needed to get Monsignor Keating to perform the duty. I said to him: "Are you going to let a little five-year-old boy die without the last rites? If so, then don't bother coming."'

Thompson arrived within minutes. Meanwhile, the ambulance officers were working on Colin junior, trying to get oxygen into his lungs. They didn't realise their oxygen cylinder was empty.

'It was harrowing,' Mary says. 'They got my brother back for a moment. Bill worked out the tank was empty and ripped out the fixed tube from Colin's throat. It was suffocating him.'

During the entire poolside emergency, the boy supine on the concrete, Bennett cradled his son's head and shoulders beneath his left arm. Eileen led the children in prayer, then joined her husband, kneeling at the boy's feet, touching his legs.

In a desperate attempt to save the boy a full oxygen tank was retrieved from the car of the *Courier-Mail*'s police roundsman, who had subsequently arrived on the scene. As the ambulance left for the hospital, Bill Fleming broke down, inconsolable.

Colin junior was pronounced dead shortly after.

During the inquest into his son's death Bennett got an early taste of the malevolence awaiting him in broader political life. His enemies – and there were many after a decade as a Brisbane city councillor and a lawyer of unimpeachable ethics, who went out of his way to fight for human rights, whatever your social status, and abhorred corruption – attempted to lay blame for the boy's death on Bennett and his wife, citing parental negligence. At the election in May 1960, Eileen would be berated at a polling booth by a Liberal–Country Party supporter, implying that Colin junior's death was a consequence of being associated with the Labor Party.

Bennett tried to protect his children from the inquest and its publicity. He took to hiding the daily newspapers during the hearings.

The coroner's findings were inconclusive. Colin had been born with a strangulated hernia and was constantly in and out of hospital. It was nothing, Mary recalled, to come home from school and find out their brother had yet again been admitted overnight.

The family discussed the possibility that Colin may have had a heart attack – stemming from his multiple illnesses over five years – that led to his drowning. Or that the act of drowning had brought on an attack to an already damaged heart and caused his death.

Bennett put on a brave face.

At the funeral at St Mary's later that week, mourners filled the church and spilled from side and front doors, the crowd covering the small lawn and pressing towards the gates facing Peel Street.

'It certainly did change him,' Mary says of her father and his response to the tragedy. 'Dad became, in a sense, frenetic. He had to find something else to focus on.'

She later overheard her father saying to a friend that 'it would be easier if I didn't have the other children'. 'I was initially very hurt by this,' Mary says. 'But later I realised he was probably referring to taking his own life. It was because of us that he just had to get on with things.'

Colin Bennett was poised to become one of the legendary fighters of Queensland parliamentary history, its bare-knuckle conscience.

But at the dawn of 1960, with his family tucked away safely in their old Queenslander at 20 Paradise Street, Bennett's thoughts were dominated by one thing – the death of an innocent.

1960s

Dear Sir, I Have Been Directed to Inform You

At the start of the new decade, with his brush with demotion and humiliation over the Leigh Hamilton incident still fresh, Detective Lewis trod quietly and carefully.

In those first few months of 1960 he arrested, among others, a boy who stole a bicycle, and a man who shoplifted a small tin of tobacco.

And while he'd had some experience with Bischof's Bodgie Squad a couple of years earlier, it was clear that this rock'n'roll phenomenon was not going away. It, and the arrival of television, had an instant impact on Brisbane.

Suburban and city teenage dances proliferated; and along with the dances came a new wave of home-grown bands, their managers, and their bouncers – the latter usually disaffected young men from the suburbs who had found, by chance, a way to be remunerated for their natural taste for thuggery and violence.

The biggest band in the city in 1960 was unquestionably The Planets. And their bouncer was the huge, oafish John Bell. Bell went everywhere with the band, organised illicit alcohol for backstage parties, and provided his own version of law and order for the actual performances.

In the early, exciting days of rock'n'roll in Brisbane, The Planets were different. They were trained musicians who shunned the city's established promoters and organised their own affairs – from the takings to the publicity and venues. They were so popular they started their own club – Birdland, in the old Centennial Hall in Adelaide Street – where they would play a weekly gig.

John Hannay, a menswear attendant at Myer department store, became their manager. He had a talent for networking before the term was invented, and looking after The Planets began a long association between Hannay and the nightclubs of Brisbane.

Ultimately, the relationship between Hannay and the band soured.

As band member Len Austin recalled in *It's Only Rock'n'Roll But I Like It*: 'John Hannay used to do the banking at the end of the night. It was a considerable sum of money in those days. He came into us and said, "Someone's got into the boot of my car and all our money is gone." No one actually believed him. We're all pretty sure that he did it himself.'

It was this music phenomenon that gave rise to a small petty criminal set in Brisbane.

Another bouncer at the time, John Wayne Ryan, remembers the police struggling with the new clubs, the bodgies and widgies, and the whole roiling medusa of rock'n'roll.

'I was bouncing one night in the Valley and this big black Ford pulled up,' he says. 'Out stepped Murphy, Hallahan, and Lewis. They confronted a group of bodgies and they literally ordered them to take their shirts off and gave them white shirts and ties to put on. It was unbelievable.'

Police Commissioner Bischof frequently gifted troubled young men with respectable shirts and ties during his Saturday counselling sessions.

'He never had any children,' recalls Lewis. 'I think the job was his life, like others, and he used to – he got ridiculed in the media for it once – showing leniency towards young people . . . I don't know how this came about but he got some boy who got into trouble and got the mother in and presented him with a shirt or some such thing. And of course that was ridiculed by some.'

Meanwhile, Lewis was living with Hazel and their now four children in a high-set Queenslander at 28 Ellena Street, Rosalie, two houses up from the local Baptist church, and a few hundred metres downhill from Government House. They'd shifted there from a small house in Fifth Avenue, Coorparoo, in June 1957. Ellena Street cost them 3300 pounds.

Their home might have been on the floor of the little valley created by the ridges of Latrobe Terrace and the top of Baroona Road, where the older and finer homes and the red-brick churches and presbyteries perched, and it may have abutted Rosalie's clutch of old worker's cottages in Beck Street, but the Lewis family was incrementally moving in an upward direction.

The house was also closer to CIB headquarters than any of their previous homes, and Lewis would take the short tram ride through Rosalie village, past the barber's and the butcher's and the petrol station and the small picture theatre, and into work.

In mid-June 1960, Lewis received a letter in the post from nearby Government House, regarding the presentation of his bravery medal over the Bahnemann arrest and conviction.

'Dear Sir,' Lewis read, 'I have been directed to inform you that His Excellency The Governor, Colonel Sir Henry Abel Smith, K.C.V.O., D.S.O., intends to hold an Investiture at Government House, Brisbane, at 11a.m. on Friday 1st July 1960, at which he would be pleased to present you with the Insignia of the George Medal awarded to you by Her Majesty the Queen.'

On that sunny winter morning, Lewis, wearing a dark suit, white shirt, loud checked tie and felt hat, received his medal. He is pictured in the newspaper reports of the ceremony with his attractive wife, Hazel, she in a woollen dress and white gloves, proudly holding the medal pinned to Lewis's chest and looking admiringly at him. Behind her in the same picture is a young and handsome Hallahan, his own George Medal affixed beside a dark handkerchief in his left breast suit pocket. The picture caption read: 'Mrs Lewis admires her husband's gallantry award while Detective Hallahan looks on.'

Also honoured that day were Constables Shearer (British Empire Medal) and Morris (Queen's Commendation for Bravery) from Wynnum police station. Both were regaled in their standard issue police uniforms and white helmets.

All four men appeared on the cover of the June 1960 *Queensland Police Union Journal.* UNDER FIRE! read the headline: 'It is unfortunate that sufficient and proper publicity is not given in the Public Press to actual valour performed by zealous and courageous members of the Police Force . . . The coolness and courage displayed by Detectives Hallahan and Lewis and Constables Morris and Shearer in disarming a demented migrant after being fired on at point-blank range was deserving of the highest reward.'

The Dog with Two Tails

Just months after the drowning of his young son, Colin Bennett threw himself with an almost manic energy into the state election campaign of 1960. The work was a balm to the grief.

Bennett would arm wrestle former premier and Queensland Labor Party candidate Vince Gair for the seat of South Brisbane. While he had some political experience as leader of the Labor Party in the Brisbane City Council, he had failed to win the seat of Kurilpa at the 1952 state election and had not run for higher office since.

Late in the 1960 campaign, Police Commissioner Bischof launched a huge and costly public relations exercise, assuring Queenslanders that their police force was right on the job.

Given the election was just eight days away, and he had the Liberal–Country Party to thank for his top position, why not comfort voters with some friendly advice and assurances on how hard the police were working for their safety? Why not suggest how the Nicklin government cared about the wellbeing of every citizen of Queensland?

Alongside the police minister, Ken Morris, an immaculately groomed Bischof launched an anti-crime brochure entitled 'ATTENTION! Here is a Police Message'. The pamphlet featured a front-page photograph of Police Commissioner Bischof in full uniform. It had a first print run of 100,000 copies.

'Every householder in every community centre of the state will receive a call from a member of the Police Force carrying a booklet,' Bischof told the press. The one hundred anti-crime tips in the document included, 'If you must leave money for the milkman, put it in an inconspicuous place known only to you and your milkman. Change the "hideout" frequently.'

On Tuesday 24 May, the Labor Party's federal deputy leader, Gough Whitlam, dropped in on the campaign to help his state colleagues. Premier Nicklin described Whitlam as a 'would-be Labor bogy man in spats'.

Days before the election – set for Saturday 28 May – south-east Queensland was in the grip of a major rain event. Candidates traditionally conducted their impromptu street-corner meetings with prospective constituents throughout their electorates. In Brisbane, they did this huddled under umbrellas.

The poll would be Australia's inaugural television election campaign. Channel Two broadcast a pre-election forum that was hosted by Sydney presenter George Baker and featured a smattering of party figures as talking heads. No candidates took to the airwaves.

During the campaign, Bennett caused a stir by utilising what the *Courier-Mail* described as 'a modern, loud twin-speaker van' and hailing 'from a microphone on the footpath'.

Bennett's unique speakers were cobbled together by a local shop owner, Labor Party supporter, and electronics fanatic – a 'Mr Earwacker' – and the flatbed truck was borrowed from another South Brisbane supporter.

'They were loud,' daughter Mary Bennett says of the speakers. 'You could hear them five or six streets away . . . People would either stand around or sit in their houses and listen to these speeches.'

In another first, Bennett introduced to Queensland politics the idea of doorknocking every house and business in the electorate. South Brisbane contained around 11,600 voters, and the Bennett team developed a time-saving strategy.

'He had teams of supporters, including my mother, out there on Saturdays and Sundays,' Mary recalls. 'They'd pull up and target one street, then they'd go along the houses and tell voters that Colin Bennett was across the road, or next door, if they needed to talk to him. They all threw themselves into this big mission . . . Mum got involved with every ounce of her being.'

The effort was worth it.

At around 9 p.m. on the night of the election, Vince Gair, chuffing on a cigar, left his seat beside the radio in his Annerley home and gathered friends and family in the lounge area.

After twenty-eight years as the member for South Brisbane, he had been defeated.

'Don't be downhearted – I'm not,' he told his supporters. 'I am only geared to greater efforts. I'm not making excuses, nor am I whingeing. I accept the decision of the people as a true democrat.'

Two suburbs north, in Highgate Hill, the Bennett family celebrated. As had been the tradition with Bennett's council election victories, kegs of beer were brought up from the Coronation Hotel, not far from the Killarney brothel.

The next day the *Sunday Mail* ran a front-page story: 'Brisbane barrister Colin J. Bennett is just about the hero of the Australian Labor Party . . . How did he feel last night? Well, like a dog with two tails . . . The ALP had hoped for this result to break the back of the QLP but had not been sure it would happen.'

Bennett told the newspaper, 'My win just goes to prove that you cannot win an election with slander. That sort of thing will just not be accepted by a fair-minded population.'

In the newspaper photograph of a jubilant Colin Bennett and his wife, Eileen, it is evident that the new member for South Brisbane had, in just five months, aged considerably since the loss of his son.

But even Premier Nicklin's return to government couldn't take away Bennett's victory over Gair.

They celebrated long and hard in Paradise Street that night, and within months Bennett would be tearing into his favourite subjects – Police Commissioner Frank Bischof and corrupt police.

The Passion Pit

With the city's brothels padlocked, sex literally came to the streets of the Brisbane CBD. And if you wanted some female company, you could find it at the National Hotel and the Grand Central Hotel.

The Grand Central – just down Queen Street from the Wintergarden Theatre, and next door to Bayards department store (specialty: dresses and materials) – already had a dubious pedigree before the likes of Shirley Brifman and her friends Lily Ryan and Val Weidinger – all expatriates of Killarney brothel – used its bars and lounges as their business offices.

Lewis, during his days in the Consorting Squad, says he made several arrests in the Grand Central.

'Most of the prostitutes [you] used to get in Queen Street, the Australian Hotel, or the main one was the Grand Central,' he recalls. 'It used to have a bar in Queen Street and a lounge and an alleyway at the back. It was a favourite spot for prostitutes because we used to go and talk to them and pinch some of them.'

In *Johnno*, David Malouf recalls the Grand Central of his youth in Brisbane. 'It had a ladies' lounge on the second floor . . . known as the

Sex [or Passion] Pit, since it was the special preserve of Brisbane's most flamboyant tarts. They occupied a table apiece, wore glossy patent-leather shoes, carried glossy patent-leather handbags, had their hair lacquered and piled up in sculptured jet-black, peroxide or chestnut curls, pencilled eyebrows, vivid scarlet mouths . . .'

The shift from Killarney brothel made no difference to Bischof's collect boys. They continued to pick up their payments, regular as clockwork.

Brifman was even kicking back to a distant cousin, Detective Syd Currey: 'He used to work from the Grand Central one-out,' she later recalled in a police interview. 'He knew what he was there for and you would go into Bayards and meet him there . . . You would wait and pay Currey.'

He also hit up Val and Lily.

'Ten pounds was the limit,' Brifman said. 'He was the small asker. That's not bad, anyway – twice a week – three girls, ten pound each girl. The big boys were the big askers . . . Bauer was connected with the brothels. The payments would have been going from the collect boys to Bauer to Bischof.

'Norm Bauer. He'd turn to me in a half-stupor – that Sundown murder. He used to rave on and on about it.'

Brifman added that 'if Murphy wanted anything he just got it . . . Actually, there was always an excuse for Murphy: "I have to paint the house. The car is going to cost so much." There was always a reason. The children. They were tutored – the whole lot.

'Murphy was always there. He was at the hotel, everywhere. On duty when he should have been somewhere else, he was with me. He would carry on his duty at the office and make me sit on the desk.'

Tony Murphy's family emphatically denies this ever happened. His wife, Maureen, says, 'She was an informant of his. I know it's hard to understand but they have to do this . . . I knew Tony had used her. She used to ring the house occasionally.'

Another acquaintance of Brifman from her early days working in Brisbane was David Young. Then in his late twenties, Young was a barman in the Passion Pit and he got to know a wide variety of Brisbane's prostitutes, though he had left the Grand Central to work at the National Hotel before Bischof ordered the closing of the brothels. It was during this time that he was accused of illegally selling beer to police on a Sunday.

Lewis wasn't having such fun. After the Leigh Hamilton incident with Hallahan, he was seconded to the Company Squad. Forget beer and girls – he was up to his neck in forged cheques and false pretences.

He was partnered with Detective Jack Cain and his old friend Abe Duncan.

'I found it interesting . . .' he remembers. 'Someone might pinch a cheque book and start cashing them up and down the state.

'I went and introduced myself to accountants in the major banks, and asked them to let us know if they came across a run of bad cheques. In that way we could follow the trail.'

As for the Big Fella – Police Commissioner Bischof – he was enjoying regular lunches and dinners at the National Hotel with his good friend and proprietor Rolly Roberts and Rolly's brother Max.

Greg Early, a young constable at the time, says Bischof was one of a long line of 'signing commissioners'. He'd sign documents when he had to, and that was about it: 'He didn't take any active part in the running of the police force; that was done out of Legal Services. Police qualifying exams, questions in parliament, ministerial files, communications – it was all done from Legal Services, which was very powerful.

'Those types of commissioners didn't do much. They'd go out to lunch.'

Bischof loved the power and pomp of the job. He was always accompanied by two police officers as big as himself, and he went around town in his flash commissioner's car – a two-tone, automatic

Ford Customline. And that car was always driven by his loyal driver, 'Slim' Somerville.

'He was the only fellow who drove it,' recalls Lewis. 'He was a lovely bloke. Never drank. Never smoked. Never did anything except be a loyal driver and [the car] was looked after like a baby.'

Early was sometimes called upon to chauffeur Bischof when Slim went on holidays. To drive the commissioner's automatic was a dream: 'We only had manual cars at that stage and I always thought I was like a rat with a gold tooth.'

That car, too, was often seen heading out to the racetrack.

Police Commissioner Bischof, as it turned out, was a compulsive gambler. It was nothing for him to lay bets of up to 2,000 pounds at a single race meet. Often, he'd back three horses in a single race with hundreds of pounds on each nag.

Bischof laid all his bets as credit bets. Bookmakers ascribed the bets made by Bischof to a 'Mr B'. If Bischof's horse won, the bet was later filled out in full as that of 'Bischof'. If he lost, another surname was penned after the 'B'. His losses were usually attributed to 'Mr Baystone'. The ruse was well known to the city's SP and paddock bookmakers.

Mr Baystone, without question, was Brisbane's worst punter.

Meanwhile, near the end of 1960, Detective Tony Murphy was set to go on four months' long service leave. He had some relatives to visit in north Queensland, and a brick patio to build at the Murphy family home in Coopers Plains.

Detective Glen Hallahan struggled with his health through most of 1960. He had undergone a kidney operation in late 1959 and spent much of the next year getting back on his feet, taking several weeks of intermittent sick leave.

Down at the National Hotel, Hungarian immigrant John Geza Komlosy had begun work as a night porter. On his first evening on the job, he witnessed so much prostitution and drinking beyond legal hours that he brought up the matter with Max Roberts. Komlosy was told not to worry about it, the hotel was being sold and they were cashing up.

On another night, two detectives brushed past the porter, saying, 'It's okay, we're friends of Max.' It was Murphy and Hallahan.

Komlosy regularly saw the pair at the National after that, with Murphy often staying until after midnight. The porter also began to work out the regular prostitutes who frequented the hotel, either soliciting trade or using the premises for their business.

In some instances, Komlosy saw prostitutes sitting on men's laps in the bars and lounges and openly engaging in sexual intercourse. There was even a rumour that some of the rooms at the National were being used as pornographic photography studios. Komlosy got to recognise Val, Lala, Mary, Christine, and, of course, the pretty and petite Marge (Shirley Brifman).

He often witnessed Police Commissioner Bischof drinking at the hotel and attending parties in Max's private flat on the first floor. Komlosy was even asked to serve drinks to occupants of a squad car parked outside the hotel, while other police officers drank the night away inside.

Komlosy also noted the hotel's curious and unusual use of its room register sheets.

In March 1960, for example, fourteen rooms were booked out for a full week without the names and details of the occupants being entered into the sheets. This mystery continued throughout the year, culminating in October, when nineteen nights and numerous rooms were secured for fifty-eight unnamed guests. The National was as busy as ever – the bars packed, the rooms booked – but most of the people who stayed there didn't have names.

And for whatever reason, Room 35 was one of the most popular on the booking sheets. It was often secured more than once on a single night.

Komlosy, the father of three children, was confused. He had come to Australia from Hungary for a better life, and was now the night porter for what appeared to be nothing more than a fancy brothel.

He quickly adapted, selling liquor after hours to make a few extra quid, and keeping the names and personal details of prostitutes that frequented the hotel in the back of his porter's notebook. If a guest needed a lady, Komlosy was the man to see.

In a few short years, he and the National Hotel would be front-page news.

Attack Dog

Colin Bennett, the new member for South Brisbane, might have been in parliament for less than five months, but he was wasting no time in establishing himself as the Opposition's go-to attack dog and a whistle-blower in the making.

He settled quickly into state political life, and while he might not have had the sartorial elegance of government ministers like Treasurer Thomas Hiley – who wore three-piece suits, a carnation in his buttonhole and brandished a walking cane – he had an intelligence and a focus that needled at the Liberal–Country government.

Bennett also found an early ally in cane farmer Edward (Ted) Walsh, the member for Bundaberg. Walsh liked a good steak and a Bundy rum, but he also relished a verbal brawl in the parliamentary chamber.

In early October 1960, and working almost as a tag team in parliament, Walsh and Bennett took on Police Commissioner Bischof, the CIB and the police minister, Ken Morris.

Walsh called for a commission of inquiry into police corruption, and accused officers, especially the CIB boys, of 'parading around like Hollywood stars'. He could quite reasonably have had the dapper Glen Hallahan in mind, let alone the splendidly dressed Bischof.

Then Bennett entered the fray. He accused members of the CIB of presenting false evidence in court 'without raising an eyebrow, giving a blush or turning a hair'. This, again, would have fitted Hallahan to a tee. There was a running joke among some members of the force in the 1960s concerning a picture framing business in the city, near to CIB headquarters. Officers passing the framers would point to it and say, 'That's Glen Hallahan's office.'

Bennett, himself a legal powerhouse, went on to say that the behaviour of CIB officers in court could virtually convince anyone present that part of their training was to offer evidence in keeping with the prosecution's indictment rather than the true facts at hand.

He also voiced a belief that many officers knew to be fact: Queensland police were prepared to swear to anything on oath in order to secure a conviction. Bennett was attacking the tried and true police 'verbal', slang for the police fabrication of confessions.

He noted that 'very few voluntary confessions' were extracted from suspects being interviewed at CIB headquarters when 'customers' were accompanied by parents, relatives or friends; yet, in their absence, full confessions miraculously appeared, worded in such a way 'that one would think the confessors were lawyers'.

Ken Morris was adamant there would be no inquiry, and Police Commissioner Bischof generously offered any member of the public with a grievance to call him direct at any time.

One Saturday Night in Hendra

On Saturday 22 April 1961, Detective Lewis reported for duty at CIB headquarters at 7 a.m. and commenced duties.

According to his police diary and arrest log, he and Detective Price took a squad car and went to the home of a jug-eared, jut-chinned thirty-six-year-old man who lived in a Queenslander on busy Newmarket Road in inner-city Wilston. He was charged with attempting to defraud another man of fifteen pounds and taken to CIB headquarters, photographed and fingerprinted. He pleaded guilty in the Police Court later that morning and was fined five pounds.

Lewis was back home in Ellena Street, Rosalie, by 3.30 p.m.

Later that day, a race day, one of Jack Herbert's colleagues in the Licensing Branch up at the police depot – Alan Pembroke – raided a house at 299 Nudgee Road, Hendra (two streets from Doomben racecourse) with Sergeant Ron Donovan and other police.

Inside, they found Neil Cruickshank and Clarence Parsons conducting an SP bookmaking operation.

Cruickshank, caught red-handed, asked if he could take the full brunt of the charges. He didn't want Parsons involved.

'This fellow wants to take this on his own,' Pembroke informed Donovan.

'No, charge both of them,' Donovan said.

Both men were conveyed to the Brisbane city watchhouse and their betting sheets and equipment were confiscated as evidence. Bailed, Cruickshank and Parsons were ordered to appear in court the following Monday.

After their appearance, Parsons approached Pembroke and asked him if he could look at the seized betting sheets. He explained that clients were claiming they'd made bets on certain horses when he knew they hadn't.

Pembroke returned to the Licensing Branch offices and sought advice from Sergeant Gorrie, who approved the request, so long as none of the sheets went missing.

Later, Pembroke met Parsons in the bar of Lennons Hotel in George Street. Parsons took the sheets into the men's room and returned soon after. They shared a round of drinks.

As they left the hotel, Parsons asked, 'Can I get protection?' He had heard from a friend that it was possible. He suggested ten pounds per week.

'I told him I didn't know anything about that,' Pembroke later recalled. 'I would check it up for him and I would get back to him.'

Later, back at Licensing, Pembroke took the matter up with his colleague and friend Graeme Parker. Could he protect Parsons?

'That'll be all right,' Parker said.

Soon after, Pembroke and Parker drove an unmarked squad car to Anderson Street, not far from the gothic Old Brisbane Museum on the fringe of Spring Hill, to meet the two bookies.

They parked the squad car in front of Cruickshank and Parsons, who got out of their own car and joined the officers. They hopped into the back seat.

Parker was gruff and forthright. He told the bookies that their phone number for race day had to be phoned in to him or Pembroke. They weren't to 'move around' on race day. They had to stick by that phone number. And their protection agreement had to remain confidential.

They were to pay twenty pounds per fortnight. One fortnight Parker collected the money. The next, Pembroke.

Cruickshank and Parsons had joined a growing list of about thirty protected SP bookmakers.

Behind this tangled but efficient web was Jack 'the Bagman' Herbert. It was testimony to his organisational skills that Pembroke never had a discussion with Herbert about the protection racket, and in turn saw or heard nothing to suggest that Herbert, the mastermind, was corrupt.

Pembroke, when he got on board with the Joke, could only speculate about who else in the Licensing Branch might be corrupt, by monitoring who got along well at work. If several men were friendly with Parker, then it was highly likely they were a part of the protection rackets.

The genius of the system was to maintain silence between participants of the Joke, isolate them, keep them guessing. From day to day no one knew who was on the take or not. No one knew who they could trust. That, in itself, was a very powerful form of insurance.

Herbert, meanwhile, was never mentioned. Never implicated. Never suspected. He was deeply embedded, the watermark on the bank note.

Terry Moves House

By the end of 1961, and still knee-deep in the Company Squad, Lewis was finding the Ellena Street house a bit of a squeeze with four children. Hazel Lewis, who had a keen eye for real estate, had spotted a house for sale up on nearby Garfield Drive, in the shadow of the Bardon water tower.

For decades, reaching back into the nineteenth century, Garfield Drive had been the address of politicians, bank managers and surgeons. It was premier inner-Brisbane real estate, the drive itself running crookedly across the top of what was once referred to as Archibalds Hill. At one hundred metres above sea level, it commanded spectacular views across the CBD and out towards Moreton Bay to the south-east, and from its north-west aspect it took in Ashgrove, The Gap, and beyond to the hills of rural Samford.

Just a dozen or so houses were positioned on Garfield Drive, and for the Lewises it was socially a light year from the occasionally flooded floor of Rosalie, just a few hundred metres away. It was the sort of place where ladies held card afternoons to raise funds for the local church.

In November 1961 Terry and Hazel purchased 12 Garfield Drive for 5,500 pounds – an old Queenslander with views away from the CBD and sitting on tall stumps on the northern rump of the hill. They had sold Ellena Street for 4,250 pounds. Garfield Drive proved to be an extremely canny investment.

Lewis's police diaries reveal that he went on extended leave on 4 November presumably to give him time to move his family and their chattels up the ridge to their new home. He did not return to work until 1 January 1962.

He says: 'We were on the left [entering from Macgregor Terrace]. The rich side was on the right, looking over the city and the university.'

He may now have had surgeons and company executives for his neighbours, but in the CIB in the city Lewis must have wondered, in the New Year, where his future lay in the police force.

He was still close to Bischof, and the likes of Murphy and Hallahan, but nearing thirty-three years of age, with a large family and two years already served in the Company Squad – his office a pokey room in an outbuilding at the back of CIB headquarters, next to the even smaller office of the Motor Squad and a stone's throw from the commissioned officers' toilets – he must have pondered the opportunities available to rise through the ranks.

Lewis was clever, cunning, and fiercely ambitious. He did not need his picture in the newspapers – unlike Bischof and Hallahan, and to a lesser degree Murphy. If there was an alternative route to higher rank where he could fly under the radar and progress without attention or fuss, he would find it.

He had come a long way for a boy who left school at twelve. But he had to go further. He needed to work longer hours to show Hazel and the children how much he loved them.

He needed to be smart. Smarter. And it may have been in that small Company Squad room that it occurred to him that education just might be that path to glory. A single university degree would, in one fell swoop, make him one of the most educated men in the force.

The End of the Affair

In September 1962, Police Commissioner Bischof, with offsider Senior Sergeant Cedric Germain, jetted out to the thirty-first Interpol

General Assembly in Madrid, Spain. Bischof had been selected to be Australia's representative at the conference – a meeting of the world's top police officers.

The Big Fella loved to travel. And he had judiciously chosen his travelling companion. Germain, from the police commissioner's Legal Services – a small group of officers not legally trained but who worked as the boss's general dogsbodies – was as tall and imposing as Bischof, and always presentable.

Germain's job in Madrid from 19 to 26 September – and later in the United Kingdom and the United States on their six-week trip – would be to sit in conference presentations and take notes on proceedings, while Bischof did as he pleased. 'Cedric was a very decent fellow,' Lewis recalls. 'If Bischof asked him to jump, Cedric would ask how high.' Bischof was not the conference type.

Prior to the Interpol gathering, however, Mrs Mary Margaret Fels was feeling more than a little slighted. Her affair with Bischof had continued uninterrupted for almost five years. He had taken her on holidays to the South Coast and promised her overseas trips.

Now Bischof was planning to wing his way around the world, all expenses paid, with Germain. Had he at one point in early 1962 vowed to take his lover to Spain? And had he, at the last minute, reneged?

Whatever the reason, it began to dawn on Fels that Bischof was a liar, that he was using her, and that he would never leave his hearing-impaired wife, tending her cacti garden over in Ashgrove.

So Fels approached the secretary of the Police Union, Clyde Behm, a powerfully built former detective with a reputation as being a bit of a ladies' man himself. Behm had been married to Calliope Claire Behm, who had drowned in the Brisbane River in 1958.

Terry Lewis was acquainted with Calliope. They had both worked for the US army at the Bulimba shipyards during the Second World War.

'She was very pretty and I remember Behm, a big policeman then, coming in and talking to her at that time,' Lewis says. 'I heard from other people that he liked the ladies and that he had a reputation for violence . . . The story was that she jumped in the river to get away from him and drowned.'

Soon after, Fels sat down and penned a three and a half page summary of her life and times, since 1957, with Frank Bischof, Queensland Commissioner of Police. She detailed the sex. She outlined their clandestine meetings. She revealed his broken promises to her. She was not only accusing the 1959 Queensland Father of the Year and the state's symbolic moral gauge of flagrant infidelity, of being a no-good philanderer, but she was, conversely, exposing herself to the same charge. She was still living on the small family farm in Underwood Road, Eight Mile Plains, with husband Alfonso and six children.

In short, her rage must have been of sufficient depth and heat that she was prepared, in a conservative city, to destroy her own reputation and, by proxy, that of her entire family.

Behm took the statement to well-known Brisbane solicitor Arnold Hopgood, brother to Merv 'Hoppy' Hopgood, Lewis's friend and regular partner in his Consorting Squad days.

'Bischof had been rooting her and promising her everything . . . to take her on this trip overseas on a fact-finding tour – it was going to be a fuck-finding tour, we all said,' says former detective Ron Edington. 'Anyway, Behm takes the statement and Bischof finds out about it.'

Bischof hauled Behm into his office. According to Edington, the police commissioner said, 'I understand you had an interview with Mrs Fels.'

'Yes, that's right,' Behm replied. 'I've got the statement and it's in my safe.'

Bischof replied: 'In my safe I've got a file here where your wife was drowned in the Brisbane River and she had several bruises and I've since found out that you had a lot of domestic disputes. I suggest that you keep that statement locked in your safe and I'll keep my file locked in my safe.'

Soon after, Behm resigned as secretary of the union and was replaced by Merv Callaghan.

Fels's damning and salacious statement was signed by two witnesses. Solicitor Hopgood subsequently arranged a meeting with himself, Fels and the member for South Brisbane, Colin Bennett.

Bennett promised to give the document 'due consideration', and tucked it away in a desk drawer. And there it stayed.

'Throughout my sixteen years of public life I have never failed to deal with a complaint and I have always had such complaints, whether large, small, complicated or simple, properly and suitably investigated,' Bennett said of the incident in private correspondence. 'This one was a particularly difficult one and I decided to give it consideration before taking any precipitate action.'

Since joining the Queensland parliament in May 1960, Bennett had never shied from attacking Bischof and what he considered an increasingly corrupt police force. But the case of Fels was more than just a political opportunity to bludgeon the police commissioner.

As a Catholic with seven children, he understood the sensitivity. Here was Fels – a married woman of longstanding with six children of her own. Her public exposure in the affair – even at her own urging – would bring a lightning strike of shame and disgrace to the Fels family. Fels would be pitted against one of the most powerful men in the state, a man with infinite resources who was not afraid to use them. Then there was Dorothy Bischof to consider. She, too, would be hurt and aggrieved.

This wasn't a case of police drinking after hours or taking protection money from prostitutes and SP bookmakers. This could potentially decimate two families.

And once the press got a whiff, it would detonate as a huge public scandal.

Bennett, always ready to swing a punch on behalf of the voiceless, sat on the Fels case and pondered. Here was information that could demolish reputations and ruin lives, but it also had the power to severely damage the Liberal–Country government, and potentially bring it down.

Mrs Fels, growing more indignant towards Bischof by the day, pushed for action.

'During this time I was besieged with phone calls from Mr Callaghan, Mr Hopgood and Mrs Fels (sometimes before breakfast) demanding I do something,' Bennett reflected. 'Mrs Fels on one occasion even suggested that I might have "cold feet".'

Bennett was aware that if he didn't do anything, it might come back to embarrass him, so he made an appointment to see Premier Frank Nicklin. After reading Fels's document, Nicklin agreed it was 'a serious matter'.

'I informed him that I did not want to use the matter politically, or to have any public attention drawn to it, but suggested that it was something that should be investigated at Cabinet level with which he readily agreed,' Bennett said.

'I also made the comment or commenced to make the comment: "Hell hath no fury like a", and he finished off, "woman spurned".'

Bennett assured the premier that he had 'no personal animosity' towards Bischof, but as a Catholic man 'and as a man who demands certain standards of conduct', he believed that Bischof was 'wholeheartedly unsuitable for his present position'.

Bennett waited more than two months for the premier to act. Nicklin did nothing. As a last resort, Bennett brought Fels to Parliament House in George Street to meet with the premier. He refused.

The member for South Brisbane felt he had no option but to air the matter on the floor of the parliamentary chamber.

Fels had telephoned Bischof before he flew out to Madrid, warning him to expect the details of their affair to be outlined in state parliament.

On Wednesday 24 October 1962, Bennett did just that, though he didn't name Bischof and Fels.

'A certain allegation in writing containing three foolscap pages was made against a top member of the Police Force,' Bennett told a shocked house. 'The information was widely circulated and known throughout the Police Force and unfortunately the great majority of those who know of it believe it.

'It is a very serious allegation. Contained in the same report is a suggestion that the series of offences, committed over a long period of time, was committed in premises owned and controlled by the leading and well-known operator of a chain of houses of ill-fame in this city.'

Bennett further titillated parliament by exposing a series of questions he recently posed to Police Commissioner Bischof, and the answers he received.

Bennett: Would you say cohabiting with other people's wives is not
           very serious?

Bischof: I said it was a serious matter.

Bennett: Would you say a police officer who cohabits with another
           person's wife whilst on duty would be committing a serious
           offence?

Bischof: I would say so. His conduct on and off duty should be
           exemplary.

Bennett: Would you say a police officer who cohabits with another
           person's wife whilst on duty and in uniform should be
           dismissed from the police force?

Bischof: If there were no extenuating circumstances I would say that
           might be an appropriate penalty.

It was a brilliant Bennett strategy. He had embedded the answer to the riddle – who was the senior Queensland police officer sleeping with another man's wife? – in his parliamentary bombshell.

The affair was the talk of Queensland. Bennett pledged to name the philanderer in state parliament at his next opportunity – Tuesday 27 November 1962.

Then Bischof made his move. Forty-eight hours before Bennett's parliamentary appearance, the *Sunday Truth* splashed with an eye-popping front-page exclusive. A third of the page was filled with a photograph of Bischof, his hair brushed back and neat, his tie, shirt and suit coat immaculate.

Another third was the headline: I AM THAT MAN.

Bischof had outed himself.

'The Police Commissioner, Mr Frank Bischof, revealed that he was the "senior police officer" in the Bennett case,' went the story, written by journalist and Bischof's friend Ron Richards.

'Mr Bischof [said] . . . he had been pestered for years by telephone calls from the woman concerned. He said there was not one scrap of truth in the allegations it was claimed she had made.'

Bischof added that he had read Bennett's parliamentary speech on the issue when he returned from Madrid, and he revealed his relationship with Fels, who was unnamed in the *Sunday Truth* report.

'About five or six years ago a woman, then unknown to me, came to my office at the Criminal Investigation Branch and enlisted my aid in a family upset. I was able to help her and her family,' he recounted. 'My wife and I were afterwards invited on a number of occasions to their home . . . Later the woman commenced to telephone me at my office and I had occasion to remonstrate with her.'

He then said the woman had started phoning him at home.

Bischof was congratulated by the *Sunday Truth* for his courage in stepping forward and 'removing an intolerable slur from any member of the Police Force' who might be considered Bennett's 'senior officer'.

The newspaper also declared the Bischof incident 'one of the major political crises of the Nicklin Government'.

The soap opera continued. The next day Bischof lodged a Supreme Court writ against Mary Margaret Fels for alleged defamation. It had the effect of instantly gagging public discussion – everything was now sub judice – and exposed Fels to the public gaze.

It didn't deter Bennett. He was prepared to stand in the chamber the next day, as planned, and let loose with more damaging allegations against Bischof, but a last-minute meeting of Labor's central executive – led by the member for Brisbane, Johnno Mann, known to have close, and possibly corrupt, ties with police – muzzled Bennett.

The Speaker ruled that any debate over Bischof would be sub judice.

In the chamber, Bennett expressed his disappointment at being silenced. Bischof himself was there in Parliament House that night, sitting in a lobby with a police legal adviser not far from Bennett in the chamber.

Incredibly, the front page of the *Sunday Truth* for 2 December had yet another scoop on the saga. This time it was a huge photograph of Fels, affectionately touching the cheek of her husband, Alfonso.

I AM THAT WOMAN, the headline read. FARMER'S WIFE SPEAKS!

The story described Alfonso Fels as 'a shiftworker in the city', who also had a strawberry and cucumber farm. Fels said she'd be leaving the defence of the writ in the hands of her solicitors.

The farmer's wife actually didn't speak. There were no direct quotes from her. But there was a single, sad exclamation from Alfonso.

'This has been a very trying time,' he said. 'I would like to see the whole mess thrashed out and over and done with.'

With Bennett gagged in parliament, the press silenced by the Supreme Court writ, and the Felses, out on their small farm off the Pacific Highway, left to deal with the pressures of public shame and years of waiting for the case to reach court, the scandal disappeared.

The personal fallout, however, was immediate. Mary Margaret Fels changed her name by deed poll to deflect attention. So did some of her children. And the marriage remained externally intact but behind closed doors was essentially over. The saga's impact would tremor for decades into the future.

Meanwhile Bischof had yet again secured a victory against those who would slur his good name.

The next time he appeared in the local press, he was warning the good citizens of Queensland to take care on the roads.

Conferenceville

Commonwealth Police Commissioner Ray Whitrod, having been in the top job for a few years, was offered a unique view of policing across the country courtesy of the annual Police Commissioners' Conferences.

Whitrod was entrenched in Canberra, a city that suited his temperament and his intellectual interests – here he developed his skills as a bureaucrat, studied economics and later sociology at the Australian National University (ANU), and reshaped the Commonwealth force on the back of tenets he would later attempt to apply to the Queensland police force: education and training.

Even in the early 1960s, Whitrod worried over the public perception of state police forces as populated with uneducated rednecks. In building his Commonwealth unit, he also had to establish meaningful cooperation with the individual state forces if his national vision was going to work. Whitrod would need their help.

How, though, could he overcome the reality of the situation? When he sat down with the top state commissioners, he was virtually the only one in the room with a tertiary qualification, let alone a university degree. When he then met with federal government bureaucrats and ministers to discuss and debate Commonwealth police business, everyone at the table had higher education qualifications. He needed to find a way to build bridges with the states.

The annual conferences – through the prism of the state commissioners – gave him at the very least a thumbnail sketch of those disparate forces, courtesy of the individuals who were running them.

It was how he first came into contact with Police Commissioner Frank Bischof.

'Big, tall, imposing man,' Whitrod recalled in an interview. 'Never, never volunteered much at police commissioners' conferences. Never contributed much in the way of new ideas . . . Seemed happy with the world. [We] spent most of our weekends at conferences, but he would go to the races . . .'

Another senior officer who attracted Whitrod's attention at the conferences for all the wrong reasons was Fred Hanson from New South Wales.

Whitrod set up a number of senior police executive workshops for investigating the future of policing. He recruited into the workshops a number of academics from the ANU; his aim was 'to interest these pragmatic deputy police chiefs in an intellectual task'.

It was onerous. 'Try as my academic friends would to interest [Hanson], he sat most of the time looking out the window.'

One of Whitrod's great friends and mentors was Police Commissioner Brigadier John G. McKinna of South Australia. McKinna had had a distinguished military career and experience in business. After the war he worked at Quarry Industries – a local operation that would grow into a national quarry, asphalt and concrete concern. He had a degree in engineering from the University of Adelaide.

When he joined the South Australian police force as an older recruit in 1956, he was met with some suspicion, but soon became one of the force's most admired and respected figures. He was made police commissioner in 1957.

Another Whitrod supporter was Chief Commissioner Major General Selwyn Porter of Victoria.

'The three of us were interested in introducing businesslike management practices into our forces,' Whitrod recalled. 'The other commissioners were very much in favour of the status quo.

'They had risen through the ranks and were now comfortably positioned. The world was their oyster, so why change it? Why indeed when, in some cases, the world was supplying an income considerably greater than that normally earned by the head of a police force?

'At the time I had little understanding of how entrenched corruption was in the eastern states and I don't think McKinna or Porter were any better informed.'

Indeed, as Whitrod slaved away with his academic and business template for future police forces, his horse-loving acquaintance Frank Bischof was about to face his greatest challenge – the first-ever royal commission into police corruption in Queensland.

Courtesy of the Author

Gunther Bahnemann, the crazed German gunman from Whites Road, Lota, had in the meantime settled into prison life at Boggo Road gaol and kept himself busy.

Before he allegedly attempted to kill Glen Hallahan on that strange night in late 1959, Bahnemann, as unconventional as ever, had been struggling with a memoir of his time in Rommel's Afrika Korps during the Second World War. With boats to build, wives to divorce, and minor run-ins with the law, he never got traction on the manuscript.

In gaol, though, with seemingly infinite time on his hands, he returned to his literary career. He dubbed his cell the 'publishing office', and finally produced *I Deserted Rommel*. It was released to acclaim in 1961 and serialised in several Australian newspapers, including the Brisbane *Telegraph*.

Detective Terry Lewis, on publication of the book, paid Bahnemann a visit in prison and got him – the man who had attempted to kill his colleague Hallahan with a shot from a .303 rifle – to inscribe his copy.

Why would a senior detective take the time to visit a thwarted cop killer? Lewis says: 'I don't know. He had been a soldier . . . he took up with a prostitute and that didn't do him much good . . . I don't know whether I was at the gaol for something else and went and said hello out of a feeling of . . . I don't know . . . not withstanding what he did, you can still think the poor bugger's in gaol. I didn't have any motive, or anything I wanted him to do or not do.'

By 1963 – four years into his sentence – Bahnemann was finishing off his next bestseller. The novel *Hoodlum*, 'a dramatic expose' of the bodgies, widgies and teen gangs infesting the Western world on the back of rock'n'roll, purported to be based on true stories told to Bahnemann by young offenders incarcerated in Boggo Road gaol.

THIS STORY IS BASED ON FACT! the Horwitz Publications paperback screamed. 'You have never read a story quite like this!' Here was Larry Loring, the jean-wearing, leather-jacketed hood who lied, cheated, stole and fought to get whatever he wanted. Here was his woman, Kathy Morris, Jonno the prisoner, Lorna, companion to bodgies in her tight sweaters, and Detective Sergeant Jason, 'a tough but fair policeman battling with his fellow officers against the hoodlums . . . to make the streets safe'.

Bahnemann dedicated the book to Boggo Road gaol chaplain Brigadier Harold Hosier, and he inscribed Lewis's copy thus: 'To Terry Lewis, Yours is a difficult job, Terry, may you succeed in your department, Gunther Bahnemann.'

The bard of Boggo Road, however, was not popular with other inmates. They claimed that he was being treated with 'kid gloves'. That he was given the privilege of daily hot showers and unlimited visiting rights. In his cell he had a typewriter, desk and stationery. He also had the opportunity to develop and patent a marine engine.

Bahnemann was released on parole in May 1963. He told the press he had no animosity towards Lewis and Hallahan: 'I hope to go up to police headquarters sometime and say hello to Glen.'

Shortly after his release, Bahnemann wrote Lewis a letter, addressed to CIB headquarters, from a friend's home on Old Cleveland Road in Belmont.

'Dear Terry, this is just a brief note enclosed with a copy of my book "Hoodlum". I am presenting you with this autographed copy because

I remember a man with courage – namely YOU – who did not feel too big to come into prison some years ago and ask for an autograph when my first book appeared on the market.

'That, Terry, after what had happened – or did not happen – at an earlier stage, took all of a man and moral courage to boot.

'I can only ask you to look upon the past as being "past" and therefore let us concentrate on the future . . .'

Why would Bahnemann ask Lewis to move on from the past, over an incident that happened 'or did not happen'?

A Secret Meeting with the Premier

Thomas Hiley, the minister in charge of racing in the early 1960s, had a vexing problem.

His departmental staff was reporting enormous amounts of SP betting activity across Queensland, and yet according to statistics the police were securing virtually no convictions for the offence. First-time offenders were being fined, but where were the big operators behind the SP betting rings?

Hiley pondered this when, by chance, he was called on by a delegation of SP bookmakers from west of the Great Dividing Range. And they had an astonishing story to relay.

'These SP bookmakers told me there was an organised SP ring operating under a direct arrangement with the police,' Hiley recalled in an interview and statements later. 'An annual fee was set and collected from the SP operators. It was $80,000 . . . for major Queensland towns, and $40,000 for some lesser towns then $20,000 for smaller towns again.

'In return the police were to leave the bookmakers alone.'

The bookmakers believed that half the money went to local police, and the rest to Brisbane, as in Police Commissioner Frank Bischof.

Hiley asked them if they would give evidence in court. They replied, 'Mr Hiley, we'd be dead, we'd be dead.'

Hiley subsequently uncovered Bischof's 'Mr Baystone' betting scam. How could a commissioned officer on a public service wage regularly plunge 2,000 pounds on a single race at Eagle Farm?

After further investigations by his department, Hiley had enough evidence to present to Premier Nicklin. He met with Nicklin and told him the story, emphasising a lack of evidence. So they hatched a plan to bluff Bischof.

The police commissioner was summoned to George Street on a Wednesday – cunningly of Hiley, a local race day – along with Alex Dewar, the police minister.

A hijacked Bischof quietly listened to Hiley's allegations: 'Bischof caved in front of us. He made no denials of the statements that I made about the organised graft from bookmakers.'

'"What do you want me to do?" Bischof asked.

'"You started all this," Hiley responded. "You stop it."'

For a time police attention towards SP bookmaking increased dramatically. But Hiley would later admit the bluff was a grave error.

'We should have pressed home our advantage and retired him there and then,' Hiley said. 'I was silly enough to think that like a beehive, if you destroyed the Queen Bee, the whole hive will perish.'

He was wrong, he later admitted: too many officers had been exposed to the 'Bischof infection', and the 'seeds of corruption' were sown in the junior ranks.

Bischof, again, had evaded the noose.

Silent, Liar

Detective Hallahan, with his bouquet of cologne and deep voice, was his own one-man Consorting Squad on the streets of Brisbane by mid-1963.

He would be partnered with other officers on the roster sheets but even on two-man jobs he'd disappear during a shift. He seemed to have carte blanche to travel intra- and interstate on a whim. He would shoot up to Townsville in the hunt for a murderer, or down to Sydney and Melbourne on the trail of counterfeiters and safe-blowers. The keeping of detailed and accurate official police diaries was, unlike Lewis, anathema to Hallahan. Unless it suited his needs.

His impulsiveness, too, seemed to have developed – since the Sundown Murders triumph and the George Medal victory – into an aphrodisiac. It was nothing for him to pull someone out of a hotel or off the street, at a whim, and falsify evidence against them on the most minor charges. He sensed, with his self-inflated reputation and the powerful consorting laws behind him, that he had become untouchable.

It was an error of personal judgement.

On 28 June 1963, Hallahan was in the Brisbane CBD and customarily nicked another city 'vagrant' – this time a man Hallahan said he recognised as a Sydney criminal with an extensive record, Gary William Campbell, twenty-three, labourer – from the doorway of TC's, or the Top Cat Sound Lounge, in Elizabeth Street.

As a club, TC's was a sensation. When you walked in off Elizabeth Street and down a long corridor, you emerged into a large room. On the left were small platform stages with rubber bars for the go-go dancers. And straight ahead was a bar where two Greek boys from West End served freshly cooked hamburgers.

The owner, a white-suited entrepreneur from the Gold Coast, hit on a phenomenon when he opened TC's to teenagers on a Saturday afternoon. No alcohol was served.

'It was incredible,' says John Ryan, who became a bouncer and later the 'cooler', or head bouncer, for TC's. 'It was the place to go. The underage kids were hanging from the rafters. They had a DJ playing vinyl records. There were young girls everywhere.'

'Gary was a tough guy. From Sydney. We think he may have coined the word "bouncer" because when he was throwing someone out of TC's, he'd carry them down that long corridor and bounce their head off the walls as he went.'

On that winter night in June, Campbell was escorted by Hallahan to his flat, where police searched for missing blankets and pillows from Campbell's prior residence, which police claimed had been stolen. They merely unearthed several hotel beer glasses.

Hallahan told Campbell: 'If you haven't got them, you know who has and we'll charge you with having housebreaking instruments. We'll load you right up and make sure you get put away.'

Campbell admitted he only had 'five bob' in his possession, and Hallahan added that he would be charged for vagrancy.

In the magistrates court the next morning, Campbell pleaded guilty.

The prosecutor outlined the facts as provided by Hallahan: Campbell was an active criminal located in the city area; he had no money and no legitimate source of income; he'd made no effort to secure employment.

Campbell was sentenced to six months' hard labour.

Stunned, Campbell appealed. The hearing was scheduled for August. So Hallahan got busy preparing a deflection to any impending criticism from the full court, confecting his supremacy as a detective in the local press, especially with the help of his mate Ron Richards of the *Sunday Truth*.

Fortuitously, at least for Hallahan, on 8 July – just ten days after Campbell was arrested at TC's – Sydney gangster Robert James 'Pretty Boy' Walker, twenty-six, was shot down with a machine-gun outside his home in Randwick, Sydney. He suffered six bullet wounds to the torso. In the aftermath of the murder there were several wild theories as to the identity of the perpetrator.

One was Brisbane-born redhead Raymond 'Ducky' O'Connor, twenty-five, a standover man and feared gunman based in Sydney.

Sharp as a tack, Hallahan seconded the Walker killing to plant his first ruse in the local press. On 28 July 1963, the *Sunday Truth* splashed with a sensational story by Richards about how the Sydney underworld figures, or 'judges', who had ordered Walker's assassination were lying low in Brisbane and the Gold Coast.

Richards continued: 'Other information obtained in a top-secret trip to Townsville by Detective G.P. Hallahan last weekend could finally crack open the vendetta killing of "Pretty Boy", a small-time hoodlum.' The *Sunday Truth* said Hallahan had been directed to Townsville by the Brisbane CIB chief, Inspector Norm Bauer. Hallahan's old friend.

The article also stated that 'two of Australia's top detectives' had made a secret visit to Brisbane the week before, concerning the Walker killing.

One of those was Detective Ray 'Gunner' Kelly from New South Wales. Hailed as a brilliant, fearless investigator, he was notorious early in his career for either shooting criminals dead or discharging his firearm in pursuit of an arrest.

His philosophy was famous: 'If a man hits you, hit back. Hard. If a man shoots, shoot back.'

Kelly would later be found to have been heavily entrenched in corruption with his longstanding contacts in the Sydney underworld.

Kelly shared many characteristics of the young Frank Bischof and now Glen Hallahan. He always found himself in the right place at the right time in terms of major investigations. He appeared constantly in the press and cultivated specific journalists for exclusives and the lionising of his work and career.

Kelly was just a few years off retirement when he bunked down at the National Hotel during his time in Brisbane in pursuit of Ducky O'Connor. There he settled into a familial atmosphere that only the top echelon of Queensland police, in their favourite pub, could provide. He ate well and had drinks with Hallahan and Brifman and the rest of the gang.

They had only suspicion about O'Connor and his involvement in the Walker killing. But their suspicion gave Kelly a possible suspect, it publicly showed them active in the murder investigation, and it gave Kelly a chance to study Hallahan.

It was, in a sense, a meeting of master and apprentice. And Kelly clearly liked what he saw. On his return to Sydney, Kelly would mention Hallahan to Detective Fred 'Froggy' Krahe, one of the most feared and, to some, 'evil' detectives in New South Wales. He, like Kelly, had a vast criminal contact network. He was taking kickbacks from numerous corners of the Sydney underworld.

'Krahe, after Kelly meeting Hallahan, came up here on different occasions and he was told to get in touch with Hallahan,' Brifman recalled.

In the restaurants and bars of the National Hotel, the most corrupt cabal of the New South Wales police force had met its counterpart in Queensland. The doors were now open for some interstate business.

Meanwhile, Hallahan's heroics in the press continued prior to Gary Campbell's full court appeal against Hallahan's fabricated evidence.

Just two weeks after the *Sunday Truth*'s exclusive on the 'Pretty Boy' Walker killing and Hallahan's secret trip to Townsville, the young detective was on page one again, in another Ron Richards scoop.

MARIHUANA SEIZED IN SWOOP BY POLICE ON WEIRDOS, the headline read.

On the right-hand side of the page was a full-length photograph of a huge, suited Hallahan 'bundling' what appeared to be a naked man, his genitals barely covered by a white towel, towards a police vehicle. The caption claimed the man was a 'male striptease dancer'.

The story went on: 'Brisbane's seamy night life was ripped wide open early yesterday when Vice Squad detectives sensationally swooped on four secret haunts and seized marihuana reefers and other dangerous narcotics.

'In one raid at Herston police uncovered a flat full of weirdos being entertained by a male strip teaser.' The paper continued that the stripper had been entertaining 'potted' guests at midnight when police burst in.

'The early morning raids followed weeks of master planning by Brisbane CIB chief, N.W. Bauer, and Detective G.P. Hallahan of the Consorting Squad.'

It was the old Mount Isa crew, working in concert once more.

The sexy scandal did little to ingratiate Hallahan to the full court. When the Campbell appeal was heard in August and September, the judges learned that Campbell was in fact not an unemployed vagrant, but working as a bouncer two days a week at TC's when Hallahan brought him in.

Hallahan's tried and true method for securing voluminous convictions – and one of the many things, along with manufactured publicity from friends in the press, that had contributed to his standing as one of Queensland's most efficient and outstanding young detectives – had been exposed.

Justice Stanley: 'Such a disparity between truth and statement cannot be fairly reconciled with mere negligence of hasty generalisation. It is difficult to imagine a more unsatisfactory trial . . . I have come to the conclusion that, whether by deliberate intention or mere recklessness, the statement submitted to the stipendiary magistrate on this case amounted to a fraud on the court.'

Justice Hart: 'I would have gone further, and found the true story as to why Campbell pleaded guilty . . . Fraud in presentation of evidence is clear.'

The full court quashed the conviction and ordered Hallahan to pay costs.

Police Commissioner Bischof dutifully ordered an internal police investigation into the matter of Hallahan and false evidence.

Former TC's employee John Ryan claims there's no way Hallahan would have 'recognised' Campbell as a Sydney criminal when he first made the arrest: 'Hallahan was around the Top Cat all the time.

Why? Girls. Girls. Girls. He was a bit loopy at that stage, Hallahan. I politely told him once to move on. Gary wouldn't have been so polite. He would have told Hallahan to get his filthy hands off the young girls or he'd "knuckle" him. That's what would have triggered the arrest.'

Campbell, despite his victory in court, couldn't get work around town after the case concluded. Ryan believes Hallahan would have had something to do with that, too.

As for the male stripper and reefer scandal, a few weeks after the *Sunday Truth* exclusive, Colin Bennett, the member for South Brisbane, received a three-page typed letter from a concerned Brisbane citizen called T.N. Armstrong. Armstrong was the near-naked stripteaser who had appeared on the front page of the newspaper, with sales of over 240,000 copies.

He had previously written to see if Bennett would represent him in any future defamation case he may proceed with, and wrote to explain precisely what happened on the night of the 'master planned' police raids on the 'weirdos'.

Armstrong explained in his letter to Bennett, 'I was invited to the party that night by a person called Billy Phillips [William Garnet Phillips, Hallahan's closest informant]. I was warned not to go but as the flat belonged to a girl I called a friend, I decided to go.

'I was only at the Herston party for little over half an hour. I was asked to dance, having danced for quite a number of years profession-ally. I most certainly wasn't doing a striptease . . . [but a] belly and muscle control dance exactly as I have did in public before lots of people.'

Armstrong didn't know what marihuana was and had never smoked a reefer. The police rushed in around midnight and he was taken out-side by Hallahan.

'The *Sunday Truth* photographers were waiting for me,' he contin-ued to Bennett. 'I was held and told how to stand while they took at least four photos of me . . . The towel was arranged by Mr Hallahan across the front of me which when in print in *Truth* looked like I had nothing on.'

At CIB headquarters he was further photographed and provided with a single pair of 'filthy' trousers. 'I begged to be allowed to dress in my own clothes but was refused. I had nothing else on . . . and was told I could go home.'

He said since the incident he had been pulled up three times by detectives, one who asked, 'Hello, how's drugs and vice?'

Armstrong added in a 'p.s.' that he later learned the girl who lived in the flat was not home at the time of the party and not even aware it was being held. Billy Phillips had broken into the premises and organised the whole thing without her knowledge.

If Hallahan were capable of organising a break and enter for the purposes of a bogus sting and to manipulate the press and time the publication of manufactured stories for his own benefit, what else might he be capable of?

The Bum Smackers

By the winter of 1963 Detective Lewis had been back in the Consorting Squad for several months after years in the Company Squad.

While he was not specifically partnered with Hallahan, they did work together on a major job in January of that year on the Gold Coast. They prowled Surfers Paradise for criminals following tip-offs from informants and turned up several unlicensed Browning pistols along with detonators.

Later in January, Lewis joined Tony Murphy and others on a case of multiple break and enters, and in April he was again working with Murphy, this time at Eagle Farm racecourse. Later that month he was back with his former consorting partner Hoppy Hopgood.

On Monday 13 May 1963, however, Lewis's career was literally about to change overnight.

He arrived for duty at the new CIB headquarters in Makerston Street at 5.45 on that brisk morning, having travelled down from Garfield Drive, and met his partner, Hopgood. In Car 12 they patrolled Spring Hill and the south side of the city, arresting two men for being vagrants with insufficient means.

They returned to CIB headquarters and saw Inspector Bauer, then had their lunch.

Lewis was then called to Police Commissioner Bischof's office. He recorded the encounter in his police diary: 'Commissioner advised P/W Yvonne Weier and I to commence work there tomorrow, in Juvenile Aid Bureau . . . Off duty at 4pm.'

The next day, at 8.45 a.m., Lewis again turned up for work at Makerston Street. The old Queensland Egg Board building, constructed in the 1930s, was the new home to the Queensland police, and its four floors absorbed the CIB from down at the church buildings in Elizabeth Street, Traffic Branch, Legal Services, and virtually every other police department. Bischof's office was moved from the old police depot to the third floor of the building. The police commissioner had a view of Makerston Street, and possibly a glimpse of a bend of the Brisbane River.

Juveniles would often pass the building and shout out, 'There are some bad eggs in there!'

Lewis, on his first day in charge of the Juvenile Aid Bureau (JAB), was joined by policewoman Weier, the daughter of a policeman.

The attractive Weier, one of a handful of female officers in the force, was in demand in numerous departments but Lewis was pleased to have her appointed alongside him. Among her peers she would develop a reputation for being 'secretive', and 'the best person to keep those secrets' – whatever they were – contained in Lewis's JAB.

'Bischof gave me absolutely no warning I was going from Consorting to the JAB,' Lewis says.

The first thing they did was again see Bischof. Then they were off to the State Stores Department in Margaret Street to forage for equipment. The JAB was given a room next to the commissioner's office.

From its formation, Lewis's bureau was immediately known within the force as 'the bum smackers'.

As it happened, Lewis, now in his early thirties, was tiring of the shift work and demands of Consorting. He'd worked diligently around the clock for more than fourteen years, and had missed a significant portion of his own children's early years. The JAB gave him a more civilised routine, with weekends off, but he continued to work longer hours than his time sheet demanded.

The JAB was, importantly, Bischof's baby. Over the years the police commissioner had carefully cultivated a reputation for caring for the community's disadvantaged and wayward children. He lectured them and presented them with nylon shirts. He had been Father of the Year. The bureau extended the childless Bischof's public image as 'father' to the state's children.

Some police were perplexed at the JAB's location, so close to the commissioner's office. Weren't there more important considerations for Bischof than Lewis and a policewoman waving a cautionary finger at naughty youngsters? Lewis says: 'I don't know why he put us on the same floor. It suited us. We could have access to him even if it was just passing him in the passageway.'

Lewis, as ever, took his orders without complaint, and began to assemble the new bureau.

'Bischof did go to England in the early 1960s and he must have had a look at a scheme that was being run by the London metropolitan police,' Lewis remembers. 'Bischof came along one day and said he'd like to start off a similar type of thing that they were doing in England.

'They give young people a chance to be spoken to, young people who were getting into trouble, not necessarily committing crimes, but getting into trouble and causing their parents and their communities concern.

'They said pick a policewoman. In those days we had a total of seven policewomen. I was lucky to get Yvonne Weier.

'Bischof said, "There's a room there, there's a couple of desks, away you go."'

Reporter Ken Blanch contends that the proximity of the JAB office to Bischof's was no coincidence. As far as the Rat Pack as bagmen went, Blanch says Hallahan and Murphy were the 'enforcers' and Lewis 'the bookkeeper sort of thing'.

At Lewis's farewell function from the CIB, many of his old colleagues raised a glass and threw some money into a hat, including Tony Murphy. Hallahan was not on the invitation list. Civilians invited were *Sunday Truth* journalist Ron Richards and Lewis's early mentor, Wally Wright from the Fuel Board. Lewis isn't sure now but thinks the function was held at the National.

Lewis, at his quiet desk in the JAB, secured a typewriter and started from scratch.

'We didn't have a thing,' he says. 'It was a matter of sitting down and thinking, Who do we need to get on side? Most of our work came from two sources – the retail stores and the high schools. The retail stores because young people go in there and knock off little bits and pieces.'

Lewis met with the city's department store security officers and asked them to let the JAB handle any incidents of shoplifting, whereby offenders would only be cautioned and their parents informed.

'Then I went around the various schools and we started on the high schools because most of the youngsters who came to our notice would be probably between twelve and sixteen. Most of the state high school principals were marvellous. Then we went on to some of the private schools . . . Everybody was pleased to cooperate.'

Lewis says 'the bum smackers' were not immediately accepted by rank and file police, despite his experience as a detective.

He adds: 'But then, after a while of course, it really was, and then everybody's sort of kids came to our notice, from university professors to prostitutes' kids to policemen's kids.'

In fact, one recalcitrant teenager who attracted the attention of the JAB in its first week of operation was a fifteen-year-old named Lorelle Saunders.

Lewis noted in his police diary for Tuesday 21 May 1963: '8.30am. Collected car. On duty with P/W Weier. To 25 Alamine Street, Holland Park, and saw Mrs Lindall Rose Saunders re: conduct of her daughter, Lorrelle [sic] Anne Saunders.'

The following morning, the diary continued: 'To Cavendish Road State High School and saw John Stephen Wilson, H'master, then Mr Gherke; Mr Brennan and Miss Parker re: conduct of Lorrelle [sic] Anne Saunders. To Holland Park police re: same. To 25 Alamine Street, Holland Park, and saw Mrs Saunders and then Lorrelle [sic] Anne Saunders, 15yrs, and then Mr Saunders.'

Lewis vividly remembers the case. 'She'd had a crush on the school teacher and he obviously didn't reciprocate, and she and a couple of others got a hose, went to his house, shoved it under his door and flooded the house.'

Twenty years later, Saunders would be, as a member of the Queensland police, at the epicentre of one of the biggest scandals of Lewis's career, and involving an attempted murder charge against Saunders, the theft of weapons, a sexual tryst and allegations from her of corruption within the police force.

Lewis, by fate or design, had begun a ten-year period in his career where he virtually went off the radar. In his warren near Police Commissioner Bischof, he quietly worked nine to five, visiting high schools, sitting down with parents and children, putting the next generation of Brisbanites on the straight and narrow.

And in that environment he began to plot his road map to the police commissioner's chair.

A Crowded Hour

Colin Bennett, in his few short years in state parliament, never missed an opportunity to strike at Police Commissioner Bischof, but by late 1963 the volume of information he was receiving from hundreds of sources about corruption in the force was overwhelming.

Since his election as the member for South Brisbane in 1960, Bennett's reputation as a straight shooter and whistleblower had grown steadily. He became the lightning rod for tales of crooked cops, verballing, perjury, trumped-up crime statistics, police bashings, kickbacks, and dodgy internal police politics.

Bennett was still juggling two careers – politics and the law – and he intentionally handled only specific criminal cases – SP bookmaking charges, theft, and the like. In this way, he could be in and out of court quickly in the morning then return to his political life in the afternoon. He avoided any cases that might keep him occupied in court for days or weeks at a time.

He was also in the unique position of appearing for police who were either appealing for promotion or against another officer's promotion. So Bennett could be fighting against the evidence of a senior officer in court in the morning, and literally representing that same officer's interests in the Police Appeals Court later in the day.

It was not unusual for Bennett, waiting to go to court on a given morning, to enter into amiable discussions with some of the many police officers he knew through his busy schedule. And many of them told him stories of what was going on behind the scenes at Makerston Street.

If you included the tales he was offered by the city's underclass during his open-house legal aid sessions down at the Inns of Court at

North Quay, and the many hundreds of letters he received each week from the public, often with titillating allegations about police and corruption (Bennett made a point of responding to each and every letter that came to his parliamentary office and law chamber), then he was receiving a substantial amount of information about Bischof and his boys.

He had also taken on an interesting new client – a prostitute called Shirley Brifman. She had sought him out for minor matters and trusted him. Her engagement with Bennett over the next ten years would become so substantial that he would dedicate a leather briefcase solely to the work he would do on her behalf. It became known in the Bennett household and at the Inns of Court as the 'Brifman briefcase'. She too would be a font of information for Bennett.

But from 1960, Bennett had relied heavily – for his parliamentary attacks – on a single police informant. Ron Edington.

Edington, since the early 1950s, had had his run-ins with Bischof. One even spilled into the public arena at a function in the late 1950s, when both men almost came to blows.

It was the Police Department's annual dinner, always attended by the police minister and other dignitaries. On this particular occasion it was held at the Moreton Bay Hotel in Redcliffe.

'Bischof hated me because I was a friend of Col Bennett,' Edington remembers. 'I was the first uniformed man to defeat two detectives on promotion appeal. I won the appeal and Col looked after me on that one.

'On the night of the dinner I got up to respond to one of the speeches. Bischof was half bloody full and he said: "Sit down and shut up."

'I said: "Distinguished guests, you've just witnessed the actions of a man who's got the recognition of being called the commissioner of police. I would like to apologise to you gentlemen for his disgusting behaviour."

'Bischof nearly went mad.'

As the two men passed each other near the function room piano later in the evening Bischof 'hooked' Edington in the stomach and said, 'You bloody bastard.'

'I hooked him in the guts with my elbow and said, "You go and get fucked",' Edington says. 'I went to work the next day and I'd been transferred to uniform.'

Edington immediately consulted with lawyers, who recommended he launch a legal action against Bischof. He planned to serve the summons himself.

When Edington and Jim Donovan – who was passed over for police commissioner in favour of Bischof, and himself no friend of the Big Fella – were entering police headquarters days later, they were stopped by a young police officer in the corridor. The officer told them that Bischof had written a negative report on Edington and had backdated it to weeks prior to the Moreton Bay Hotel incident.

Two days later, Edington sent a message to Bischof that he knew of the backdating and would withdraw his summons if the transfer was cancelled and he received an apology from the police commissioner. To avert an ugly court case, Bischof acceded to Edington's demands.

With his relationship with his boss at rock bottom, Edington actively worked with Bennett to undermine Bischof.

'Ron gave Dad a lot of information and Dad pursued it,' Bennett's daughter Mary recalls. 'He was around at the house all the time. He'd just drop in when he was working his shifts. I think Ron thought the force was as rotten as Dad did. Dad wanted a royal commission.'

At 4.27 p.m. on Tuesday 29 October 1963, Bennett stood in a nearly empty parliamentary chamber during a debate on supply, and began: 'I propose to concentrate my attention on the Police Department and the Police Force of Queensland . . .

'I believe we have a large body of men in the Queensland Police Force in whom we can have only the greatest of pride; but I further believe that those men, in the carrying out of their tasks, are being frustrated, disconcerted and disillusioned, first of all, through the lack of attention by the Government and the Cabinet, and secondly, by the example that is set for them by the top echelon of the Police Force . . .'

Bennett went on to reveal that he had concrete evidence of how various officers charged with misconduct had received different punishments within the force depending on which 'faction' they belonged to.

The department's 'Record of Punishment of Members of the Queensland Police Force' going back to 1957 – the dawn of Bischof's reign – showed numerous instances of misconduct ranging from being drunk on duty to using a squad car for immoral purposes to indecently dealing with women at the Brisbane city watchhouse. The punishments ranged from reprimands to fines. Only a handful of police were dismissed from the force, two being Constables McArthur and Murray, who were involved in the death of James Michael Jorgensen, the man who died in the Mount Isa watchhouse in 1956.

Just weeks before Bennett's address on police corruption to state parliament, both Constable M.R. Strong and Senior Constable J. Maccheroni were fined three pounds each for engaging in 'remunerative employment', namely driving motor cars from Sydney without the approval of the police commissioner.

But Bennett's concern that Tuesday afternoon was not a few cops turning up for duty drunk, or swearing at their superiors, or earning a quid on the side. He was tackling the big picture. Bennett wanted to expose Bischof and his top-level clique of officers. He wanted to rip back the veil on what would later be dubbed the Rat Pack.

'The Police Force itself is seething with discontent,' he went on. 'There are what might be termed camps in the Police Department, and police officers are in one camp or the other depending on the treatment that they are receiving from the Commissioner and some of his top colleagues.

'Unless they are prepared to bow to the dictates of those top administrative officers, they have no chance of getting anywhere in the Force and, what is more drastic and alarming, they run the risk of getting into a heap of difficulties.'

Bennett said that during 'the last three or four years' – since Bischof became police commissioner – there had been 'more trouble' in the force than under any other government or commissioner in Queensland history. 'There is something wrong somewhere, and someone must take the responsibility for it.'

Bennett went on to discuss the importance of police officers' private lives needing to be exemplary – no doubt a direct strike at Bischof over the curious incident with Mary Margaret Fels the year before.

Bennett further accused Bischof, and CIB Chief Inspector Norm Bauer, of being too active in politics, and, in particular, of leading a 'barnstorming' in support of the Liberal–Country government at the 1960 election. Bennett said of the police commissioner: 'He is meddling in politics and endeavouring to keep the present Government in office because he knows that under its regime he can do as he pleases.'

Bennett then prosecuted Bischof for his control over who appeared on jury lists, and strongly intimated there was huge potential for corruption if jurists had to be vetted by Bischof.

In just under sixty minutes, Bennett had ranged across numerous serious issues to do with the administration of the force. He discussed the existence of a protected cabal at the top of the force with Bischof at its centre, wide-ranging political interference by senior police and their potential corrupt infiltration of the judicial system.

It was a crowded hour.

But there was one paragraph – halfway through his missive – that would later receive all the attention.

'I do not wish to dally too long on this subject,' Bennett said, 'but I should say that the Commissioner and his colleagues who frequent the National Hotel, encouraging and condoning the call-girl service that operates there, would be better occupied in preventing such activities rather than tolerating them.'

It was classic titillating tabloid newspaper fodder. It was also an allegation that had a specific address. Although it was buckshot to Bennett's fusillade of heavy artillery, it was the one the Nicklin government dallied over.

Author Peter James described the impact of Bennett's parliamentary speech as akin to 'setting off a string of Chinese firecrackers at the Oriental New Year: fireworks and noise, billows of smoke and, when the smoke clears, a few scraps of paper blown by the breeze'.

Members poured into the chamber after Bennett's speech and a ferocious debate ensued. The Liberal member for Sherwood, John Herbert, said Bennett's attacks on Bischof were the 'outpourings of a diseased mind'. He suggested that Bennett produce evidence to support his charges or risk being branded 'a character assassin of the lowest order'.

The police minister, Alex Dewar, appeared caught on the hop and offered ineffectual debate. He said he had taken up the matter of the call girls with Bischof and was satisfied Bennett's allegations were the figment of an 'infantile imagination'.

Days later, the Police Union urged Dewar to conduct an open inquiry into the matter. Dewar demurred.

The following Tuesday, 5 November, Premier Nicklin – whose government just months before had been returned to power in the state elections – appealed for credible public witnesses to come forward with first-hand evidence relating to Bennett's accusations.

A single anonymous letter arrived in the mail at Parliament House. The author, later identified as former National Hotel employee David Young, was subsequently interviewed by Crown Law officers. There he signed statements listing specific allegations against police and the hotel.

Young asserted that he had served Bischof food and alcohol during and after trading hours; he often served beer to Licensing Squad members after 11 p.m., as well as Detective Tony Murphy, without payment; he sometimes took calls from police on Sundays, warning of impending raids; the hotel was used by prostitutes, some of whom gave favours to police; and police supervision of the hotel was lax.

Young's allegations were handed to the premier for perusal.

Bischof did not waste time. He immediately seconded Murphy and Hallahan to investigate Young. They, in turn, got in touch with Shirley Brifman. She had gone to Sydney mid-year to procure an abortion – she claimed it was easier than getting one in Brisbane – and had temporarily settled there. She decided at the last minute to have the baby.

Brifman was in constant touch with Murphy and Hallahan during those few months in Sydney, and their contact heated up during the debate over whether to stage a royal commission. Hallahan liked to phone. Murphy, with old-school charm, used to type a letter to Brifman about once a week. In late 1963 she was living at 195 Bunnerong Road, Maroubra.

In one letter, Murphy wrote: 'By the way Marge [the name Brifman used when working as a prostitute, and appropriated from her sister Marge Chapple], I would like to reassure you that anything you tell me in confidence will always be kept that way by myself, and so consequently, you need have no fear of my repeating anything you tell me in your letters to anyone, for I am only too well aware of the position that it would put you in. If you are worried over anything in that regard, you can leave it to me to see everything is always covered, as I have in fact already done at all times.'

Murphy promised to give her and husband, Sonny, a ring when he was next down in Sydney.

Murphy also wrote asking what she knew about David Young. Brifman had been acquainted with Young when he worked briefly as a barman at the Grand Central Hotel in Queen Street, Brisbane.

'In particular I was pleased to learn what you knew about this person

David Young,' Murphy wrote. 'You may well realise my surprise to learn that he had accused me of certain misconduct. I'm still not sure what he has alleged against me.'

He later explained to Brifman: 'We have gotta finish David Young. We have got to get something on him.'

On Friday 8 November, the *Sunday Truth* received a letter from a man called John Komlosy – the former night porter at the National Hotel. He too made allegations against Bischof, certain police and the hotel along the same lines as Young.

On Monday 11 November, after the government's weekly Cabinet meeting, Premier Nicklin announced a royal commission into the allegations. It was a page-one story for the *Courier-Mail* the following day.

JUDGE TO INQUIRE INTO CHARGES AGAINST OUR POLICE, the headline read.

The next day it was revealed that Justice Harry Gibbs would be the commissioner of the inquiry, and the terms of reference were released.

Down at Makerston Street there must have been a sense of relief, perhaps cause for celebration. The terms of reference were so narrow and so utterly containable that the exposure of Bischof's corruption was not under threat.

Author Peter James observed that the terms of reference limited investigation to a handful of police associated with a single hotel, relying on the evidence of one witness, David Young. Bennett's controversial parliamentary speech ranged across corruption throughout the entire police force, yet the royal commission stemmed from one sentence about booze, call girls and the National Hotel.

Colin Bennett said he was 'disgusted' with the terms of reference, adding that the government was 'not game to have a full and open inquiry into police administration'.

Lewis says the allegations that formed the basis of the royal commission were false, especially those against Bischof drinking late at night at the National.

'There might have been the odd prostitute [who] got in there from time to time, but I never saw one and I didn't know anybody who did see one and we didn't pinch any from there that I know of. Whereas from the Grand Central we pinched quite a few . . .

'And Bischof had a very unusual car. He had that as commissioner when it was sold . . . Rolly [Roberts] bought it and . . . in those days you could bloody park anywhere and it was parked in front of the National regularly.

'Somehow the rumour was put around that Bischof was there at all hours of the night drinking grog and then the National got a reputation which was almost completely undeserved.'

The royal commission was set to have a preliminary hearing on 20 November 1963, followed by Justice Gibbs and the inquiry team's inspection of the National Hotel.

The first regulation sitting day was scheduled for 2 December. David Young would be the first witness.

Digging for Dirt

Lewis might have been working for the greater good of Brisbane's troubled teenagers in the JAB with policewoman Weier, zipping across town to high schools and private homes, meeting government officials and university academics, but an old friend came calling when the royal commission was announced.

Tony Murphy was responsible for shoring up the police case, and that meant gathering data – incriminating or otherwise – on the two primary witnesses, Young and Komlosy. He sought Lewis's help.

The day after the inquiry was announced, Lewis recorded in his police diary: 'To Brunswick Street, N.F. and saw Attila Kury of 8 Eva St, Deagon re: Komlosy. Saw Commissioner re T.V. show on Sunday.'

A month later Lewis's duties with the JAB went out the window for the day: 'With D/S Murphy to Canberra Hotel and saw Mr Toombs re Komlosy employed there about May to July 1957. To Commonwealth offices, Adelaide St., to see Mr Killen, M.H.R., [federal member for Moreton] and saw his secretary re Komlosy. Off duty 5pm.

'Then with D/S Murphy checked Prints and M.O. Sections re females mentioned by Komlosy. To St. Patricks, Valley and saw Fr. Miklos re Komlosy. To Carlton Hotel and saw Mr Shapley and then to Lennons Hotel and saw Mr J. Walker re: Komlosy. To Office and sent messages to Sydney and Tasmania. Checked criminal files and histories of females. Off 10pm.'

The next morning he had a meeting with Bischof and spent much of that day with Murphy, digging into Komlosy's past.

Hallahan also got in on the act.

Witness David Young lived in a low-set Queenslander at 31 Beck Street, Rosalie, in the city's inner west, in the shadow of the nearby Marist College.

On the night of 19 November, Young received an anonymous phone call at his home. The caller told Young that police had made a thorough check of his background and outlined the allegations about his past that would be aired in public if he gave evidence to the inquiry. He added that police were waiting for him 'with open arms'.

Young suspected the caller was a police officer intimately acquainted with the royal commission, but had no proof. Later, on hearing Hallahan give evidence at the inquiry, Young found the identity of his mystery caller. It was Hallahan, with his deep, slow, dulcet tones.

Komlosy was also intimidated, and received a death threat letter, postmarked Cowra in New South Wales. 'Keep off the police or we will get [you] as they do in Hungary. If you value your life, say no more. Don't show this to anyone. It will not pay.'

Young and Komlosy were about to discover what it meant to cross Bischof and his trusted boys.

First Steps to the Big Chair

With Murphy, Hallahan, and Jack Herbert set to be called as witnesses before the royal commission, Lewis took his first concrete steps towards the commissionership. He decided to get educated.

In the latter part of 1963, Lewis was indefatigable, on behalf of the JAB, in developing contacts and forging links with government, community and educational bodies.

One was Dr Elsie Harwood, a senior lecturer in psychology at the University of Queensland.

Ever on the lookout to better himself and gain a qualification, Lewis took up a course in general psychology given by Harwood for Brisbane's Board of Adult Education. He consulted her about the latest psychological literature as he steadily pieced together the work of the JAB.

He also asked her about the possibility of studying at the university.

Harwood observed a 'conscientious and thorough student' in Lewis. '[He] availed himself of the opportunity in his own time to study . . . in the special fields of child and adolescent development, delinquency, criminality, and personal adjustment,' she would later write in a reference for Lewis.

He then wrote to J. Edgar Hoover, director of the Federal Bureau of Investigation in the United States, about printed material dealing with how the FBI managed troubled juveniles. The literature was forwarded to him in his little office in the old Queensland Egg Board building by the Brisbane River.

Lewis was working hard and working well. Given the proximity of the JAB to Bischof's office, it would have been surprising if Lewis was not aware of a small court matter involving a juvenile by the name of Daniel Fels, seventeen, labourer, of Underwood Road, Eight Mile Plains. Daniel Fels was one of the children of Mary Margaret Fels, Bischof's ex-lover, who was being sued by the police commissioner for defamation and was, by late 1963, still living under the pall of a future court case.

Incredibly, or coincidentally, a CIB summons issued against Daniel Fels over the alleged theft of a pair of sunglasses was listed for hearing in the Police Court just two days after Premier Nicklin ordered the royal commission into the National Hotel.

The incident allegedly occurred in early March 1963 – less than four months after Bischof had lodged his defamation writ against Fels. Following a fatal car accident in Eight Mile Plains, Daniel, who happened to be in the vicinity, was interviewed by investigating officer Detective Hoppner and accused of stealing a pair of sunglasses from one of the wrecked vehicles.

He was issued a summons for theft more than two weeks after the accident.

The boy's father, Alfonso, subsequently made the trip into headquarters to discuss the matter with police.

Alfonso would later allege that Hoppner told him that instructions had come from 'the top' to prosecute Daniel.

Renowned lawyer Dan Casey represented the boy in court and vigorously cross-examined Hoppner.

Casey: Did you tell Mr [Alfonso] Fels the day he saw Sub-inspector Rockett [at police headquarters] that 'instructions had come from the top' and you couldn't do anything about this prosecution?

Hoppner: No, sir. I told him that other lads involved would be charged, and we couldn't make fish out of one and flesh of another.

Casey: What, stealing a pair of sunglasses?

Hoppner: Serious in the nature of the offence – stealing from a car in which one person was killed.

Hoppner explained that Alfonso Fels had tried to get the charge quashed.

Casey: And that was when he was told instructions had come from 'higher up' that his son must be prosecuted?

Hoppner: No, sir, to my knowledge, the matter never went past Sub-inspector Rockett.

Casey: How would you know?

Hoppner: As I said, not to my knowledge.

Casey: I am putting it to you that the real reason why you did not serve this summons until seventeen days after the alleged offence was that you did not intend to proceed with the matter until you were compelled?

Hoppner: No, sir. That is not so.

Casey: Why did you take [Daniel] into the presence of his mother and father against his wish?

Hoppner: So as to obviate his arrest and proceed by summons.

Casey: That had nothing to do with it, did it?

Hoppner: Yes, sir, it did.

Casey: You surely would not proceed by way of arrest over a pair of sunglasses.

Hoppner: No, I would not, in the circumstances.

Casey: Well, I take it you have made arrangements for Mrs Fels to be called to give evidence in relation to conversations?

Hoppner: No, sir.

Casey: Why?

Hoppner: I discussed the matter with Sub-inspector Hambrecht, and I did not.

Casey: Again, then this case is being directed by an authority higher up? You have not had a free hand in the preparation of the prosecutor's brief?

Hoppner: No, that is not so. It was Sub-inspector Hambrecht who queried me as to why I had not attempted to get a statement from Mrs Fels and it was decided that at that stage it would not be proper to approach her.

Casey: Why wouldn't it be proper?

Hoppner: That was the reason.

Casey: But why would it not be proper?

Hoppner: Fels was being defended and pleading not guilty and no doubt Mrs Fels would receive certain advice.

Hoppner said he had never met the Felses before the incident, but when he took Daniel to the family home to confront his parents, his mother admitted she was the woman Bischof was suing for alleged defamation.

It was just another one of Bischof's usual pincer movements against his foes. He kept building pressure. And he used his closest allies in the force – his personal foot soldiers – to execute his tactics.

The Inquiry

In the months leading up to Christmas, it was Detective Murphy's habit to buy young chickens and ducklings and prepare them for sale during the festive season.

Murphy would religiously collect scraps and leftovers from the city's restaurants and fatten up his birds back home. When they were plump enough, he killed and dressed them and sold them to restaurants for a small profit. His family says it was a way for the struggling suburban father to earn a few extra bob.

In December 1963, he would have had little time to prepare his poultry.

The royal commission opened for business on 2 December in a Brisbane District Court and instantly became the biggest show in town. It potentially had it all – a call-girl network, a lid lifted on the peccadilloes of upstanding Queensland husbands and fathers having a night out at the National, corrupt police, and a police commissioner who enjoyed the largesse of mates in the hotel business after hours. In terms of police, the hotel and prostitution, Justice Gibbs and his royal commission would reveal the worst kept 'secret' in Brisbane.

Murphy, Bischof, the Roberts brothers, alleged prostitutes (covering their faces with handbags), witnesses and well-appointed legal counsel were all photographed by the press coming and going through the ancient iron gates outside the courts.

Inside the hot court room with its poor acoustics, Bischof, immaculately dressed as ever, took his seat at the bench immediately behind the bar table, and its eleven barristers, and farthest from the witness stand. He appeared carefree and jovial, and was regularly in animated conversation with his senior counsel, future governor of Queensland Walter Campbell, QC.

More than 120 people filled the gallery on the opening day. They were not disappointed.

The first witness, David Young from Beck Street, Rosalie, gave evidence that detectives, including regular Tony Murphy, indeed drank at the National after hours, that prostitutes were booked for clients from the lounge – there were several to choose from in the four-storey building, including the Sovereign and Westminster rooms on the first floor, the Skyline room on the third, and the Twilight and Roof Garden rooms on the fourth – and the hotel was warned of impending police raids.

There was a barrage to come – Young would allege he had seen prostitutes in bed with men and had once entered a room where all three beds were occupied by naked couples. One of them he recognised as Marge (Shirley Brifman), who would confide in him that she gave 'favours' to a senior Queensland police officer. Murphy would later claim that no prostitutes were ever discovered and arrested at the National, and that, while he knew of Brifman, he had no proof she was a working prostitute.

What caught the imagination of the press on opening day, however, was Young's anonymous threatening phone call prior to his appearance at the inquiry.

The *Courier-Mail* reported on the front page the following day: PROBE WITNESS WILL TELL OF THREAT. On page three were photographs of a beaming Bischof in suit and hat, and another of chief witnesses Young and Komlosy, a short, balding man carrying a briefcase.

The details of the anonymous caller's forty-five-minute conversation with Young were aired before the inquiry, including Young having procured an abortion for a girl in Sydney, that he had had an affair with a married woman, and that he had somehow arranged for a prostitute to be arrested by police.

From day one, these spurious allegations against Young were entered into the transcript, into the inquiry's landscape, and would be repeatedly used to strike back at the barman's character and veracity. It couldn't have been a better start for Bischof and his crew.

The following day, Young's barrister told the inquiry that the cross-examination of Young could 'turn the inquiry into an inquiry into Young'. It was a prescient observation.

Justice Gibbs ensured that he would take steps to stop such a development if it went beyond the hypothetical.

Yet Murphy and Lewis's muckraking came into immediate play, and Young's employment history and moral fibre were vivisected.

Under cross-examination, Young admitted he had had sex with Brifman's friend Val Weidinger in a room at the National, and that he'd also had intercourse with a co-worker in Brifman's Spring Hill flat. His infidelity to his wife was held up by some counsel as a measure of the man's integrity. Here was someone not to be trusted, who was making allegations against the morals of police, and yet was enmeshed in the same murky world he was trying to expose through an inquiry for the betterment of the community.

Counsel Eddie Broad – for Weidinger and Lily Ryan, another friend of Brifman – convinced Young to withdraw his allegation that both women were prostitutes, having never physically seen them receive money from men for services rendered.

As the days progressed, the commission once again informed the inquiry that the hotel's guest books had been requested. None had been forthcoming.

Following Young's evidence, a cavalcade of witnesses passed through the inquiry, all denying his allegations.

Night porter Komlosy was next in the firing line. He claimed to be shocked at the late-night drinking at the National when he first started work there in the winter of 1960. He often encountered Murphy and Hallahan drinking after hours, usually beyond midnight. Further, he claimed several prostitutes practically lived at the hotel, including Weidinger and Brifman. He saw Bischof at the hotel often, once at a party in Max Roberts's flat. Komlosy also named 'top executives' in the city who partied at the National. Several would later be called before Justice Gibbs and deny the allegations against them.

Komlosy, a Hungarian immigrant who had settled in Australia in 1951, having served time in a Russian prisoner of war camp during the Second World War, gave a singular reason for appearing as a witness at the inquiry. 'I lost my country and everything dear to me; there were so very few people who spoke up for the truth. I don't think that should happen in this country.'

If Young felt he had been drawn and quartered under cross-examination, it was nothing compared to what Komlosy was about to experience. Murphy and Lewis had done their job well.

Justice Gibbs, too, failed to stop his royal commission becoming, at this point, an inquiry into Komlosy himself. The former night porter told the commissioner that he might lose his job as a storeman if he were engaged by the inquiry for a lengthy period.

Counsel for the government immediately exposed that Komlosy had been dismissed from a former job at Queensland Railways for absence of duty. It didn't stop there.

'Do you remember threatening to throw a man under a train?' counsel asked Komlosy. And: 'You were convicted under the *Aliens Act* in 1957, were you not?' And: 'You presented a fraudulent cheque to Qantas in New Guinea?'

Counsel for the Police Union continued: 'Is it not true that you were sacked from the C— Hotel as night porter because you stole the master key and entered a female employee's room?'

The purpose of the accusations, as with Young, was to prove him an unreliable witness.

Komlosy was also closely questioned about his association with Tony Murphy at the National Hotel. Komlosy claimed he saw Murphy often and liked the man.

What followed was a classic Bischof-inspired Rat Pack manoeuvre. Counsel asserted that Komlosy had only met Murphy once, at Brisbane airport a year after he ceased employment at the National. Komlosy had taken his two sons to the airport to see Prime Minister Menzies arrive on a visit to Queensland, and said he saw Murphy there and introduced the detective to his children.

Murphy had been at the airport to arrest a homosexual arriving from Sydney, and by chance was approached by the federal member for Moreton, James Killen. Killen alerted Murphy to a 'suspicious character' on the periphery of the prime minister's party.

Murphy then allegedly approached Komlosy and said, 'We're from the CIB and we've been told that you may attempt to harm or interfere with Mr Menzies. What is your business here?'

Komlosy then supposedly told the detective he'd brought his sons out to see Australia's biggest political gangster, Mr Menzies. 'In my country we'd put him against the wall and shoot him.'

Murphy gave Komlosy a warning, and Komlosy then allegedly asked, 'What is your name?'

'I am Detective Murphy.'

This scenario shared more than a few characteristics with the Gunther Bahnemann incident years earlier. Here all over again was the formal language concocted from thin air, the suspected violent potential of a 'foreigner', the threat by an outsider to the Australian way of life, upheld by ever-vigilant, honest Queensland detectives. The clear implication, too, was that the two men did not know each other – and Murphy still didn't know Komlosy's name – until this moment.

Murphy later produced his police diary, in which he'd written: 'Interviewed man Kom Losy at Brisbane Airport . . .' Murphy said the incorrect spelling of the surname proved that he did not know the night porter.

Komlosy was getting fed up with the trashing of his personal life. 'Not one gentleman has asked me anything about the National,' he said, exasperated.

Komlosy did lose his job. He told the royal commission he intended to leave Australia with his family in a couple of months. Murphy and crew had destroyed his new life and robbed him of a future in his adopted home.

Murphy appeared as a witness on Friday 13 December. He was the first police officer called.

John Hay of the *Sunday Mail* described the moment: 'Sergeant Murphy is unmistakably a policeman. Tall. Erect. Forthright in speech, with a seemingly precise memory indicating years of training and experience.'

Murphy said he felt 'in jeopardy' when the inquiry was called and believed it was necessary to investigate Young's background.

When asked about specific prostitutes, particularly Brifman,

Weidinger and Ryan, he said he had spoken to them on suspicion of their being prostitutes but had no proof. None of the women had a police file.

Brifman later admitted: 'Between the Grand Central and the National, I lived in the two of them . . . It was a habit to go from one hotel to another.'

In fact, Murphy went as far as to say that he had never seen a prostitute at the National. According to official police statistics, a meagre eight had been arrested there over a period of four years.

'Well, there was one woman who could've been. Yanka or Yanku . . . Hallahan arrested her,' Murphy said on oath.

He was also questioned about Young's anonymous threatening phone call. 'If there was any such phone call, I don't think the caller was any friend of mine,' Murphy said.

In a contradiction to Murphy's testimony, another officer – Detective Sergeant William (Bill) Osborne of the Licensing Branch – told the royal commission that in the course of an investigation in 1962 into whether a Grand Central waiter was procuring women for prostitution, he interviewed Brifman and Ryan. Osborne said that both had indicated to him that they worked as prostitutes in Brisbane but only operated out of the Grand Central, not the National.

Brifman later recalled that Osborne was an 'honest' cop, and he told her that he had been persecuted in the job because he was one of the men who initially objected to Bischof's appointment as police commissioner in 1958.

The inquiry adjourned on 20 December and resumed on Monday 13 January 1964.

The next day, Hallahan was called before the inquiry. Just the previous Wednesday he had been suspended from duties over his 'fraud on the court' matter regarding so-called vagrant Gary Campbell, pending an internal Police Department investigation.

Hallahan claimed he was ill – presumably related to his kidney condition – and hoped his testimony and cross-examination could be expedited swiftly.

He said he could never prove Weidinger and Ryan were prostitutes. Brifman? 'Not a reputed prostitute.' Yanku? Hallahan had taken no notes after he pulled her out of the National following a phone call from Rolly Roberts.

Hallahan called in sick the next day. Meanwhile, Young was re-examined and he explained he had come in to the inquiry to specifically hear Hallahan give evidence and to solve the mystery of the anonymous caller. He said he believed Hallahan was the man. Young's claim was later dismissed by the commissioner.

When Hallahan resumed his testimony, he said he was shocked to hear Komlosy describe him as a regular after-hours drinker at the National, as his kidney problems precluded him from taking alcohol. He admitted he had made some queries into Young's background for Murphy, concerning break and enter charges, but nothing came of it. It was more damning hearsay entered into evidence against Young.

After Hallahan, the Big Fella swore on the Bible and took the stand. He had appeared briefly earlier in the inquiry to outline his friendship with Max Roberts ('Slight,' he said), but now he came armed with ten statements from senior police claiming no illegalities in relation to the National and its operations.

Bischof denied all of Young's allegations. Showing the sort of agility he demonstrated in shutting down Mary Margaret Fels, he told Justice Gibbs that he first heard of Young's allegations through his own anonymous phone call. 'Two ALP members skived on their mates to tell me, Inspector Bauer and Detective Murphy about it.'

Bischof repeatedly strained credulity. He said he was unaware of the contents of Bennett's attack in state parliament that had sparked the very inquiry in which Bischof sat.

He was further quizzed on his use of Rolly Roberts's beach house on the South Coast and his attendance frequency at the National. He recalled a party thrown by Rolly to farewell him prior to his trip to the Interpol conference in Spain. Bischof grew heated when it was suggested there was an intimate 'after-party' to that function.

Justice Gibbs quizzed Bischof on the definition of 'suspected prostitute', and the police commissioner replied that they would be associated with other suspected prostitutes.

He was also asked about the rules concerning the keeping of official police diaries, as Hallahan's and Murphy's had revealed possible breaches of departmental regulations.

'After the Royal Commission started,' Bischof added, 'I had all the records doubly checked to make sure that [Young's] allegations couldn't be correct.'

People were out to get him, Bischof decried: 'I think it was said two thousand years ago, "Forgive them, for they know not what they do." I say it again now.'

It would have been difficult to beat the comedy of Bischof's comparing himself to Jesus Christ, but for shock value the appearance in late January of Shirley Brifman trumped everything at the inquiry.

Unbeknown to Justice Gibbs and most counsel, she had been well and truly coached prior to her stint in the witness box. Murphy and Hallahan had been in touch with Brifman virtually every night during the inquiry hearings, to get her up to speed on the evidence.

On the day she was due to appear, Brifman and Ryan met a 'client' at Lennons Hotel and took him back to Ryan's flat in Spring Hill.

'Lily and I entertained him on Scotch at Bradley Street,' Brifman would later recall. 'Tony rang up when the court adjourned. He said, "Don't come to court – you're drunk."'

She duly appeared, nevertheless, in a white dress and broad-brimmed white hat.

'I talked to Tony before I went into the witness box,' she said. 'I talked to him that night. He kept telling me things I had to say and things I didn't have to say.

'[Hallahan and Murphy] didn't actually tell me what the questions would be. They told me they would see the barrister and tell him the questions to ask me and I was tutored on the questions and answers.

'I got into the witness box and took the oath. I think somebody read the oath to me. I recall it was an oath to tell the truth and I didn't tell the truth.

'Hallahan and Murphy told me that I had to destroy David Young and that I had to deny what Detective Sergeant Osborne had said, that I was a prostitute.'

Brifman did more than that. She said she was appearing at the inquiry to refute allegations, like the one from Osborne, that she was a prostitute. She further told the royal commission that she had only been in the National six times in the past four years. She admitted knowing Young, and was asked what had transpired when they once met in Brifman's flat.

She answered, 'David Young done an abortion on me.'

The response from Justice Gibbs and leading counsel was apoplectic. 'Just a minute!' the commissioner shouted.

He ruled that the evidence not be recorded.

Why did she give such blatant false evidence to the royal commission? She later reflected: 'For a start I didn't want my family to know [she was a prostitute] and I had to protect Tony and Glen and them. If I was a prostitute they would have been gone. I did know all of them. I even knew their wives.'

Lewis now says there is no doubt that police drank after hours at the National. But would Murphy coach Brifman on her evidence before the inquiry? 'I wouldn't doubt that.'

Young had been demolished, and Komlosy was so aggrieved at his treatment he planned to flee the country.

The inquiry concluded on 24 February. It had sat for thirty-four days, featured eighty-nine witnesses and received 167 documentary exhibits.

Justice Gibbs presented his almost two hundred-page final report to Premier Nicklin on Friday 10 April 1964.

In short, Justice Gibbs found no evidence of a call-girl service being run out of the National Hotel, Petrie Bight, nor was there anything to suggest that Bischof and his cohorts drank there after hours.

'To sum the matter up,' the commissioner concluded in his report, 'although the law relating to the sale and consumption of liquor on licensed premises after lawful trading hours was broken on many occasions over a period of years at the National Hotel, and most of those breaches remained undetected by the police, there is no acceptable evidence that any member of the Police Force was guilty of misconduct, or neglect or violation of duty in relation to the policing of the hotel, the conduct of the business or the operations or the use of the hotel, or the enforcement of the law in respect of any breaches alleged or reported to have been committed in relation thereto.'

Justice Gibbs did recommend that official police diaries supplied to detectives be 'examined, initialled and dated' once a week by the officer in charge.

Both Bischof and Murphy were awarded costs.

Years later, former Queensland treasurer Thomas Hiley remembered a story told to him by various policemen after Bischof and his boys were exonerated: 'In the victory party that night . . . Bischof, by this time, is as full as a kite and he's up on the mini-stage – it was the band area where the bands used to get up about one step off the floor – and he's got these three fellows [Lewis, Murphy, and Hallahan] up on the stage and he's doing his best to put his arms around three necks at once, rather a hard task, and he said, "I want you all to know that these are the boys who got me off this rap," and he said, "I want you all to know I'm going to look after them." He said, "You won't stop until you go right to the top."'

The party was held at the National Hotel.

Lewis says: 'I don't remember the party, but there could have been one. I was never at a party at the National Hotel when Bischof was present. And he would never put his arms around my neck, never, no matter how much he loved me.'

Empire Building

While the city's attention was drawn to the royal commission and its colourful cast of characters during January and February 1964, Lewis continued to quietly shore up his future.

On Monday 20 January, as Bischof, Murphy and Hallahan were masterfully manipulating the inquiry, Lewis headed over to the University of Queensland in pretty inner south-west St Lucia and 'saw Dr Harwood and then Dr Rawson re application for entry in Dip., Public Admin. Course'.

But he had not forgotten his mates. His police diary shows that on Tuesday 4 February, he arrived at the office at 8.30 a.m. and attended to files. He then 'attended Royal Commission in Supreme Court with Detective Murphy'. 'Off duty 5pm.'

February 14 saw Lewis back at the university, where he met Harwood and picked up his faculty handbook. He later 'paid fees and submitted enrolment forms'.

Lewis went on two weeks' leave from Wednesday 19 February, and by early March was back at the JAB, uncovering cases of child neglect in the city, responding to the discovery of an obscene letter at a high school, checking on reports of children in various stages of undress misbehaving in St Lucia, tracking down runaway kids, and generally delving into the domestic battleground of parents and their teenagers across Brisbane.

Meanwhile, Shirley Brifman had experienced enough of Sydney to understand that she could earn more than a decent living in the Emerald City. Moreover, after the publicity surrounding the National

Hotel inquiry, it would have been close to impossible for her to continue practising her trade in Brisbane, even with the clandestine support of Murphy and Hallahan. The inquiry, though a triumph for Bischof and his boys, had marked her as a suspected prostitute and something of a city identity, albeit a morally bankrupt one.

Incredibly, given the circumstances of the inquiry, Murphy and Hallahan each pleaded with her not to permanently move south.

Brifman later recalled in police interviews: 'When I told Tony and Glen I was going – was there a blue and a half. They said, "The girls [Ryan and Weidinger] have got to get out. You know we have only tolerated them because of you."

'They still wouldn't wear it. They did not want me to go to Sydney. When they knew my mind was made up, they said, "We will give them a break, Shirl – five hundred pounds a piece." That was to be paid the day I was leaving to Hallahan and Murphy by the other two girls so they would stay in this city because I was leaving it. They paid. They did definitely pay.'

Brifman broke the news to the girls in Ryan's flat in Bradley Street, not far from the National Hotel. Ryan and Weidinger agreed to pay the cops to keep working, and the money changed hands in a lane behind the Port Office Hotel in Edward Street.

And with Brifman gone, Hallahan now dramatically raised the rates on payments from city prostitutes.

In Sydney, Brifman's modus operandi was identical to her work out of the Grand Central Hotel and National Hotel. Like a moth to a flame, she headed straight to her new home's traditional vice epicentre – Kings Cross – and conducted her business in the Hotel Rex, just down Macleay Street from Fitzroy Gardens with its Canary Island date palms and iconic watery dandelion, the El Alamein fountain.

The refurbished Rex was a stand-out city hotel when it was opened in 1953, and introduced to Sydney some novel features, including a 'continental-style' sidewalk café – a cramped, open-air vestibule partitioned from the street by a low stone wall and shrubbery and festooned with beach umbrellas – and an adjoining espresso bar. There were numerous places to take a drink in the hotel's 'bar block' – a saloon, public bars and a bottle shop on the ground floor, and the 'Canberra' lounge and beer garden on the top floor. It also had its own hairdressing salon.

What may have appealed to Queenslander Brifman – even a decade after its grand unveiling – was the hotel's deliberate sub-tropical atmosphere, its walls and features painted pastel pink, peach and putty.

The Rex became her base; one that she shared with several other street prostitutes.

After the National Hotel fiasco in Brisbane, she was fed up with police officers and the complications they gave to her already unconventional way of life. She had never attracted a single charge in Queensland, but Sydney, crime and vice capital of Australia, was a different story.

She soon confronted an almost mirror image of her situation in Brisbane. Sydney, too, had its tough detectives and vice squad officers who accepted a quid for protection. Where up north she had Hallahan and Murphy, down south she was to become entangled with their New South Wales twins, Ray Kelly and Fred Krahe.

Krahe was reputedly one of the most feared police officers in Australia. Like Murphy and Hallahan, he was a superlative detective and had innumerable criminal contacts, including some of the biggest gangsters in town.

In the early 1960s he visited Brisbane on business – like Ray Kelly – and got to know Hallahan. In turn, and keeping Brifman in his web, Hallahan gave Krahe Brifman's phone number at Bunnerong Road, Maroubra, when she settled in Sydney in 1964.

'I did not know who Krahe was,' Brifman later revealed in police interviews. 'I had enough of police after the royal commission . . . I was not going to get landed with the Sydney detectives. Krahe annoyed me that much with phone messages. He never gave up.'

Brifman eventually had a drink with the physically imposing Krahe in the old Hyde Park Hotel opposite the sandstone cenotaph near the corner of Elizabeth and Bathurst streets.

'Have you ever dealt in money before, Shirley?' he asked her.

'What do you mean?'

'Well, the same applies here as in Queensland.' Krahe had clearly been briefed on Brifman by Hallahan. 'You don't work in this town unless you pay.'

Krahe outlined how things worked in New South Wales: 'It's like this . . . You get mugs with the knockabouts, you get in with them, you find out about their robberies.

'When they sell their stuff, we give them one night with their money. Next morning we move in . . .'

This was another level of police corruption to what Brifman had experienced in Queensland. She was incredulous and said, naively: 'You're worse than the thief. You are letting them rob and you are getting the benefit of it and you are supposed to be a policeman.'

She told him she wasn't interested. She didn't know who she was dealing with.

'If you repeat one word of what we have said here today to the Queensland police,' Krahe said, 'I will shoot you stone dead, and anything you have to say to them, naturally they will repeat back to me.'

Later that night she phoned Hallahan and told him to get Krahe off her back.

Lewis also knew Krahe, and, on one of his visits to Brisbane, Lewis picked up Krahe from the airport and dropped him at the National Hotel.

'I went in with him,' Lewis recalls. 'You know how you put your hands on people . . . I felt he had a shoulder holster and revolvers on both sides.

'The supposition is one [gun] was your official one and the other is if you shot someone and he didn't have a gun you'd give him one. Or if you unlawfully shot someone you'd use that other revolver.'

Shirley Brifman was a long way from Atherton. And in those early days in Sydney she couldn't have known – meeting strange men in the bars at the Rex and pulling tricks shoulder to shoulder with a gaggle of other well-dressed prostitutes – that in a few short years she would be the most celebrated madam in Sydney.

Peacekeeper

Frank Bischof and his men were given a clean slate by Justice Gibbs early in 1964, but there was a lingering hangover to the celebrations. It was Glendon Patrick Hallahan, and the internal police investigation into the arrest of Gary Campbell at the Top Cat Sound Lounge.

Hallahan was facing three charges, two of preparing misleading and dishonest statements regarding the case, and failing to keep his police diary current.

The Queen's Counsel charged with conducting the case reversed the Full Court conclusions. Hallahan was simply found guilty of the diary charge, and fined. Again, Colin Bennett and others attacked the outcome in parliament.

While it was another victory for the Rat Pack member, Hallahan's appearance at the royal commission, the allegations aired against him, and now the publicity over the internal police investigation must have chafed with Bischof. Brifman was out of the way. Maybe it was time that Hallahan, too, stepped from the spotlight for a while.

In far off Cyprus, the continuing violence between Greek and Turkish Cypriots triggered the United Nations Security Council's Resolution 186, and a peacekeeping force was mobilised. It included British, Irish and Australian troops.

Australia would send forty men – a combination of Commonwealth and state police – and Queensland was asked for five volunteers. Individuals would have to express their interest to Police Commissioner Bischof, then be vetted and approved. One of those men was Hallahan. He had just turned thirty-two. The rest were young officers in their early twenties. Whether Bischof had quietly suggested to Hallahan that it might be a good idea to vanish from the local scene for twelve months will never be known.

Hallahan flew to Canberra in May for intensive training at the Royal Military College, Duntroon. The *Courier-Mail* featured a photograph of Hallahan at Brisbane airport: 'The other four Queensland constables will fly south today.'

Among those joining Hallahan in the Queensland contingent were Ray Strong and Bob 'Doc' Gillespie. They were farewelled at the airport by Bischof and Dewar, the police minister, and due to fly to Cyprus on a chartered Qantas Boeing 707 from Canberra on the evening of Sunday 24 May.

Hallahan, despite his immense experience as a detective, was at first glance an unusual fit for the job. He was a decade older than most of the others in the peacekeeping force. He would, because of his senior rank, hardly be on patrol of small Cyprian villages looking for strife. Then again, he had huge organisational skills – courtesy of his growing stable of informants – and in a sense was proven as a people facilitator.

Was there a settled home and love life to consider given the year-long secondment? He had apparently been engaged to a Sydney journalist in the early 1960s, but given his long hours and his proclivity to work the bars and clubs at night, personal entanglements were obviously not a factor.

During their training, the peacekeepers were briefly addressed by Commonwealth Police Commissioner Ray Whitrod. He congratulated the contingency and reminded them they had a job to do in Cypress. It would be Hallahan's first contact with his future boss.

In Canberra, the Queenslanders formed a quick bond. Doc Gillespie was working in the Brisbane CIB during the late 1950s when he first met Hallahan. 'He was a good detective,' Gillespie recalls. 'I got along very well with Glen.'

Ray Strong had also worked in the Brisbane CIB before serving time in Mount Isa and then relieving on the Gold Coast at the time he volunteered for Cyprus.

The contingent – with no formal powers of arrest – went over armed with .38 revolvers.

'Glen and I shared a room in a hotel in Famagusta,' Strong says. 'Hallahan was experienced as an investigator and we, being the first in there, we had a hell of a job – we had to work with the leaders on both sides. Glen being Glen, he had know-how. He made sure everybody did their job.

'I don't think there's a person in the contingent who had a bad word to say about him.'

Strong says Hallahan taught himself shorthand in the hotel room when he had time off: 'He'd study the Pitman's manual.'

Norm Webber, also a former Cyprus volunteer, remembers Hallahan as 'a very shrewd, sharp operator . . . he had an air about him'.

'He was a very presentable fellow and gave the impression that he knew what he was doing,' Webber says. 'It was a culture shock for all of us.'

Later, Hallahan settled in the capital, Nicosia, and assisted in administration. He was promoted during his secondment.

Strong says he was familiar with Hallahan's nickname, 'Silent'. 'He was a very good source of information. Where it came from, I don't know . . . He would never divulge any of his informants.'

Hallahan returned to Australia in 1965 – he had taken advantage of a free around-the-world air ticket offered as a bonus to all volunteers – and waiting for him was a New South Wales police officer who was very keen to do business. With the Sydney underworld operating at full tilt, its crimes and characters enmeshed with several corrupt police, why not expand the empire and get Queensland into the game?

That man was Detective Fred Krahe.

Life up on the Drive

A few months before Hallahan returned to Brisbane, Police Commissioner Bischof alerted Lewis to a child-neglect case in Charleville, 740 kilometres west of Brisbane. It was decided, as head of the JAB, that Lewis would personally travel to the town, retrieve the child, and place it in government protective custody.

He was seeing more and more cases of neglect, particularly in Brisbane, and it wasn't just the province of the working classes. The kids of rich parents were also coming to the bureau's attention, left with pockets full of cash as their parents indulged in the city's nominal indulgences, particularly the races.

Lewis himself was working long days, attending university lectures at night and catching up on his study in a small office nook in the Queenslander in Garfield Drive, with its view across Ashgrove, Enoggera and beyond. Lewis seemed to be forever behind a desk.

As wife Hazel remarked: 'The children only know you by the back of your head.'

On the night of Tuesday 5 January 1965, Lewis went to the police depot and picked up a brand new Ford Falcon, designated for a senior commissioned officer. The next morning at six, he drove from home to nearby Milton to pick up Miss McHutchison of the State Children's Services Department and they headed for Charleville.

After filling up the car in Dalby, they drove for a short distance and stopped for a snack.

'Miss McHutchison offered to relieve me with driving for a period,' Lewis recorded in his police diary, 'and after ascertaining that she had a

Driver's Licence; was authorised to drive Govt. vehicles and had done so for 14 years without an incident of any sort; was familiar with driving Falcons and was familiar with the road to Charleville, I permitted her to drive.'

Having passed through Miles and approaching Roma, east of Charleville, Miss McHutchison attempted to overtake a semitrailer.

'We were alongside of it and I could see that in the truck's rear-vision mirror the glass was missing – there was no way he could see we were coming alongside him,' Lewis recalls. 'The truck wriggled a bit and we went off the road doing sixty miles an hour. We went headfirst into a tree.'

The driver had cuts to her face but Lewis's head went through the windshield and his body bounced back into the Falcon. He had fractured his pelvis and was bleeding profusely.

By good fortune, a vehicle coming behind them stopped. The driver was a RAAF man and his wife was a nurse. She stabilised Lewis before he was rushed to Roma hospital.

The next day a battered and bruised Lewis was taken by ambulance all the way back to Brisbane's Princess Alexandra hospital. He was expected to be off work for six months. He was back in three.

'In hospital my legs were up in the air,' he says. 'Everybody and his dog came to visit – Mr Bischof, Buck Buchanan.'

Lewis was back on duty at 8.15 a.m. on Thursday 8 April, bearing the scars of the accident on his forehead.

A man keenly tethered by routine, Lewis slotted straight back into life in the JAB and Garfield Drive. On Sunday evenings he would religiously buff and polish his four children's school shoes so they were ready for Monday morning. On his way to work he would drop off his daughters, Lanna and Loreen, at the prestigious All Hallows' Catholic boarding school in the city.

On Saturday nights the family would often attend the Paddington Picture Theatre down on Given Terrace ('I knew the man who ran the theatre – Ted James – and he'd let me know what was coming up,' remembers Lewis) and went to mass every Sunday at the imposing red-brick St Brigid's at nearby Red Hill.

The house, though still more spacious than their previous residence down the hill at Rosalie, remained a squeeze for the young family, especially with four children.

It had a main bedroom, a small side bedroom for the girls, and another slightly larger room for the boys. There was a lounge, dining room, kitchen and an upstairs internal lavatory.

In the steep yard out the back, Lewis tied an old tyre to a tree for the children.

Meanwhile Hazel, an excellent cook, was doing some part-time work as a cooking demonstrator.

It was a full life for Lewis, especially studying for his diploma in public administration. He saw the diploma both as a tool to seek promotion through police ranks, and to better understand his work in the JAB. By 1965 he had five full-time staff.

'I was dealing with a lot of doctors, psychiatrists, psychologists, social workers and all sorts of professional people,' he says. 'I thought it was wise to learn a little bit about what they were involved in. The diploma had eight different subjects that ranged across many of these areas.'

The JAB and study had also lifted him out of the predictable cycle of drinking in the city after a shift with other officers.

'I was very happy to leave that,' Lewis adds. 'Occasionally I'd have a drink with some of them. But a lot of police officers then, particularly detectives, were very heavy drinkers. For the sake of my children, I was glad I had so many years in the JAB.'

It did not escape anyone in the upper echelons of the force that Bischof, while appearing robust, was suffering from hypertension. Lewis heard it second-hand from the greatest source of all, Bischof's driver, Slim Somerville.

For the first time in his long career, the Big Fella's powerful presence was showing some hairline cracks.

To the Satisfaction of Both Parties

More than two years after Mary Margaret Fels was exposed as some deranged and obsessive Brisbane housewife harassing Police Commissioner Bischof, his defamation writ against her was finally set to appear in court.

Just a year after the sensational, though ultimately anti-climactic, National Hotel inquiry, the city was ready for another titillating insight into the conduct of their controversial top policeman.

In early 1965 the press revealed that Bischof was seeking twenty thousand dollars in damages from Fels for defamation. The hearing was set down for 22 March in the Supreme Court.

Bischof's claim asserted that between February and November 1962, Fels 'falsely and maliciously' wrote – and published or caused to be published – to the general secretary of the Police Union, Merv Callaghan, and the minister for education and migration, Jack Pizzey, certain defamatory statements. (Pizzey's portfolios now also incorporated the Police Department.)

The crux of the defamation was Fels's allegation that Bischof 'had intercourse' with her 'on diverse occasions from early in 1957 until in or about August 1960, at Jeays Street, Fortitude Valley, and Underwood Road, Eight Mile Plains [the Fels family home]'.

Bischof claimed that the allegations had 'seriously injured' him, that he was 'likely to be injured in character, credit and reputation', and that he had been 'brought into public scandal, odium and contempt'.

Fels was represented by the legendary Brisbane barrister Dan Casey.

But come day one of the hearing, Bischof was nowhere to be seen.

Bischof's counsel, John Aboud, told the Supreme Court that the police commissioner was in Mount Isa on official police business.

Despite Fels's annoyance at the adjournment, the matter was stood over for the next Civil Sittings.

Three months later – on 21 June – the defamation case was abruptly settled. The Acting Chief Justice was told that the matter had been settled 'to the satisfaction of both parties', and the action was struck out.

Bischof, his nerves fraying after years of seemingly relentless public scandal, may have felt the ghosts of his past were catching up with him. Given that Fels's counsel requested, in the March appearance, that Bischof be ordered to pay costs for the untimely adjournment, and her angry phone calls to Colin Bennett years before, urging him to take up the sex scandal in parliament, it would appear she wanted the matter heard once and for all in a public court, and her former lover to be held to account, at last, for his actions.

Whatever the reason behind the settlement – that the police commissioner had agreed to pay Fels's mounting court costs may have indicated a weakening confidence – Bischof was once again saved embarrassment in a court of law.

His position, though, in the eyes of the public, some of his men and a mounting number of members of parliament, was showing signs of becoming untenable.

Silent Gets Rowdy in the Emerald City

It was a different Glen Hallahan who returned to Brisbane from peace-keeping duties in Cyprus in 1965.

While he was admired for his professionalism and organisational abilities overseas by the many men who worked with him in the peace-keeping force (though one detractor described him not-so-cryptically as an 'entrepreneurial' policeman), he landed back in the Consorting

Squad with grander ambitions. He wanted more illegal income, and he could only get that by teaming up with the big boys in Sydney.

As usual, he was given enormous latitude by his superiors – Bischof and Bauer – and literally did as he pleased.

If he desired to head down to Sydney, he found cases with a Queensland hook to swing into. And a local link was not even always required: in 1967 and 1968, for example, he would use the investigation into the disappearance of Prime Minister Harold Holt to visit Melbourne to afford his expertise to the case – and catch up with friends.

His sojourn overseas may have given Hallahan time to reflect on future plans. He began to gravitate to Sydney and his old friend and lover Shirley Brifman, who was still trading her body successfully out of the Hotel Rex in Kings Cross.

Brifman recalled in later police interviews: 'After Glen came back from Cyprus and I threw him into Freddie [Krahe], he was never away from Sydney.

'Freddie knew I had Brisbane in the palm of my hand and he wanted Glen Hallahan. I had a hold on Glen. Glen would do what I wanted . . . I put Freddie and Glen together. They were two top men in different states . . . and Glen trusted me.'

Instantly, the two men were a potent mix. Krahe controlled pockets of the Sydney underworld. He could use Hallahan to help expand criminal empires into the comparative backwater of Queensland. And Hallahan wanted to make more cash. Their ambitions dovetailed.

In Sydney, forging his friendship with Krahe, Hallahan invariably stayed at the Hotel Rex. There he entertained Brifman, other known prostitutes, their bludgers, and an assortment of Sydney criminals.

Once, Brifman was in Hallahan's room at the hotel, packing the detective's bag for his return flight to Brisbane, when Krahe arrived. 'What would Glen do without you?' Krahe remarked. Krahe then drove Hallahan to the airport.

Their plan was to organise robberies – sharing criminals for interstate jobs – and then divvy up the proceeds. It was a far cry from Hallahan hitting up Brisbane prostitutes for protection money. He had struck a rich, albeit dangerous, vein with Krahe.

There were parties. Restaurants. Dinners at the Mandarin Club and a French eatery in Potts Point. Then Hallahan would invariably fly home and return to his small bachelor flat in a red-brick block of six in St James Street, Petrie Terrace, directly across the road from the Normanby Hotel, and a short and pleasant walk to the old police depot and CIB headquarters in the city.

It was common knowledge in the police force that Bischof gave his boys – Lewis, Murphy, and Hallahan – an unusual degree of free rein. This was flagrantly exploited by Hallahan and Murphy.

While all officers had to report to a senior sergeant when they went out on a job, including its location and what squad car they'd be travelling in, not so the Rat Pack.

Ron Edington recalls: 'They'd walk past the senior sergeant and he'd say, "Where are you going?" [Then they'd reply] "Aw, it's got nothing to do with you, it's a private job." The sergeants were starting to oppose them, you know, to resent them . . . these three blokes were walking over the top of them.'

Edington says their unaccountability extended to interstate travel, especially to Sydney. He says a system evolved whereby Sydney criminals coming to Queensland had to pay 'rent' – about one thousand dollars a week – to Hallahan. The reverse applied to Krahe and Queensland criminals in Sydney.

'This is where the corruption started,' says Edington. 'They were planting bloody guns on blokes and . . .'

In one instance, a criminal was pinched. He had eight guns in his possession, but was only charged over a single firearm. Hallahan and Murphy kept the other seven. When Edington asked Murphy why the bloke was only charged with carrying one gun, he replied: 'We're keeping them [to plant on] seven other cunts!'

As business with Krahe intensified, so did Hallahan's Sydney visits. He was soon dropping down at least twice a month.

Mary Anne, Shirley Brifman's daughter, was a schoolgirl when Krahe and Hallahan's partnership really took flight. She remembers the Brifman family home at 25 Maitland Avenue, Kingsford, being used as a 'store house' for the proceeds of various robberies – everything from cash to transistor radios to women's clothing.

'There were kids running in and out, there were four of us,' Mary Anne recalls. 'We had a full-time housekeeper. We'd come home from school and they used to [be there] divvy[ing] everything up . . .'

Brifman said the splitting of protection and other monies between Krahe and Hallahan was 'just an everyday occurrence'. She said it usually happened in the lounge of her home.

Mary Anne says she knew all the Queensland and New South Wales players because they all came to the house – Murphy, Hallahan, Lewis, Krahe, and the rest. Lewis denies he ever went to Brifman's house in Sydney.

'Mum actually believed them to be her friends,' Mary Anne says. 'Workmates. They were a team of people, and my mother was a very important part of that team . . . They needed someone they could trust. My mother wouldn't steal. But she was still a naive country girl.'

As for Hallahan, he was in a peculiar sort of relationship with Shirley Brifman. The Atherton prostitute had fallen for him, and the feeling was mutual. Hallahan confided his deepest secrets to her.

'Hallahan . . . he had some conscience, and he struggled with that,' remembers Mary Anne. 'My mother talked about that. Because she was emotionally involved with Hallahan, he would yield to her.

'She had a very soft spot for him, and her soft spot was built on compassion for him. There was not that about Tony Murphy from her, ever . . . Hallahan couldn't cope, emotionally and mentally, I don't think, with what he'd done. I think it affected him gravely.

'I really do believe she was having proper affairs with Tony Murphy and Glen Hallahan. The chemistry with Glen Hallahan became a problem for Tony Murphy.'

There were other minor problems for Murphy. Fellow senior officers were beginning to resent the Rat Pack's charmed life under the protection of Police Commissioner Bischof. After the National Hotel whitewash, the 'untouchable' attitudes of Murphy and Hallahan, in particular, were beginning to chafe.

Senior Detective Don (Buck) Buchanan couldn't stand Murphy. It may have involved a bit of professional jealousy from the senior cop, but the animosity was so pronounced that Buchanan refused to speak to Murphy, even when the latter offered a simple 'good morning' at CIB headquarters.

'Everybody knew about the Rat Pack in the 1960s,' says one former officer who worked closely with senior detectives at the time. 'Tony was on the take. I knew he was. I let him know I knew and he just laughed. They were that bad. They used to laugh about taking the oath and telling lies in court.'

For this officer, whatever decent 'kills' the triumvirate brought to the table through legitimate police skills, their good work was undermined by the hypocrisy.

He recalls: 'It was obvious what Glen was up to. Tony covered his tracks better. As for Terry, when he got into the JAB, to all outward appearances he was pure – saving children's souls.'

Murphy, meanwhile, was on his own new trajectory. He left Consorting in 1966.

'Tony had been trying very, very hard to get into the Licensing Branch,' Brifman remembered. 'When he got in . . . he said to me, "Shirley, I'm sitting in the place where I've wanted to be for years. The place where I can make money."'

On his first day in the new job, he was approached by Jack Herbert, now a virtual veteran of Licensing and the supreme organiser of the Joke.

Herbert claimed that he'd learned from a fellow officer that Lewis and Murphy had been paying a corrupt Licensing Branch detective to protect a baccarat game in South Brisbane run by entrepreneur, and their friend, Tony Robinson Senior.

Herbert recollected in his memoir: 'We went around to the police canteen and we had a meal. I told Tony Murphy there was a Joke on in the office and would he like to be included. I had money there to give him straightaway. I recall his exact words when I said, "Do you want the money?" He said to me, "Watch your arm."'

Lewis recalls: 'I could never imagine why Murphy went into the Licensing Branch.

'I suppose if you look at it sensibly, Murphy was a detective sergeant first class, and if [the Joke] didn't have Murphy in the caper, and Murphy being a hard worker, it would have been impossible.

'I can't say Murphy was a crook. But it mightn't have been only Jack Herbert who told me lies. Murphy might have told them too.'

Herbert said that within weeks Murphy approached him and suggested Terry Lewis be included in the Joke. Despite running the JAB and being of little use to Herbert and Co., there was Lewis's friendship with Bischof to consider.

Herbert remembered meeting Lewis socially a few times after this, in company with Tony Murphy: 'I recall the conversation getting around to payments of money . . . and Terry Lewis saying to me – he thanked me on a number of occasions and he said, "Little fish are sweet" . . . He would just thank me and say, "Little fish are sweet".'

Bombs and Brothels

Hallahan's informant, the well-known Brisbane tattooist Billy Phillips, lived in a dingy, rundown Queenslander on a steep ridge at 29 Earl Street, Petrie Terrace, with his de facto wife, Tracey, three little children, and any number of friends and associates who happened to drift by.

By the late 1960s the imposing, bearded Phillips was doing it tough. He had Tracey on the game, and was dabbling in the sale of illegal firearms.

Just a hundred metres away to the east from his dilapidated home stood the block of flats in St James Street where Detective Hallahan lived. (His private phone number was 25051.) They were, quite literally, neighbours.

'You've got to understand,' says bouncer John Ryan, a former friend of Phillips and Tracey, 'that Hallahan was just as much a gangster as he was a cop. These guys lived near each other, they worked together, they used each other. That's the way it was back then.'

Phillips was running his tattoo business out of the Earl Street house. He had a lengthy criminal record, primarily for assault, and was struggling financially when he was Hallahan's informant.

Still, he had gained a reputation for being able to procure handguns and shotguns, and was the first port of call for interstate criminals looking for a weapon: 'I know Hallahan dropped off a few police issue .38s to Billy's place,' Ryan claims. He was also a competent fence, often receiving stolen goods – from both local thieves and crooked police – in exchange for tattoos or money.

'He was a brilliant artist,' recalls Ryan, who was first tattooed by Phillips in the 1950s. 'He could look at something and freehand draw it. He became the best known tattooist in the southern hemisphere, but a lot of his clients were dancers and prostitutes. They'd pay him with sex some of the time.'

And, like Hallahan, he had an insatiable passion for cash.

'He was going to own houses,' Ryan says, 'and rent them out. Hallahan was also mad for money. I'd bump into Hallahan over at Billy's house and all they ever talked about was money, big money.'

According to Ryan, Phillips started mixing with 'some very heavy characters' around 1966 and '67. At the same time he was feeding information to his neighbour Hallahan. Sometimes Billy sent a girl over to Hallahan's flat. Other times the detective dropped by Earl Street to smoke marijuana.

'I saw Hallahan sitting on the couch smoking a reefer and I just couldn't believe it,' Ryan says. 'This guy was a cop, and here he is smoking marijuana. I'm thinking, this cop's going to knock him off.'

Then things went foul.

Phillips began offering Hallahan false leads in order to distract attention from some of his own criminal activities. Hallahan wasn't pleased. According to Ryan, Hallahan started spreading the word that Phillips was a 'dog', or police informant. Given Phillips's new associates, it was potentially a death sentence.

On the morning of Monday 9 October 1967, postman Jonus Mickus, in his Postmaster-General-issue shirt with the sleeves rolled up above the elbows, and wearing his wide-brimmed hat, lugged his post bag up Earl Street, dropping off the mail.

At 8.50 a.m. he delivered a small package to the Phillips home, and continued on his route. Ten minutes later, working Belgrave Street, parallel to Earl, Mickus heard a tremendous blast issue from number 29.

He vaulted their back fence and rushed through a rear door to the house. He found Phillips's wife, Tracey, twenty-three, screaming and writhing on the bedroom floor, Phillips, then twenty-six, unconscious beside her, and their five-month-old son, Scott, knocked out on the bed and bleeding from facial wounds. Bomb shrapnel was embedded in the victims' bodies. Two other Phillips children were wandering about the house, dazed.

In a rare and disturbing event for Brisbane, the Phillipses had been sent a letter bomb. Addressed to Billy Phillips and clearly intended for him, Tracey had innocently opened the parcel, the size of an alarm clock and wrapped in brown paper. The explosion blew off her left hand and mangled her right, and her upper torso and face were mutilated.

Police later learned that the bomb contained a nine-volt battery detonation system and gelignite. It was housed in a small, Asian-style trinket box made of magnolia and birch.

One of the first detectives assigned to the investigation was Glen Patrick Hallahan.

Did the assassination attempt stem from underworld knowledge that Phillips had been working as a police informant? Or was it more personal, related to Phillips's multiple infidelities with women, particularly sex industry workers?

'I recall Billy telling me that he and Hallahan had these big plans,' Ryan says, 'They were going to be the big boys running guns, women and drugs. I was over at Billy's one Saturday morning and a young prostitute turned up. The next minute she's putting out for everybody for a tattoo. Billy said to me, "You never knock it back, John."'

Surgeons were unable to save Tracey's right hand and she was also blinded. Her face was disfigured. And it was discovered she was pregnant and lost the baby. Phillips and his son recovered.

Hallahan shot down to Melbourne to investigate the bombing, and also went to Sydney to interview known criminals. Naturally, he contacted Brifman. He went to her home at Kingsford and later they went up to his room at the Rex. He had something to show her.

'I had a few beers with him upstairs . . . then he said, "Have you ever seen forged money, Shirl?" It was ten-dollar notes. He said, "Do you want some, Shirley?"

'I said no. I said, "What are you going to do with all them?" He said, "I'm going to use some myself and the rest I'm going to load up crims I don't like."'

Ever the opportunist, Hallahan had picked up the notes off a criminal associate in Melbourne while he was making his Phillips bombing inquiries.

Hallahan also discussed the bombing with Brifman. He said an informant had told him that Phillips's former wife, Vickie, had allegedly set up the bombing from Melbourne.

Some years earlier, Vickie and Billy had had an extremely acrimonious split, according to family friend John Ryan. 'He was sprung
having sex with two women,' Ryan says. 'Vickie always threatened to
kill him. He was expecting retribution from her for years.'

Brifman recalled: 'Tracey copped the bomb. Glen told me that Billy
stood at the door and said to Tracey, "Don't open that, it will be a
bomb." He had been expecting it for about three or four years. Being
a sticky beak, she did open it.'

When Hallahan prepared to fly back to Brisbane, it was Fred Krahe
who drove him to Sydney airport.

On another occasion in 1967, Brifman was in Brisbane staying at
the Treasury. One night she went over to Hallahan's one-bedroom flat
for a drink.

'I remember I picked up a cent off the floor and handed it to him
and I said, "Put it in your money box."'

Hallahan then opened a wooden wardrobe and inside Brifman saw
bundles of genuine cash bound with rubber bands.

'Well, you don't need the cent piece,' she remarked.

Hallahan replied: 'I have never been short of money since I went
to Sydney.'

They sat and drank for a while and the phone rang around 11.30 p.m.

'Forget about the bank robbery tonight,' Hallahan told the caller.
'I've got a friend up from Sydney.'

Off the phone, Hallahan explained to Brifman that a bank robbery had been arranged at Capalaba, south-east of the CBD towards
Redland Bay.

He said, 'I put if off because you're here. When it's done I'll charge
another couple of chaps with it.'

Around this time, Brifman remembered what Tony Murphy had told
her about Hallahan: 'Shirley, you have got to be careful with Glen. The
trouble Glen is getting into lately. We're trying to drop off Glen.'

Brisbane was getting dangerous. And so was Detective Hallahan.

The Stockbroker with the Gold Limousine

Of all the men Brifman met in the course of her work as a prostitute, there was nobody quite like Robin Corrie.

Corrie was a flamboyant Brisbane-based stockbroker with Corrie and Co., a broking firm that was an institution in Brisbane, founded by his grandfather in 1877.

Corrie was short and wiry, a prankster and a daredevil, a self-publicist and showman with ferocious energy. As a teenager in 1935, he made the news pages of the *Courier-Mail* when his dinghy sank in Bramble Bay, off Redcliffe, and he and a companion were rescued after spending more than two hours in the water. With youthful bravado, he told the reporter that he didn't feel in danger at any point but was hesitant about his mother finding out about the mishap.

As a successful broker, he pulled stunts and subsequently attention to himself. He had a grey Rolls Royce (it had a tow bar, in case Corrie wanted to take off with his caravan) complete with capped chauffeur.

Corrie's son, John Corrie, recalls being excruciatingly embarrassed when his father dropped him off of a morning at Eagle Junction State School.

'We'd be dropped off in front of seven hundred screaming kids . . . The chauffeur with cap would open the door to let us out. Where could you go? There was nowhere to go.'

Corrie also had a Ford Fairlane that he painted gold to bring notice to his belief that gold stocks were on the rise. The act earned him a fine from the Brisbane Stock Exchange.

He was also a man who knew how to spend serious money. While he had a passion for yachts, he also had a taste for marijuana and the wilder fringes of life. He was well known to management and staff at the National Hotel.

In the late 1960s, the Corries – wife Barbara, three children and a Labrador – lived in what the press described as a 'mansion' in the well-heeled suburb of Clayfield. The house featured a marble foyer, a wading pool with a waterside bar, and a maid's room. Corrie also owned a large beachfront getaway house in Hedges Avenue, Mermaid Beach.

For all intents and purposes, Corrie was a wealthy man with a happy home life. He had been a pioneer with oil stocks in Queensland, was well connected to government, and was nationally respected for his good business judgement.

Behind the scenes, he was worrying about the future of his company and was mentally starting to fray. His lifestyle didn't help. He smoked at least six packs of unfiltered Benson & Hedges cigarettes a day. His children remember him lighting up while still in bed and half asleep.

After Corrie met Brifman in Sydney, he would often fly her up to Brisbane for 'big money' and put her up in a hotel in the city.

Both Hallahan and Murphy knew of Shirley's lavish client and their interstate arrangements.

'He used to discuss all his problems with me,' Brifman said. 'There was nothing I did not know about Corrie.' One of the last things Corrie confided in her was that he had exercised poor judgement over a share purchase that 'went wrong' and had received criticism from those who took his advice.

While in Brisbane, Brifman dined with Corrie at the fashionable Lennons Hotel on the corner of Ann and George streets. At one end of the hotel foyer was a large clock and a map of the world, emphasising the establishment's 'cosmopolitan' atmosphere. It was all leather banquettes and cut flowers, and a far cry from the National down at the Bight with its bawdy clientele.

Brifman called Corrie 'the professor', and he offered her his wisdom and worldly advice. She visited the Corrie family home in Clayfield, and he would send each of the Brifman children forty dollars every Christmas.

In April 1968, Corrie flew to Sydney to take possession of a new yacht – a twenty-three-foot Hood he planned to sail home from Sydney. But he had some partying to do first.

'He rang me,' Brifman remembered. 'He came in and played up with Ann Marie Stevens that night. Ann Marie was coming up to Surfers. He said, "When you come up, give me a ring."

'After playing up with her that night he wouldn't have anything more to do with her. She got the brush-off. Robin told me that he went home this night and his first wife was very upset. She said a girl had rung and said, "Do you want to know who your husband is playing up with in Sydney? It will cost you so much."

'He had to put on the defensive. Naturally, he said, "Tell [this woman] to come forward and front me." His wife believed him. Ann Marie rang back and Mrs Corrie told her she did not believe her.'

Corrie's association with Brifman – one of the best connected prostitutes and madams in Sydney – was starting to blow back into his private and professional life.

And with Hallahan monitoring Corrie's illicit activities – not just squandering cash on prostitutes and drugs, but on Brifman, who had been intimate with Hallahan for years and was deeply interconnected with corrupt police and criminals in two states – it was destined to end badly.

The Traveller and the Travel Agent

Lewis was his usual punctual self on Tuesday 24 October 1967, and arrived at the office forty-five minutes early, at 8.15 a.m., to an exciting surprise.

A telegram waiting on his desk announced that his application for a Churchill Fellowship had been successful. He was off on his first trip overseas – to the United States and Europe – to learn the latest techniques in policing juveniles.

For whatever reason, that morning he walked down to the Wintergarden Theatre and saw *Danger Grows Wild*.

The film was an anti-drug spy and action flick produced by the United Nations. Did he think it his duty to see a film about the heroin trade in Afghanistan, as it was potentially harmful to young, impressionable Brisbane teenagers?

Afterwards, Lewis saw Bischof about the fellowship and immediately typed an application for special leave.

He was still plugging away at his degree, but the Churchill honour gave him even greater kudos. He had proved he worked hard, now here was recognition from the prestigious Churchill Trust, established in 1965 in memory of former British Prime Minister Winston Churchill and based on merit rather than academic qualification. The fellowships aimed to offer overseas experience to applicants whose 'pursuit of excellence' had been exhausted on home ground. Lewis was Queensland's first Churchill fellow.

And in executing an international tour of juvenile policing, he was emulating Bischof, who had undertaken a similar study tour early in his own career. It gave a sign to Lewis's friends and foes in the force that Lewis was heading for greater things.

In theory, the fellowship would look good on his curriculum vitae. But prior to taking the global trip – devised through research conducted by Lewis himself – he learned that not only was the daily allowance for travelling expenses minimal, but he would only attract a half-salary back home for the six-month duration of the expedition. With a wife and four children to support up on Garfield Drive, this was the cause of much anxiety.

He considered handing back the honour.

'It caused me more financial stress and heartbreak than anything I ever did,' Lewis recalls. 'I was given an economy-class airline ticket and eleven dollars a day expenses. It was very, very tight.'

Yet another police function was held at the National Hotel, to help raise money for Lewis's travelling expenses.

He flew to Europe with Qantas on Wednesday 1 May 1968. Lewis admits he was daunted at the prospect of his first trip overseas, and especially with so little money to make it work for him.

Lewis distilled the trip to three months, travelling to Germany, Denmark, France, the United Kingdom, and the United States, bedding down in the cheapest rooms he could find, keeping an eye on food expenses along the way. 'It was a cup of coffee and a bun for breakfast,' he says.

Shirley Brifman later claimed that she met with Lewis around this time. 'I saw Terry off when he went to England on the Churchill Fellowship,' she said. 'He rang me on the way back, at Sydney, and I went out and saw him.'

Lewis adamantly denies this: 'I landed in Brisbane. Why would she come to the airport to see me? I never had anything to do with bloody Brifman.'

He was relieved to be back at his desk on Tuesday 23 July, where he saw all of his JAB staff then the police commissioner 'about his overseas observations'. *Telegraph* journalist Pat Lloyd phoned for an interview.

It is possible that Lewis, in preparing his trip earlier in the year, might have crossed paths with local Dalgetys travel agent Gary Venamore, thirty-five, a gregarious socialite and man–about–town who lived with his mother in Rawlins Street, Kangaroo Point?

As a child, Venamore showed a talent for singing and on special occasions performed in his local church – the old stone Wesley Methodist in Linton Street, just seven streets from Venamore's home. On Christmas Day in 1943, the Wesley congregation was treated to a solo performance by 'Gary Venamore, nine-year-old boy soprano'.

As an adult, his friends called the bisexual Venamore '. . . the gay, witty, exuberant life of the party'. He also liked to hop bars and clubs.

One barman acquaintance said of him, 'Sometimes his jokes were a bit naughty . . . but he was the type who could tell them to just about anyone and get away with it . . . If he wanted a drink it wasn't just a case of asking for a beer or whiskey – it was always, "Peel me a grape, love."'

While he enjoyed the hobnobbing of the Old Bailey Bar at Lennons Hotel, he would gravitate later in the night, and after consuming more alcohol, to the seamier National Hotel and a nearby club, the Playboy.

The Playboy, a venue with a risqué reputation where you could see drag queens and strippers, had a large bar upstairs that, while unlicensed, did a roaring late-night trade. In the early- to mid-1960s the club hosted a restaurant cabaret by young talent Bernard King, who would later make millions as a camp television chef and talent show judge.

It was King who spotted a young singer, Judi Connelli, and gave her a start on the small, cramped stage of the Playboy.

She remembers it as a bit seedy, but unique in Brisbane at the time for its eclectic clientele: 'It was the first time I'd ever seen a man dressed as a woman. They were gorgeous people. You'd bump into canecutters from north Queensland who loved coming down to the city and dressing up as women at night.'

This was Venamore's midnight milieu, edgy and bawdy.

On Tuesday 5 November 1968, Venamore met up with a friend, Richard Billington, at the bar of Her Majesty's Hotel in Queen Street for a round of drinks right on 5 p.m. Billington observed that Venamore was carrying a roll of notes. They were met by another friend, shipping clerk David Peel.

At 6 p.m. they left the bar, and Venamore proceeded alone to Lennons Hotel in George Street to meet other friends. Billington knew Venamore well: he would continue drinking, possibly heavily, into the night.

Peel later joined Venamore at the Old Bailey Bar in Lennons with another friend. An hour and a half later, Venamore made motions to move on.

'He intimated to us that he should be going home, and he left us about 8.30,' Peel said. 'I did not see him again.'

As the night deepened, Venamore found his way down to the National Hotel precinct, with its lovely views of the Brisbane River and the Story Bridge.

He may have gone in for a drink at the National. He was known there to manager Jack Cooper, and was probably acquainted also with the hotel's famous tourist attraction: Warren Dennis, who ran Warren's Bar within the hotel and dressed in drag. For the era, he was a scandalous curio, a spectacle, in his sequined dresses, silver wig, painted fingernails and jewellery, pirouetting as he pulled a beer off the tap.

By around 10.30 p.m. Venamore was at the Playboy, north of the National at the intersection of Queen and Adelaide streets. He told club doorman Reg Durston: 'I've got no brass.' It was arranged for him to cash a five-dollar cheque.

What happened between his arrival and when he left with two men at 2.20 a.m. remains conjecture. The club was known by police to be frequented by homosexuals, but they gave the Playboy little official attention.

Detective Ross Beer says of Venamore: 'He was a sort of Jekyll and Hyde . . . He was a ladies' man when he was sober, a playboy and very dapper. He'd mix with the social set. But when he got on the drink he was a raving homosexual. He'd make approaches to people.'

Taxi driver Jack Sangster picked up Venamore and the two men at 2.25 a.m. near the club and drove them to a block of flats in nearby Maxwell Street, New Farm, not far from Lighthouse Wharf. A witness remembered hearing a loud and prolonged scream from a man between 2 and 3 a.m.

Just after 6.10 a.m., a ferry launch master spotted a body floating face-up beneath the Story Bridge, a short distance towards Petrie Bight from the Lighthouse Wharf. It was a brutally bashed Venamore, his body shifting with the tide back towards the CBD. Ironically, anyone awake and taking in the fresh morning air on the balconies of the National Hotel that day may have seen it.

Detective Beer and Glen Hallahan were called in to investigate the murder.

'He was really badly bashed about,' Beer says. 'Someone had taken to him with a fence paling or something like that.'

The coroner would find that Venamore had a .23 blood alcohol reading, and that the cause of death was drowning, a ruptured liver, haemorrhage, and multiple injuries. He had wounds consistent with being kicked around the head and being struck with a blunt instrument. There were also bruises on his wrists and ankles, suggesting an unconscious Venamore was then swung and thrown into the river by two people.

The estimated time of death was 4 a.m. The suspected motive was robbery, as Venamore's watch – given to him by his late father – was missing.

Beer and Hallahan interviewed seamen from the twenty-one ships docked in Brisbane that night. They also questioned members of the homosexual community: 'We learned that a number of them had been bashed over a period of time,' Beer recollects, 'but they had a fear of coming forward to report the incidents.'

Hallahan flew to Sydney to follow up the seamen angle. As always, he hooked up with Brifman: 'He brought up the photographs to me. I saw all the marks on [Venamore's] face. No motive of robbery.'

Brifman said the murder had given Hallahan a business idea – blackmailing homosexuals.

'So they put . . . TV cameras on the Eagle Street toilets,' Brifman said. 'He said, "Shirley, the businessmen who are homosexuals, you would not believe it."'

Hallahan and his cronies brought the surprised men in for questioning and threatened them with the show reels in which they featured. If Hallahan was to be believed, it was a good old-fashioned sting.

Venamore's murder – violent, shocking, sudden – was uncharacteristic of Brisbane. It was a killing that would not be out of place in Sydney or Melbourne. Like the brutal rape and murder of Betty Shanks in 1952, was it epochal for the city?

Despite rewards offered and the promise of new clues, by August the following year the newspapers were comfortable printing that 'police were not following any major leads concerning the murder of Gary James Venamore'.

The case was never solved. But the murder, in hindsight, would prove to be a mere prelude, an opening refrain, to a wave of violence and crime never seen before in Queensland.

Shirley, Businesswoman

Shirley Brifman had been making a comfortable living working as a prostitute out of Sydney's Hotel Rex when, in February 1968, she had a major disagreement with the management and was barred from entering the premises.

She, in turn, issued them with a letter of demand that she be permitted to return or she would proceed with a defamation writ. Detective Sergeant Mick Phelan, to whom Brifman had been paying protection money for some time, intervened. She could not take on the Rex, he told her. He had been protecting them, too, since the early 1950s, and turning a blind eye to prostitutes trawling the bars and lounges.

Phelan had another idea. He told her that he would procure on her behalf if she set up her own place. Soon after, Brifman opened for business in Earls Court, Flat 23, Earls Place, a seedy back lane behind Darlinghurst Road and just around the corner from the Rex. She took with her about twenty-five prostitutes from the hotel, which had to close down its hairdressing facility as a result of the sudden loss of trade.

And it was at Earls Court that she began to also pay off the notorious Detective Fred Krahe so she could run her brothel without impediment from the Vice Squad.

'I would ring him or he would ring me,' Brifman said. 'He would usually come up and have a couple of drinks . . . I was intimate with him. It started the second day after he came to Earls Court. We were intimate about once or twice a fortnight.' Hallahan, whenever he was in town, also stayed at Earls Court.

Then Brifman's business took off, and with the cash flowing in she was beginning to attract attention.

'The brothel got too big,' she said. 'Fred told me that he would protect me against them if I paid him. I have got to give him credit, he did. Fred got keen on me.'

Within a year she would open more brothels in Wylde Street, Potts Point, and in the fashionable Reef in Ithaca Road, Elizabeth Bay, with its view of Sydney Harbour. In a very short time she was establishing herself as the premier madam in inner-city Sydney. And while her protection outlay, which grew to more than thirty-five police in Queensland and New South Wales, was substantial, the two brothels at Wylde Street alone were bringing her in, after wages and expenses, more than five thousand dollars a week.

Brifman was now effectively running a large business. 'She was bright and quick, she had a good mind,' says her daughter Mary Anne.

In addition, Brifman was using her brothels and private home as storage and distribution warehouses for stolen goods and cash, she was often acting as a go-between with gangsters and corrupt police, and was paying off, and sleeping with, some of the most dangerous police on Australia's east coast.

She was inextricably bound up in a volatile social mix that included the likes of Lennie McPherson, George Freeman, Abe Saffron, Stewart John Regan and Raymond 'Ducky' O'Connor.

Then there was Joe 'the Writer' Borg, the king of the Palmer Street brothels.

Borg, whose East Sydney brothel network extended to twenty premises, was a fanatical animal lover. He was also a reputed gunman and thief. Police believed his operations brought in up to ten thousand dollars a week in clear profit.

By the autumn of 1968 the fabulously wealthy Borg was in mourning. The previous November he had lost his wife to a drug overdose. She went by several names, including Anne Borg, Anne Brown and Anne Williams. In another life, north of the border, she was known as Ada Bahnemann, ex-wife of convicted German gunman Gunther Bahnemann.

Borg himself didn't have to mourn for long. On 28 May 1968, he hopped into his car outside his house in North Bondi to go to the hardware store for some interior house paint when a massive gelignite bomb exploded under the driver's seat. It decimated his lower body and he died en route to hospital.

It was a blast that Brifman must have felt over in Potts Point or Elizabeth Bay. A rival had lost his life, but who was gunning for Borg and his business? And would they come for her?

The Borg assassination also put brothels and prostitutes onto the front page of newspapers. Sydney was shocked by the killing. It suddenly wanted to know all about the machinations of the underworld.

And soon, the press would be knocking on Shirley Brifman's door.

The Haunted Mind of Frank Bischof

By 1967, having endured a royal commission, a personal sex scandal, the private exposure of his corruption before the premier, and decades of heavy drinking, Bischof's health was falling apart.

On 17 April he was admitted to St Andrew's War Memorial hospital on Wickham Terrace and treated for hypertension. The sixty-two-year-old was discharged two weeks later and recuperated on the Gold Coast before returning to his big desk and chair in early June.

Days later he fell ill again and was rushed to the Mater hospital in South Brisbane.

According to the *Courier-Mail*, the news of this latest turn 'caused a sensation in police and Government circles'. Premier Nicklin ordered a medical report into Bischof's condition.

What the public didn't read about was the alarming deterioration in Bischof's mental health.

Thomas Hiley, now retired from parliament, heard whispers of Bischof's peculiar behaviour during his hospital stays. Hiley was convinced that Bischof's exposure before Premier Nicklin many years earlier – over the SP bookmakers' delegation from western Queensland – fed the former commissioner's hypertension.

Hiley said that in hospital Bischof became 'a victim of his own fears': 'He'd hide in the laundry rooms, he'd hide in the ironing rooms. He'd hide anywhere. And there were search parties out . . . trying to find Bischof after dark, you see, and when they'd get him he'd be a quivering, shaking morsel: "They're after me, I can hear the voices, they're after me . . ."'

Mad or not, when he finally got back to work he held a closed-door conference at police headquarters with twenty of his top officers and gave them a fierce dressing down.

He claimed that he knew the names of the 'assassins' who were hoping to read his 'obituary and obsequial rites', and were planning his successor during his last bout of sickness. He accused them of suffering 'blabberitis'.

The *Courier-Mail* reported that several of the officers present were 'visibly shaken' when they left the meeting.

Bischof was clinging on. But for how long?

Enter the Country Bumpkin

Frank Bischof wasn't the only figure of power in Queensland suffering the strains of office.

In January 1968, at the age of seventy-two and after ten and a half years as premier, 'Honest' Frank Nicklin announced his retirement. He handed the reins of the state over to his loyal deputy, fellow Country Party stalwart Jack Pizzey.

Pizzey was the logical successor. Born in Childers, 325 kilometres north of Brisbane – renowned sugarcane country – he was educated, loved cricket, had worked as a school teacher in rural Queensland and had been an effective education minister under Nicklin. He was widely recognised as the premier's right-hand man.

Pizzey, too, had a major health concern looming over him. He had already suffered one heart attack in office, and, though he had fully recovered, it led political commentators to hint at the importance of the selection of Pizzey's Country Party deputy, should his health deteriorate again.

Mines and Main Roads Minister Ron Camm was the favourite. Lands Minister Alan Fletcher was also in the race. So, too, was the fifty-seven-year-old works and housing minister, Johannes Bjelke-Petersen, the peanut farmer from Kingaroy. Bjelke-Petersen won with a majority in the first ballot.

Despite having been in parliament for almost twenty-one years, little was known about Bjelke-Petersen, except that he was a God-fearing man, he flew light aircraft, and tore down scrub with the use of tractors and chains.

In the first Pizzey ministry – with Liberal Gordon Chalk as deputy premier and treasurer – Bjelke-Petersen held onto his portfolio and added another: ministerial responsibility for police.

By July, Pizzey had settled in well to the premiership and had the coalition on course for the next state election, due in May 1969. He made important trade trips to Europe and Japan.

On 31 July 1968 Pizzey suffered a second major heart attack and died close to midnight in Chermside hospital.

That night, the increasingly paranoid police commissioner, Frank Bischof, was attending the annual police ball at the iconic Cloudland Ballroom in Bowen Hills. Bjelke-Petersen was also present.

According to the *Courier-Mail*, as the balloons were to be released from the ceiling, the news of Pizzey's death arrived at Cloudland.

'Mr Bischof called for a minute's silence in the memory of the former Police Minister and senior policemen stood with bowed heads,' the newspaper reported. 'Couples who seconds before had been dancing stood to attention in silent tribute.'

On 1 August, Deputy Premier Gordon Chalk, a Liberal, was sworn in to the top office. His tenure would be fleeting, with the Country Party holding twenty-six seats in the Legislative Assembly, and the Liberals nineteen.

The Country Party would not hand over what it saw as its right to the premiership. On 7 August, Bjelke-Petersen was elected as leader of the government. The next day, Chalk resigned as premier – he had lasted eight days – and Bjelke-Petersen and his ministry were sworn in. Chalk, again, was relegated to deputy. The new premier also became minister for state development and he retained the police portfolio.

Queensland, historically lumbered with singular premiers for lengthy terms, had now had two in six months, and a third counting Bjelke-Petersen.

Bischof, meanwhile, had made the decision to retire. There was talk that he was shoved from the commissionership because of his ailing health and the many controversies that had dogged his reign.

The *Police Acts* stipulated that the police commissioner 'continue in office during such period he is of good behaviour [a notion repeatedly questioned by Colin Bennett] and until he reaches the age of sixty-five years when he shall retire from office'.

Bischof had accumulated 240 days' leave, despite his sporadic trysts in the Roberts brothers' beach house on the South Coast. If he formally went on leave on 14 February 1969, and acquitted those holidays, it would take him to 14 October, two days after his sixty-fifth birthday and official retirement age. As in all things, the canny Bischof had done his maths.

Bischof would be replaced by Brisbane CIB chief Norm Bauer, Hallahan's mentor from his Mount Isa days, and a loyal lieutenant to the Big Fella for decades. A fellow Mason, Bauer knew the ropes. More importantly, he knew where the bodies were buried in the police force.

His retirement meant the Big Fella would not be a thorn for Premier Bjelke-Petersen, as he had been for Frank Nicklin.

Interestingly, there was early liaison between the new premier's office and the officious head of the Juvenile Aid Bureau, Terry Lewis.

By late 1968 the JAB chief had completed his Churchill Fellowship report and was binding it himself with a borrowed stapling machine. He planned to disseminate it to as many people of influence as possible, both within and outside the police force. The fellowship, too, had made him an increasingly popular speaker at schools, Rotary, Rotaract and Lions clubs and Christian and charitable institutions like the Salvation Army Ladies' Home League. His profile in the media was on the ascent.

On Monday 13 January 1969, he recorded first contact with the office of Premier Joh Bjelke-Petersen in his police diary: 'Phoned Det. Sgt. Linthwaite re: tour with Premier. Saw Commissioner re: statement that Premier will visit J.A.B – he approved my contacting Premier's office re: suggestion of visit to J.A.B. by the Premier. Off duty at 6pm.'

The following day, there was further contact: 'Mr Shaffer, Premier's Office, phoned to advise that Premier will probably visit J.A.B. in about three weeks.'

Then, on Wednesday 15 January, Lewis was further emboldened: 'Report with Fellowship Reports to Commissioner and Premier.'

On Bauer's orders, in early February he helped Bischof's driver, Slim Somerville, pack up the outgoing commissioner's office.

According to Somerville, they discovered among other things a revolver, a wig and a paper mask. Lewis apparently bundled them into a suitcase, and later Tony Murphy asked Jack Herbert to temporarily secrete them, which Herbert says he did, behind some fish tanks under his house. Lewis says he can't recall finding the unusual objects.

Bischof finished up on Friday 14 February 1969. Did he enjoy the patronage of his old mates down at the National Hotel? It is likely he indulged in a long lunch: Lewis, Bischof's protégé, noted in his police diary that he finished work that day at 11.30 a.m.

Bauer's commissionership was nothing more than a temporary measure – Bauer himself would turn sixty-five in 1970. But he was an old hand, was intimate with Bischof's corrupt infrastructure, and was close to all the major players. The Joke and its adherents now had over a year to engineer a sympathetic replacement.

But a major spanner – greater than the National Hotel royal commission – was about to enter the works.

Allan Maxwell Hodges, member for Gympie and minister for works and housing, convinced Bjelke-Petersen that a premier holding a police portfolio could potentially be a dangerous thing. Any strife in the force and it would stick to the top dog.

Hodges could see that the police were getting on top of Joh. He met with the premier and in May 1969 was granted the police portfolio.

He immediately faced obstruction, indifference and inaction from Bauer when Hodges promoted various changes within the force. It quickly became evident to the new police minister that the only way to instigate reform would be to get Bauer out of the way and commence real work on slotting a smart, honest and efficient man – without a history with the old boys' network – into the commissionership.

First, Hodges toured Victoria and South Australia with Bauer, gleaning ideas for a reformed force. He was most impressed with South Australia, under the commissionship of Brigadier John McKinna.

Following the interstate tour, Bauer was duly sent on a five-month, all-expenses-paid study tour around the world – what he would have done with his newly acquired knowledge, with less than a year left in the force, was debatable. Now Hodges could get to work.

In a small but vital – and ultimately historic – victory for Hodges, Cabinet approved that McKinna visit Queensland and conduct a full audit of the force, including its education and training components.

If the National Hotel inquiry was unable to find any corruption and wrongdoing within police ranks, perhaps Hodges and McKinna could deconstruct the corrupt network from the ground up and start afresh.

Deep down, Hodges knew he had to disconnect the old circuit of commissioners and their bagmen, to dismantle a complex culture involving generational graft, verballing, and myriad corrupt practices that even extended to taking bribery money from stationery suppliers in exchange for contracts providing notebooks and pencils to the Queensland police force. He needed some fresh, honest eyes. And someone with a moral compass.

With Bischof gone, and with Bauer in a brief holding pattern as police commissioner, Lewis needed some new footholds to find his way forward. He pinned his hopes on a long-time friend getting the top job: honest officer Abe Duncan. There was little to suggest, at that moment, that the old ways wouldn't continue, business as usual.

But first Lewis needed to get acquainted with the new police minister, and get the measure of the man.

In mid-August 1969, with wife Hazel (four months' pregnant with their final child, John), Lewis went on seven days' leave to Sydney. He noted in his police diary: 'Spent considerable time with Det. Sgts. Krahe; Smith and Day of the Breaking Squad.' He had known Smith and Day from the 1950s. But what of Freddy Krahe? What was the reason for spending 'considerable time' with one of Shirley Brifman's corrupt lovers? (Lewis says he doesn't recall meeting with Krahe on that trip.)

There may have been a good reason. Not only were the old, familiar police networks in Queensland about to face fresh scrutiny from an energetic new police minister, but the New South Wales side of the equation was also set to disintegrate.

Shirley Brifman — the petite prostitute who used to work out of Killarney brothel on a bend of the Brisbane River, and now one of Sydney's biggest madams, embedded with dozens of corrupt police from commissioners down — was garnering unexpected and unwanted media attention. And she was making some very tough and very senior police in both states extremely nervous.

If Brifman went down, they'd all go down.

As it happened, Brifman was in Wahroonga hospital when the Lewises visited Sydney. She had a substantial addiction to sedatives, particularly the barbiturate Tuinal, and with her history of poor health since childhood, her nerves were going. Did Lewis pay his respects while she was recuperating? Did he go to the Brifman household and say hello to Sonny and the children?

Whatever transpired, Lewis was again back at his desk in the JAB on Monday 25 August.

Just over a week later, Hodges' first wife passed away in Gympie. Lewis and Ross Beer, along with Police Commissioner Bauer, attended the funeral in Gympie on 1 September.

Two months later, Lewis would personally meet Hodges for the first time, at the Coorparoo State High School annual speech night, where the minister was guest speaker.

He would make further attempts to get a private audience with Hodges, including hijacking the minister on his annual Christmas vacation on the Gold Coast.

But why was Lewis so desperately anxious? Did he fear the end of his stellar promotional run under Bischof? Or the exposure of the Joke? Or both?

On Thursday 13 November, he had a special visitor to his office: 'Saw Brigadier J. McKinna re: functions of the Juvenile Aid Bureau.'

Reform was on its way, and people were getting edgy.

As for Detective Glen Hallahan – who at the end of the 1960s was 'up to his eyeballs in major crime', according to reporter Ken Blanch – he quickly identified the source of all looming troubles.

It was his confidante and lover, Shirley Margaret Brifman. She knew too much, and she had recently become a lightning rod for the press.

He would have to keep a very close eye on her.

The Wise Bald Man

In 1969, in an uncharacteristically rash decision, Ray Whitrod left the Commonwealth police force, which he headed out of Canberra, to become commissioner of the Papua New Guinea police force. He and his wife, Mavis, were stationed in Port Moresby.

Whitrod had enjoyed respect in the Canberra job and had seen his children grow and marry. He was in his mid-fifties when he went to Moresby, having travelled the world, guarded royalty, accepted the confidence of prime ministers and turned himself into a quasi-academic with several degrees.

When Papua New Guinea's incumbent police commissioner, Bob Cole, approached Whitrod, a friend, seeking help to find his replacement, Whitrod mulled over suitable candidates but came up empty. Respecting their friendship, he ultimately accepted the position to help out Cole.

Why did he leave all that he knew to take on a challenging position in a country moving towards independence and the potential strife that that entailed?

'I don't know,' Whitrod later said in an interview. 'Partly, I think, because I felt that I'd largely achieved what I'd set out to do, that is, establish a Commonwealth police force, and I was working on my master's thesis, which involved native cultures at the time, and partly, I suspect, because I wanted new . . . new fields to conquer. I don't know. I never really examined my motives.'

Soon after arriving in Papua New Guinea, he contracted malaria.

McKinna, scrutinising the Queensland police force, didn't waste any time compiling his reports. They were done by the end of 1969, and they were the old police guards' worst nightmare.

In short, he proposed the removal of the time-worn promotion path by chain of superiority. It would be replaced by promotion on merit. He also encouraged multi-skilling, external studies for officers, and the division of the state into four regional police commands.

Along with a revision of existing police examination methods and a reduction in officers performing tasks for other government departments, he was recommending a total overhaul of the force. The past was to be detonated.

McKinna, an Adelaide boy, also told Police Minister Hodges that Whitrod was the only man for the job.

When McKinna got back to Adelaide, he phoned Whitrod in Port Moresby and urged him to apply for the role of Queensland police commissioner. Having just begun his post, Whitrod declined.

McKinna rang once more but Whitrod again said no.

Then David Mercer, Hodges' undersecretary in the Department of Works and Housing, phoned Whitrod. The answer was still no.

In a last-ditch effort to secure Whitrod, Hodges and Mercer flew to Port Moresby and stayed for two nights.

They got their man.

Ray Whitrod had no idea of the hell that awaited him in sunny Queensland.

Shirley, the Wife's Best Friend

Just a few hundred metres from Macleay Street, Potts Point, down Greenknowe Avenue towards the harbour, there had always been a seemingly invisible division that separated the sex, sleaze and turmoil of Sydney's Kings Cross from the mannered gentility of waterfront Elizabeth Bay.

Here – among the grand old stone piles with turrets and yards that ran down to the harbour, and huge blocks of red-brick apartments with cage-door elevators – brothel madam Shirley Brifman reached the apotheosis not just of her empire but most probably of her life.

The dirt-poor kid from a family of timber workers set up a new premises in the Reef, a modern, half-moon-shaped apartment complex on Ithaca Road.

The swank apartment was Brifman's crowning achievement, and it was Detective Fred Krahe who encouraged her to celebrate and host a housewarming party.

The function was set for Friday 9 May 1969, and aside from Krahe she sent out invitations to up to ten other local police. Many were officers she'd been paying off for years, others not.

Krahe didn't know he would be mixing with other police, among the businessmen and call girls.

As the party raged into the night, photographs were taken, many with Krahe in the frame.

Somehow, Sydney's *Sunday Mirror* got hold of them a week or so later and Krahe found out. He was apoplectic. If they were published, he needed a bogus excuse for his attendance at a party with some of Sydney's best known prostitutes. Krahe asked Brifman to see New South Wales Police Commissioner Norm Allan: 'He wanted me to explain away his presence at the party.'

The meeting with Allan was arranged on the pretext of another concern, namely that Brifman had heard of plans to unseat the police commissioner and felt compelled to share them with him. Courtesy of that Trojan Horse, she could 'explain away' Krahe and the booze-up at the Reef.

Allan had been police commissioner since 1962. He was tall, fair-skinned and wore heavy, horn-rimmed spectacles. He was renowned as a superb administrator but had old-fashioned, often intractable views, particularly regarding the death penalty, which he thoroughly supported.

When Robert Askin was elected premier in 1965, the police commissioner struck up an almost immediate and seamless working relationship with the state leader, just as Bischof had cultivated with Frank Nicklin in Queensland.

Allan left illegal gambling and SP bookmaking alone, as did his Queensland counterpart in the 1960s, and corruption within the force flourished.

Despite the demands of his position, Police Commissioner Allan obviously had the time to see Sydney's leading madam.

Allan and Brifman discussed the potential coup against him, which he said he already knew about. Furthermore, according to Brifman, he told her that she could 'carry on' her business and that anyone who touched her would 'have to answer to him'.

It didn't stop the press.

In early June, the *Sunday Mirror* ran with the story of the cops in the bordello. 'When it was published everybody panicked,' Brifman said. Over the next six weeks the newspaper ran two further stories on Brifman-related activities.

In an aftermath, she was put in touch with Peter Grose, who had recently founded the Curtis Brown literary agency. His office was a couple of rooms in the basement of his house in Paddington. They discussed her extraordinary story. He wanted to sell her memoir and call it *Shirley, the Wife's Best Friend*.

Grose recommended to Brifman that she appear on national

television to stop the flow of newspaper stories coming out of the *Sunday Mirror*. Grose confirms that the meeting with Shirley and Sonny Brifman took place. He says: 'She approached me. I met her and Sonny, but no book materialised.'

Hallahan was highly agitated over the newspaper stories. Brifman said: 'He was in a panic . . . He told me that the taxation men were in Brisbane investigating all the police I had been connected with. Glen and I fell out not long after the papers in 1969.'

And although she never fell out with Murphy, their regular contact ceased after the publicity.

The storm died down. Brifman continued to successfully run her brothels, despite increasing spells in hospital for her health. She continued to pay her crooked police friends, and she went on working as a prostitute herself.

She was still only in her early thirties but had packed at least two lives into one; everything was taking its toll on Shirley Brifman.

By New Year's Eve 1969, the central phone number for her brothels – 35 38 37 – was still ringing off the hook and was known, by her own account, to 'millions of men'.

Shirley Margaret Brifman, protected by police in two states and earning a fortune, was unaware that she was finished. The forces that made her were set to break her.

At the dawn of 1970, she had less than fifteen months to live.

1970s

Before the Storm

On the eve of 1970, the respected Brisbane criminal lawyer Des Sturgess found himself in Port Moresby, Papua New Guinea, on a case.

He knew the place well. Straight out of university, and armed with a law degree, he went to work in Port Moresby in 1953 to cut his legal teeth. His first ever case was a rape. The third, a murder.

Sturgess had of course heard of Whitrod's appointment as commissioner-elect of the Queensland police force. Sturgess himself had had a handful of encounters with one of Whitrod's predecessors, Frank Bischof, and found him gruff and self-interested. But Sturgess liked Terry Lewis, and especially Tony Murphy. He occasionally drank with the detectives at the Treasury in the city.

Once, he was stunned at the tenderness of Murphy. Queensland's big detective with a capacity to instil fear by his sheer presence had sought Sturgess's advice on a matter that was extremely unsettling to Murphy. The man who had solved murders and personally taken on gangsters and heavies up and down the eastern seaboard was fretting that one of his teenage daughters may have surreptitiously taken up cigarettes. Sturgess was agog at this different side to Murphy.

Whitrod was not due at Makerston Street until April 1970, and was still in Papua New Guinea when Sturgess landed in town.

One night, a friend of Sturgess invited him and Whitrod to dinner.

'I remember the occasion well,' Sturgess later wrote in his

part-memoir, *The Tangled Web*. 'Whitrod bounced in to surprise me with his immediate affability.

'I began some congratulations [over his appointment] which he interrupted.'

Whitrod asked: 'What do you think of the job?'

'Among the hardest in Australia,' Sturgess warned.

Whitrod laughed. 'Why?'

'You won't know the goodies from the baddies.'

'You tell me then,' Whitrod said, seriously.

Sturgess said he was taken aback at Whitrod's request. Sturgess had meant by his remark what constituted a good and bad policeman, and Whitrod had misunderstood.

Before Sturgess fully appreciated the misunderstanding, Tony Murphy's name fell to mind, and when he mentioned it Whitrod's face wrinkled with distaste. Whitrod said he'd already been warned against Murphy and Terry Lewis.

So Whitrod, prior to even packing up and leaving for Queensland, had been informed of the reputation of some members of the so-called Rat Pack.

In January, Whitrod flew to Brisbane for an interview with Premier Bjelke-Petersen's Cabinet. On arrival at the airport, he held a press conference that would ultimately colour his entire future commissionership. It was page-one news the next day.

WHITROD VIEW. MERIT KEY TO POLICE RANK, the *Courier-Mail* announced. 'Queensland's prospective new police commissioner, Mr. R.W. Whitrod, believes promotion in the police force should be by merit, not seniority.'

Whitrod said: 'Seniority is of value only when the man who is most senior is the most valuable and useful. If he is not, there is something wrong with him. I do not believe in time-serving.'

Here, he took a leaf directly out of McKinna's textbook on modern policing. Whitrod added that his personal philosophy was 'continuous training all one's life', and that training should apply to all ranks of police. Whitrod said men with higher education qualifications would also be welcomed into the force. He promised, if given the position, he would engage administratively rather than 'being a man who worked the beat and tried to do the job himself'.

Whitrod's remarks went off like a grenade within police ranks. Here was an outsider – not even a Queenslander – saying he was prepared to ditch one of the time-worn pillars of the force: a steady climb to higher ranks with incrementally increased pay, then retirement and a pension. A system whereby all police, on being inducted, knew their future career and, in turn, their life road map.

Promotion by merit? Higher education qualifications? Training? Since 1843, when Police Magistrate John Clements Wickham first commanded Chief Constable William Fitzpatrick and four other regular constables in Brisbane, these concepts were unheard of.

It was a tactical mistake from Whitrod. And his apparent imperiousness in that single interview instantly ignited prejudices that belonged, in part, to the Queensland psyche – a suspicion of outsiders, particularly an educated one, a loathing of airs and graces, and a fear of change.

The Police Union executive immediately fired off an urgent telegram to state Cabinet: 'The union feels that any suggested departure from the present promotion system is a veritable condemnation of the ability of the present leaders of the force.'

His enemies gathered before Whitrod was even formally approved the commissionership.

He returned to New Guinea, and waited.

Meanwhile, the new Queensland Police College was officially opened on Thursday 12 February 1970. The head of the college was Inspector Val Barlow. Sub-inspector Norman (Norm) Gulbransen was also on staff. Lewis attended the ceremony in Laurel Avenue, Chelmer.

The existence of the college, and its opening just two months before Whitrod's expected arrival, was no coincidence. The future police commissioner would be rigid when it came to a properly educated force, and here was this fresh palette of an institution, just seven kilometres west of the Brisbane CBD, opening its doors, as if just for him and his ambitions.

The college might not have eventuated if it hadn't been for Police Minister Max Hodges who, fortuitously, was also minister for works. There's little question that Hodges got it up and running in time for his new reforming police commissioner.

Whitrod would discover to his horror in the first few months in his new job that more than sixty per cent of police in the Queensland force had left school at primary level, and that only three in the three-thousand-strong force had actually matriculated from high school.

Meanwhile, Lewis was doing a little exploratory work on his future boss. His police diary entry for Thursday 19 February: 'Read address given by Mr Whitrod in Canberra in August 1967 on "The Prevention of Crime – A Community Problem".'

Additionally, it appears that Lewis was trying to work out the shape of the Hodges–Whitrod nexus via the grapevine. On 16 March, he fielded a call from a Mr Semple of the Queensland Teachers' Union 're a recent interview he had with Mr Hodges, Minister for Works and Police'.

Clearly, Lewis was fishing about for any scrap of information he could gather.

It was frustrating for a man who'd always had – certainly for the past thirteen years – the ear of the police commissioner, and in turn his minister. He had been favoured by Bischof. Yet Lewis struggled to communicate with Hodges prior to Whitrod's arrival. And Whitrod would fly in as a largely unknown quantity.

Worse still, the new police commissioner had seemingly formed an opinion about Terry Lewis before he landed in Brisbane.

'[Allegations of corruption] had to have been said to Whitrod by Hodges,' says Lewis. 'Hodges was an opportunistic grub.'

If Lewis intuited that his career and his life were about to change, he was absolutely right.

A Quiet Word in the Squad Car

At police headquarters, young officer and devout Christian Kenneth (Ken) Hoggett worked in Legal Services. He was a sharp, no-nonsense young man with a quick wit. He had joined the force in 1960, along with his good mate Greg Early. A master of shorthand, Early was also in Legal Services.

Both men had made a verbal pact at the outset of their careers – they would always remain friends, they would never become corrupt, and they would never relinquish their integrity.

On Sunday 12 April 1970 – the day of Whitrod's arrival – Hoggett got a call from his inspector, Cedric Germain (Bischof's travelling companion to the Interpol conference in Madrid in 1962).

'Ken, Whitrod needs to be picked up from the airport,' Germain said. 'Why don't you go?'

Hoggett took an unmarked Ford Falcon squad car and headed out to Eagle Farm.

By chance, he had been in touch with his future police commissioner before. Like Whitrod (a Baptist), Hoggett was a member of the Police Christian Fellowship, and some years earlier the young man had written Whitrod a letter about church services. Hoggett was also aware of Whitrod's reputation – honest, intelligent and trustworthy.

In a masterstroke of career manoeuvring, Hoggett and another young officer, John Dautel, aware of Whitrod's intention to educate the force, had already drafted, prior to his arrival, a police arts and sciences course syllabus. 'He thought it was great,' Hoggett recalls. 'Even more so that we'd been thinking about it.'

At the airport, Hoggett finally met the pudgy but genial Whitrod, and his wife, Mavis.

'Welcome to Queensland,' Hoggett said. 'We're very pleased you're here.'

That Sunday afternoon Hoggett drove the Whitrods to Clayfield, a short trip west from the airport, where they had temporary accommodation in a unit. Whitrod was expected to report for duty at police headquarters the following morning as commissioner-elect, and take over as acting commissioner on 27 April, by which time Police Commissioner Bauer would have embarked on his global study tour. Bauer would retire in October.

En route from the airport, Whitrod turned to Hoggett and asked which department he was from.

He then said: 'Do you believe there is corruption in the police force?'

'Yeah, I do,' Hoggett replied forthrightly.

Hoggett says he doesn't recall if he specifically named the alleged members of the Rat Pack during that brief but – in a small way – historic car ride. 'I don't remember that I did name Murphy, Lewis, and Hallahan, but I did subsequently.'

On the day Whitrod started his new job, Lewis was out at the police college attending a course. As Whitrod met other officers and organised his work space, Lewis was sitting through lecturettes on safe driving techniques and reducing the road toll. There was also a talk on 'loyalty to the department'.

That week, Whitrod turned fifty-five.

The *Courier-Mail* reported on Thursday 16 April: 'Mr Ray Whitrod will spring out of bed this morning, accept happy birthday greetings from his wife, and then begin planning his next ten years. He will have exactly a decade to make his mark as Queensland's police commissioner . . . Yesterday he was not quite sure what his mark might be. "I don't even know Brisbane yet, let alone Queensland, and it will take me quite some time to settle in," he said.'

Whitrod told the reporter that he'd like to get out into rural Queensland to find out what the citizens want of their police force. He added it was unlikely as a 'new broom' that he would take to 'sweeping vigorously' through the various police departments. He said any initiatives he might make would take at least five years to 'bear fruit'.

What makes a good policeman, he was asked.

'Honesty, honesty, honesty,' Whitrod said. 'I have no time for a bloke if he is a liar. How can you hope to have honest law enforcement if you have dishonest lawmen?'

From 27 April, Whitrod was essentially running the Queensland police force.

He also moved into Bauer's office.

One of his first acts was to phone Inspector Germain.

'Send Hoggett down to see me,' Whitrod said.

Hoggett went straight over.

The police commissioner had always had an open-door policy. That had been the tradition, forever. Also, the deputy commissioner had his own separate office – this had certainly been the case with Bischof and his deputy, Donovan.

Hoggett, in nearby Legal Services, had for years seen the comings and goings in Bischof's office. Throughout the 1960s until Bischof's retirement, he says Lewis, Murphy, and Hallahan, as a group, visited Bischof at least twice a week, sometimes more.

'They were in there at least a couple of times a week, which was pretty strange to see three detective sergeants going in and out seeing the commissioner when nobody else did,' says Hoggett. As for the deputy police commissioner, Jim Donovan, passed over for the top job in favour of Bischof in the late 1950s: 'He was never given any work. Never produced any work.'

Whitrod immediately changed office protocol.

Whitrod said to Hoggett: 'I want you to be my personal assistant and move into the deputy commissioner's office.' He said the door to the commissioner's office would be locked: 'No one will come through that door. Only the people you think I should see, I will see. If there's a matter out there you can solve, then solve it.'

With the commissioner's office door locked, Hoggett was installed in the deputy's office, which had access to Whitrod's via a side entrance. Whitrod would soon install a couch and coffee table for visitors. At least, for those visitors that Hoggett allowed to pass through the gate.

Word of the new arrangement flashed through police headquarters.

Whitrod had erected, in Hoggett, a stubborn barrier between himself and the rest of the force. Those wishing to see Whitrod had to express their reason for doing so to Hoggett. And Hoggett began issuing instructions in person and on the phone 'on behalf of the commissioner'.

New in town, Whitrod did make time to cultivate some friends in the local press.

Reporters Ron Richards and Ken Blanch, now both in senior positions at the *Sunday Truth*, invited the police commissioner for lunch on his second day in town.

They dined at the Commercial Travellers' Club on Wickham Street, Spring Hill.

Both Richards and Blanch had been professionally close to Bischof; he leaked stories to them, as did Hallahan and Murphy. They drank with Bischof, drove him around in his car when he was too intoxicated to take the wheel, and were afforded a privileged inside view of the workings of the upper ranks of police.

Now it was time to weigh up Whitrod.

During the course of the lunch, Whitrod explained to the two newspapermen his ideas on policing and how he saw the future of the force in Queensland.

'Ray,' Blanch said, 'do you understand the politics of the Queensland police force?'

Whitrod stopped, nearly dropping his knife and fork. 'What do you mean, the politics? Police forces don't have politics.'

'I feel sorry for you, mate,' Blanch replied.

Blanch and Richards went on to explain the sectarian divide in the force. Whitrod was genuinely astounded.

Blanch remembers: 'Nobody told him what he was getting himself into.' Very early in Whitrod's tenure, an anti-Whitrod faction started meeting every Friday night for drinks at the Belfast Hotel. Blanch often turned up and he says the tone of conversation was 'hatred for Whitrod and everything he was doing'. The Police Union soon began a rolling campaign against Whitrod and Police Minister Hodges.

In late May three policemen in Roma were served with summonses on charges of assault occasioning bodily harm. Here, Whitrod was showing that he was not afraid to punish his own men. Ron Edington, now president of the Police Union, called for Max Hodges to resign. Hodges fired back, telling the press: 'I am the boss of the Queensland Police Force and no one is going to tell me how to run it.'

Back at police headquarters, Lewis would soon hit the new Hoggett hurdle head on. While he was still giving talks to groups like the Geebung Methodist Ladies' Guild, and staying in touch with old friends like former Victorian police officer and then Port Moresby–based barrister Eric Pratt, it wasn't until June that the new Hoggett–Whitrod arrangement was literally brought to Lewis's door.

On Monday 28 June, Lewis wrote in his police diary: 'S/Const Hoggett brought Const C.G. Young to our office and said that he was sworn in today and is attached to the Comm's office; however, Mr Whitrod has instructed that he is to work here for almost six months.'

Lewis recorded that he saw Young, who was a patrol officer in Papua New Guinea for six years, and that Whitrod had plans to make him a liaison officer between the University of Queensland and the police. Lewis also noted that he spoke to Hoggett about the 'difficulty' in attaching temporary staff to the JAB.

Lewis had had sole operation of the JAB for eight years. Now the new police commissioner was assigning staff. Was it a deliberate slight on Lewis? And did Lewis suspect that a spy for the commissioner had been planted in his ranks?

In early August, he received a memo from Whitrod about the public appearances given by members of the JAB. The commissioner also wanted to cast an eye over the staff duty roster. Lewis had to speak with the commissioner face to face. But then, 'Hoggett phoned to say that Mr Whitrod will not see me re memo and speeches'.

Late that same month, further whispers filtered back to Lewis: 'Miss Crisp said that Mr Whitrod questioned her re functions of the JAB.'

All this scrutiny of the bureau started getting under Lewis's skin. On Thursday 8 September, he recorded in his police diary: 'Saw Snr Const Hoggett and requested to see Mr R. Whitrod.' Two weeks later: 'Saw . . . Hoggett re still desirous of seeing Commissioner'. A week after that: 'Saw . . . Hoggett re: Mr Whitrod'.

It wasn't until Wednesday 30 December that Lewis had any luck. 'Saw Mr Whitrod re staff shortage and functions of the J.A. Bureau.'

It had taken Lewis more than eight months to secure a personal meeting with the new police commissioner, when once he had enjoyed Bischof's company at least twice a week.

It was the early basis for a spectacular enmity between Whitrod and Lewis.

The Happy Gardener

To get to the Brisbane suburb of The Gap, eleven kilometres west of the CBD, you literally have to pass through 'the gap' between the slopes of Mount Coot-tha and the Taylor Range. Beyond the S-bend road that negotiates that cleft, the suburb sits quietly in the folds of both granite formations, with its established bushland, golf course, 1960s brick and timber houses, and the meandering Enoggera Creek.

Into this splendour the Big Fella, Frank Bischof, retired. He and wife Dorothy and their cocker spaniels lived in an immaculately kept home in Barkala Street, not far from a small piece of scrub that was home to an enormous, creaking stand of wild bamboo, in which neighbourhood children played and secretly puffed on cigarettes.

Bischof, with thirty-three successful murder convictions under his belt, was not built for retirement. How many times could he tend to his cactuses and trim the lawn? And how many lunches with friends, recalling old times, could he sustain at the National Hotel?

He was, in the early 1970s, a familiar figure in Barkala Street and, indeed, the surrounding streets in the shadow of the city's television towers on Mount Coot-tha. He would religiously walk his dogs at all hours.

But there were signs, even at this stage, that Bischof's hypertension from his latter years as Queensland police commissioner had quickly translated into some form of mental illness.

One neighbour says he once saw Bischof, holding his dogs on their leads, urinate quite openly in the street.

Another tells a sad but funny story about Bischof that circulated the neighbourhood at the time: 'The Ashgrove golf course is just down the hill and across Waterworks Road from where Bischof lived . . . He was sighted on several occasions taking his wheelbarrow and a shovel down to the golf course and stealing sand from the bunkers in the middle of the night . . . I have no idea what use he made of the sand, unless it was for his garden.'

Bischof would soon get a consolation job – as chief of ticket sellers for the popular Mater Prize Home raffles – a charity established in the early 1950s to assist the Mater hospital on Brisbane's southside.

Bischof told a newspaper reporter that he accepted the position because he was a 'living ball of energetic charity' and 'as fit as a Mexican jumping bean'. He added there was 'not another weed' he could expunge from his garden, not 'a blade of grass out of place'.

Despite visits from former colleagues like Lewis, Murphy, and his driver Slim Somerville, Bischof's world had gone from constant recognition, notoriety and global travel, to a small suburban block in Brisbane's west.

He would soon be giving the new police commissioner, Whitrod, the length of his tongue. And he'd also find himself embroiled in a police arrest.

This time, shockingly, Bischof himself would be the defendant.

A Confidential Meeting

In the earliest days of Whitrod's acting commissionership, Ron Edington – president of the Police Union, firebrand, father of fourteen and confidante to the member for South Brisbane, Colin Bennett – received a phone call at union headquarters at North Quay. Could he please attend a meeting at Parliament House with Police Minister Hodges and Police Commissioner Whitrod?

Edington was notorious throughout the force for his booming voice and forthright opinions. He called a spade not just a spade, but a bloody spade. He was a knockabout on the surface, but shrewd and intelligent underneath. He was also close to Tony Murphy.

Murphy often told a joke about Edington. Edington, his wife and their fourteen children are waiting for a bus. The bus pulls up and Edington ushers his wife and kids on board. There's a blind man with a metal-tipped cane waiting to get on, but the bus driver tells both men the bus is full, they'll have to take the train.

So as Edington and the blind man walk to the train station, the blind man continually taps his stick on the footpath – *tap, tap, tap, tap, tap.*

Edington, annoyed, turns to him and says, 'Why don't you put a rubber on the end of your stick?'

And the blind man replies, 'It's a pity you didn't put one on the end of yours, you bastard. We could have caught that bloody bus.'

Edington met Hodges and Whitrod at Parliament House.

'They asked me to assist them in ridding the force of the Rat Pack,' Edington recalls. 'Of course, I took to the defence of the Rat Pack.

'I told them all these corridor assassins were making up stories . . . and it was not my responsibility to investigate Murphy, Hallahan, and Lewis for any misconduct. It's the job of the administration.'

After the meeting, Edington called the three officers to his own meeting, and he vowed to defend them against Whitrod's perceptions.

Almost twenty years later, Edington would use the same phrase – 'corridor assassins' – in defence of Murphy, Lewis, and Hallahan, at the Fitzgerald Inquiry into police corruption. He now admits he lied: 'I perjured myself at the fucking Fitzgerald Inquiry.'

Nevertheless, the meeting proved that Whitrod had brought a deepened distrust of the Rat Pack with him as baggage from Papua New Guinea.

Shirley Loses Some Friends

By late 1969, Shirley Brifman had continued to expand her empire, opening two brothels in the same block of flats in Wylde Street, Potts Point, a quick stroll uphill from the navy dockyards at Sydney's Garden Island.

But her foray in the press that year had sent a collective shudder through her corrupt network of police protectors. Instead of being an asset, and a profitable one at that, she had very quickly become a potential liability.

By 1970, her old friends began to drop away. And the one she felt a strong emotional attachment to – Glendon Patrick Hallahan – was one of the first to turn his back on her.

Brifman still had regular contact with Colin Bennett. Along with Ron Edington, Shirley was a touchstone of information for Bennett, which in turn was fuel for his attacks on the Bjelke-Petersen government. He was also the lawyer and confidant she retained in Brisbane.

Hallahan, already paranoid about Brifman's appearance in the Sydney newspapers, kept his crosshair on Bennett. With talk of tax investigators sniffing about, he didn't need his name mentioned on the floor of Queensland parliament now that he had built his own corrupt network that was bringing in lucrative cash.

Despite knowing Brifman for more than a decade, Hallahan made the decision to end their association.

'I fell out with Glen in February or March 1970,' Brifman recalled. 'I fell out with him over I think Col Bennett. He was querying me about Col Bennett ringing up or coming to see me.'

Though Brifman continued to pay police, including Hallahan, for protection, it all stopped abruptly in June. The New South Wales Vice Squad – for years the recipient of her largesse – unexpectedly charged Brifman with procuring her own daughter, Mary Anne, then thirteen, for the purposes of prostitution. 'It wasn't a set-up charge,' says Mary Anne. 'It was a fact.'

Brifman was flummoxed by the betrayal.

It was the month Shirley's substantial businesses began to collapse. And for the first time in a career that stretched back into the 1950s, she had no police protection.

'My case was remanded hearing after hearing,' Brifman said. None of her old friends in the police force were doing anything to make the charge go away.

Tony Murphy's wife, Maureen, recalls: 'She asked Tony to help her. He wouldn't be in it. He strongly objected to that. I think the same thing happened in Sydney.'

While it dawned on Shirley that she could be facing some serious prison time, it also occurred to Krahe, Murphy, Hallahan, and the rest that she might start to talk.

As a form of insurance, Fred Krahe physically tortured Brifman twice in Sydney in the latter half of 1970.

Mary Anne Brifman witnessed the first incident.

'I was very distressed and not coping with all the physical pain [of working as a prostitute]. I had been very innocent up until that time. They tortured her so I'd behave.

'They were grooming me to take over my mother's business. They knew she wouldn't last long. She was overdosing all the time.'

The second occasion was more brutal. Krahe burned Brifman's feet with a cigarette lighter.

'She didn't walk for what seemed like a year,' remembers Mary Anne. 'It was a long, long time. I used to have to watch her standing on her tippy toes trying to learn to walk again. It was horrific.'

A Brisbane cousin confirms Brifman's injuries.

'The soles of her feet – I'd never seen anything like it. You wonder if they drugged her and did it. She couldn't walk. When she lost that protection . . . I remember thinking it was just too much for her. She thought she'd be able to get them off her back and she couldn't.

'Shirley had nowhere to turn.'

Her Brisbane stockbroker friend, Robin Corrie, offered her encouragement, as well as monetary assistance. He was incensed that the police had turned on her after financially gouging her for years. Corrie firmly suggested that she bring them down with her.

'You fight 'em, Shirley,' he advised. 'I know all about them.'

'I paid all these years for protection,' Brifman recalled in a police interview the following year. '[Now] I was in fear of my life. If I am going to go, they are going to go with me.'

And despite their years of intimacy, she feared Hallahan the most. 'I don't mean physical violence with Tony, but Glen would be the type. I am more frightened of Glen as far as violence goes.'

The tangible fear Brifman felt at that time did not escape her family, particularly her eldest daughter, Mary Anne, the epicentre of the charge against Brifman that would change her mother's life.

'A cold-hearted person like Hallahan, a man who can kill people and torture them as well . . . she captured his heart, yes,' remembers Mary Anne. 'I realised too late . . . that all these special people and high-ranking people and very good people in society's eyes, all were corrupt. I believed any important person was like that. I thought that was the norm. I thought the whole world understood life like that.'

With the case against Brifman adjourned over and over through 1970, she began to seethe. She'd been treated poorly. She'd been used by friends and lovers she'd trusted. And without protection, her brothels were fair game.

When she was tortured by her erstwhile lover Detective Fred Krahe of the New South Wales police, she'd reached a tipping point.

It was time to blow the whistle.

A Fiery Luncheon

As Whitrod settled into the job, his perceived pomposity and apparent need to reform the force at breakneck speed was garnering enemies at a similar pace.

If the commissioner's aim was to unsettle the old guard then he was succeeding admirably.

Over at the Special Branch – established during Police Commissioner Carroll's tenure in the late 1940s, and tasked with handling subversive activities in the state – Don Lane, friend to Hallahan from their Mount Isa days, was also beginning to chafe at Whitrod's leadership.

Norm Bauer, before going on his global study tour, and before Whitrod had taken his chair in the commissioner's office, had issued a confidential memo to senior officers throughout the force, including the Special Branch, warning that he expected to be updated on any subversive activities that 'intended to overthrow our lawfully consti-tuted Government'. He singled out the Communist Party of Australia and the National Socialist Party of Australia, among others.

Whitrod, once installed at police headquarters, swiftly removed the head of the Special Branch, twenty-year veteran Sub-inspector Leo de Lange, to general CIB duties. Rumours abounded that a new squad would replace the existing team, on the grounds that branch officers had become too easily recognised by the public, particularly demon-strators and agitators, over the years.

It may also have been a response to a phenomenon that Whitrod found perplexing – often, when he raised issues with Bjelke-Petersen, he found the premier in possession of information, siphoned from the Special Branch, before he did. Who was the premier's mole? Who was destabilising Whitrod? The rumour was it was Don Lane.

Whitrod's persistence with the education of the force also drew him into heated conversations with union boss Ron Edington.

'Whitrod wanted everyone to become an academic,' Edington recalls. 'He said, "Now I'll give you time off, departmental time, if you want to further your studies. You can go to university."

'And he says to me, "Now you being the leader of the union, you join up and do this bloody course." And I said, "Like fucking hell, I'm not going to go and listen to some poofter from the university pushing this bloody shit down my neck."

'Anytime I ever sent anything to him I used to put: *R.L. Edington. JP. NPAS* – No Police Arts and Science course.'

Lewis was also being consistently frustrated by Whitrod's staff appointments to the JAB. It directly undermined Lewis's authority, and he had little recourse to debate it.

At least this was the case until Paul Wilson, one of Lewis's aca-demic friends and contacts from the University of Queensland, was approached by Whitrod to convene a casual weekend luncheon at Wilson's home in St Lucia. Whitrod was acquainted with the young criminologist when he was head of the Commonwealth police force in Canberra.

Whitrod wanted to meet the up-and-coming young men of the Queensland police in a casual setting. He wanted to hear their thoughts, opinions and concerns.

Whitrod even set down some rules prior to the gathering – anyone, irrespective of rank, could say what was on their mind without fear of repercussion.

Wilson invited Terry Lewis.

'I also asked Ron Richards, who was chief of staff of the *Sunday Truth*,' says Wilson.

Lewis would have felt a measure of support with his old friends there at the barbecue at Wilson's house overlooking the Brisbane River. Indeed, they may have fortified him. Despite Lewis's reputation as a quiet man, he never backed away from an opportunity to forthrightly express his opinions.

Wilson says: '[It] ended acrimoniously, with both men telling me later how much they did not trust each other. I can't remember exactly why, but it was a combination of different personalities and different perspectives on what needed to be done to reform the Queensland police force.'

Lewis remembers Whitrod, in short trousers, storming off.

'So I went out there and I can still see it, in Paul Wilson's backyard and the big table. We probably had a few beers and . . . I obviously touched on something that he bloody didn't agree with, but I was very frank . . . Little Whitty. He stamped out with his fat little legs down the steps . . . He never talked to me again.

'Oh, he was a very pompous man, if that's not too rude a word.'

Lewis, in fact, offered the luncheon a scathing attack on Whitrod's managerial reforms to date. Whitrod would later tell Wilson that his aim was 'to remove the man from his job'. The gloves were off.

Not long after, Whitrod and Lewis found themselves alone in the elevator at police headquarters. Lewis, without compunction, called his commissioner a 'fat pig'.

Lewis, Whitrod thought, would eventually get his just desserts.

In Lewis's police diaries, he consistently referred to his boss as 'Mr Whitrod' or 'Whitrod'. Never 'Commissioner Whitrod'.

Stories of Whitrod's incompetence circulated.

Abe Duncan remembers Whitrod rushing into his office one morning.

The police commissioner believed that some of his men weren't happy with his appointment to the top job and were conspiring against him. In Cunnamulla in western Queensland, a prisoner had simply walked out of the watchhouse and Whitrod believed police had deliberately left the door open. He immediately sent Chief Inspector Hugh Low out to investigate any negligence on the part of police.

While Low was still out there, Whitrod burst into Duncan's office again.

'Get onto Hugh,' Whitrod said. 'Another prisoner has escaped in Hughenden. Get him to have a look at it while he's there. He can slip across to Hughenden.'

Whitrod was unaware that Hughenden was over eleven hundred kilometres north-east of Cunnamulla.

'You wouldn't be serious, would you?' Duncan asked.

On another occasion, those in Whitrod's inner-circle quickly learned that he hated to be kept out of the loop when it came to major crime incidents. He was afraid to be caught on the hop by the press. So he insisted that he be regularly briefed.

One day Duncan learned that a serious siege involving a weapon was being played out in the southern Brisbane suburb of Inala.

I better tell Whitty, Duncan thought.

He went directly to Ken Hoggett, Whitrod's minder, and insisted he see the police commissioner.

Hoggett disappeared into Whitrod's office and emerged shortly after.

'Abe, can you hang on until two o'clock tomorrow?' Hoggett said. 'He's writing his [commissioner's] newsletter.'

Duncan says: 'These were the sort of things that went on.'

Shirley Goes Live

Throughout 1970 and well into the following year, Brifman's court case over procuring her daughter for prostitution kept being set back. She was tired of the game.

Though she was still in touch with Fred Krahe in New South Wales and Tony Murphy in Queensland, she was indignant over being charged. All the while, her health was failing and she was losing weight.

In early June 1971 Brifman was finally committed for trial, and was remanded in custody at Silverwater gaol, twenty-one kilometres west of Sydney's CBD.

Granted bail, she had to wait more than a week before she was set free. She learned later that the petty criminal assigned to bail her had pocketed the money and absconded. She believed it was at the urging of the New South Wales Vice Squad.

Again she rang Peter Grose at the Curtis Brown literary agency. He told her straightaway that the ABC current affairs program *This Day Tonight* (*TDT*) had been looking for her. Brifman immediately called *TDT* reporter Gerald Stone.

It was payback time.

Brifman arrived at the Gore Hill ABC television studios by taxi between 4 and 4.30 p.m. on Tuesday 15 June 1971.

She was taken upstairs to meet with Stone, and two other *TDT* crew.

'I was assigned to do the interview and I do remember she was pissed off at how the cops were no longer doing her any favours,' says Stone. 'She was a very thin woman at this stage, very fragile. She was hardly what you'd call a stunner.'

Brifman was briefed by Stone then signed a statutory declaration. Stone said: 'This is just to protect the station.'

Brifman said that before the interview they took her down to the bar and got her 'half shot': 'I was introduced to all of them.'

TDT, which began broadcasting in 1967 and was hosted by Bill Peach, was hugely popular across the country. Brifman, with her 'unremarkable, working-class Australian voice' (as Stone remembered it), the belle from Atherton, and slightly intoxicated, was about to sign her own death warrant on live television.

Did *TDT* know that Brifman airing allegations of paying off dozens of senior New South Wales police, including an unnamed Krahe, was potential dynamite?

'Yes, of course,' says Stone. '*TDT* was an important program for an Australia in transition. Everything was outlawed still – brothels, abortion, gambling. This was huge money in the hands of corrupt police and politicians. Police corruption was a big story.'

Did Brifman tell the truth on air? 'Oh yes, there's no doubt about that,' Stone adds. 'The stories she was telling about cops and clients . . . there was no doubt she was what she was.'

Stone asked her during the interview why she had decided to step forward: 'Because I am now on charges and my children are suffering for this.

'My father brought me up the right way. He always told me to do the right thing and so, for the first time in my life, I'm doing it.'

Brifman went on to admit that she had been working as a prostitute in Sydney with the knowledge of police and had kept brothels while paying weekly protection money to a member of the Vice Squad, presumably Krahe.

Then she fired a huge shot at Hallahan and Murphy up in

Queensland, admitting that she had perjured herself at the National Hotel inquiry in 1963 and 1964, not for financial benefit but to save her life and those of her children.

Immediately after the interview, *TDT* staff took her back down to the bar.

'They gave me a beer to steady my nerves and after it was all over they said: "We've been waiting for something like this to happen and we must say it is about time someone got stuck into Frank Bischof."'

Her daughter Mary Anne remains nonplussed at her mother's decision to go on television with her allegations.

Mary Anne says: 'She mixed with corrupt police up to the premier in two states . . . Why would she think that she could tell on them and not get hurt?'

Not So in Hiding

After the *TDT* revelations, Brifman went into hiding in Sydney.

She had suffered, on a handful of occasions, the brutality of Fred Krahe, and knew what he was capable of. She had long heard the stories of his personally torturing criminals for money or information. Then there was an enraged Hallahan and Murphy to consider.

Brifman holed up in a narrow double-storey terrace at 191 Victoria Street, Kings Cross, a short walk towards the harbour from the red and white neon Coca-Cola sign. She also assigned herself a bodyguard.

Brifman's revelations were front-page news in the *Courier-Mail* on Wednesday 16 June. The report led with the National Hotel perjury angle. The story quoted her as 'Mrs Shirley Brickman'.

At 8.30 a.m. that day, respected Assistant Police Commissioner Abe Duncan, who had been taken into the trust and confidence of Whitrod, went and saw the police commissioner about the Brifman allegations.

On Friday, 18 June, New South Wales detectives Williams and Paull visited Brifman in her hideout. They interviewed her about the statutory declaration she had signed at the ABC studios earlier in the week, and asked her to check her signature – she always signed her name in full, *Shirley Brifman*, with a playful, childish loop on the tail of the 'y'. The detectives had already conducted interviews with *TDT* staff about the night Brifman appeared on television.

They told Brifman that they would be conducting in-depth interviews with her in the near future. Paull phoned Duncan on that same day, telling him that detectives planned to fly to Brisbane to continue their investigation into Brifman.

The following day, she was tracked down by a reporter for Brisbane's *Sunday Mail* newspaper. How did a journalist manage to obtain the secret address of probably the most wanted woman on the east coast of Australia – sought by both corrupt police and criminals alike – in a city the size of Sydney?

Remarkably, she granted an interview. The tone and quotes offered in the subsequent story hinted that she was either drunk or drugged, or both.

'Mrs Brifman was sleeping fully dressed in a small, starkly neat flat when the *Sunday Mail* found her yesterday,' the report said.

'"I'm supposed to be in hiding," she said as she raised herself on one elbow. "No one should know where to find me."'

She pointed to her 'bodyguard', a large man snoring on a nearby bed. 'I think I'm doing a better job guarding him.'

She told the reporter that she decided to blow the whistle on corruption when she was languishing in Silverwater gaol.

'I was worrying about what would happen to my children . . .' she revealed. 'That's the first time I have ever been in gaol and it was a real eye-opener for me.'

Soon after, she was also visited by notorious killer and psychopath John Regan. He said if she opened her mouth again she was dead.

Up in Brisbane, Tony Murphy was enraged at Brifman's squealing on national television.

He phoned Brifman's sister Marge Chapple at her home in Paddington, and went berserk.

Chapple later told police that Murphy demanded to know where Brifman was: 'Has she gone completely mad?' he said. 'There will never be another royal commission in this state. We won't allow it.'

Later, Murphy confided in Terry Lewis: 'One woman I could trust with my life. She has now brought me undone.'

The Rat Pack had comfortably negotiated the full glare of a royal commission in the early 1960s, but since then things had become more complicated. Murphy had risen in rank and stature and was now entwined with Jack Herbert in the Licensing Branch. He was also in a business arrangement with Fred Krahe and Krahe's police and criminal partners in Sydney.

Meanwhile, Hallahan had become a rogue operative. He had built a corrupt financial network with New South Wales police and was shoring up his finances with protection money from prostitutes and any other scam he could conceive of with criminal associates like tattooist Billy Phillips.

By 1971, too, he had a new potential partner, the brilliant, but eccentric, young John Edward Milligan. In the 1960s Milligan was associate to a judge in the District Court. In this capacity, Milligan crossed paths with Hallahan.

Milligan was looking at a stellar future until he was caught selling text books he stole from law libraries. It was typical Milligan – a cross between a thief and a prankster.

Colin Bennett's daughter Mary remembers him from law school at the University of Queensland. 'Milligan would eat an entire tube of toothpaste before an exam and make himself sick so he could take the exam at another time,' she says.

But in the swinging 60s, the campus clown turned his mind to drugs and importation. By the time Shirley Brifman tipped the bucket on her police friends, Milligan was mixing with some heavy characters, including John Regan.

Lewis, as he had been for almost a decade, was quietly tucked away in the JAB.

Coinciding with the Brifman scandal, the Rat Pack had fastidious, intractable do-gooder Ray Whitrod threatening to unpick a fabric of institutionalised corruption that had been decades in the making.

Whitrod, in his first eighteen months in the chair, had assembled a small cadre of officers he could trust, an inviolable unit, including Duncan, Gulbransen, Hoggett, Voigt and Dautel, among others.

Just as Brifman made her allegations, Whitrod was toying with establishing a crack investigative unit that would solely concentrate on corrupt police within the force. It was a gamble – police seriously investigating other police – but to Whitrod's mind it was another flank he could use to attack and hopefully dismantle the Rat Pack.

Brifman's public admission that she had committed perjury at the National Hotel inquiry gave Whitrod the precise fissure he'd been looking for in the Rat Pack facade.

Shirley Flees North

Despite their recent animosity, Tony Murphy urged Brifman to return to Brisbane. She was also encouraged to come home by Norm Gulbransen. If she stayed in Sydney she would be murdered.

So almost eight years after Hallahan and Murphy had reluctantly accepted her leaving Brisbane, courtesy of the National Hotel fiasco, she was again the puppet being played by the Rat Pack.

Having family in Brisbane (sister Marge Chapple) may have influenced her decision. And facing the wrath of Fred Krahe, John Regan, and whoever else stood to lose from knowing one of Sydney's biggest and now most infamous madams, would have been a major factor.

Did she trust Murphy? They had had a close relationship, and he had always been reliable in the past. 'I never actually fell out with Tony,' she said.

So Shirley, husband Sonny, and the three smaller Brifman children – Sonya, Helen and Sid – came back to Queensland in the middle of winter 1971. Mary Anne, the subject of the procurement charge, was at that point not permitted by police to leave New South Wales and stayed with a relative in Moree in the state's north, 480 kilometres from Brisbane.

The Brifmans moved into a rental property – an old Queenslander the police found for them – at 57 Vardon Street in the inner-north suburb of Wilston.

It wasn't a cheerful return to her old stomping ground. Brifman was at the brink of a complete mental breakdown.

Abe Duncan recorded in his police diary that on Thursday 24 June 1971, he received a phone call informing him that Shirley Brifman was 'in hospital from overdose of tablets'.

By 2 July, she had recovered enough to agree to meet Duncan for a formal interview in the office of her lawyer, Colin Bennett, at his Inns of Court offices in the city.

'I had no knowledge of her,' Duncan recalls. 'I never met her when she was associated with the National Hotel or Killarney brothel. I never worked on the Consorting Squad.

'She was determined to nominate many of those [police] who had personal associations with her, big shots . . . Whitrod put me on the job of contacting her and keeping in touch with her.

'She made a complaint against police from the olden days and the National Hotel. She did mention Tony Murphy and she mentioned Bischof and Hallahan.'

Duncan learned that Brifman was still on bail over the New South

Wales procuring charge and he wanted to let that court matter be resolved before further interrogating Brifman over her accusations against potentially corrupt Queensland police.

Whitrod disagreed. He needed her questioned immediately. So Duncan began a series of formal interviews with Brifman. Signed transcripts were produced.

Duncan remembers: 'She was reasonably bright and reasonably intelligent, and fairly smart when she was done up. There was no doubt she had been a prostitute from a fairly early age. And there was no doubt she had some association with some police over the years.'

The Duncan interviews with Brifman were recorded in shorthand and typed by policewoman Pat Ryan. Duncan found her a difficult interviewee. She was an emotional mess. One moment she'd be calm, the next agitated. She might appear to be cooperative then suddenly stand and walk out. Police often had to coax her back.

She destroyed her credibility with Duncan early when she told a story about Police Commissioner Whitrod himself. It was so pre-posterous that Duncan neither entered the story into the record of interview, nor ever told Whitrod the precise details. When Hallahan was a young detective in the late 1950s, Brifman told Duncan, he often flew to Sydney and Melbourne, and once, while in the Victorian capital, he was actually a guest at Whitrod's home. Brifman went on to implicate Whitrod in a counterfeit money racket.

'Whatever you say about Whitrod, there's no way in the world he'd be dishonest. She said she knew it was right.

'I've never released that statement to anybody. All I told Whitrod was – "You can't believe her because she's told me something about you that I couldn't believe."'

By July 1971, her lawyer, Colin Bennett, had already made substantial use of his dedicated 'Brifman briefcase'.

Brifman herself was exhausted. As ever that winter in Brisbane she took great care over her dress, turning up at police headquarters in a knee-length white fur coat, expensive woollen dresses, leather gloves and her customary black wigs. Still, her face, for such a young woman, was deeply lined and her eyes weary.

Just weeks after returning to Queensland she received a surprise visit at her Wilston safe house from Sydney gunman John Regan.

'He came in a little red sports car with a New South Wales number plate,' Brifman said. 'There was another chap sitting in the car, a young fellow.'

This was most probably Regan's sidekick John Edward Milligan, who Brifman would later describe as 'that blond joker'.

'Regan came to the door and said to me, "Have you got the lease of the mine they talk about in the paper?"'

Brifman did own a small mine called 'Last Chance' at Herberton, a town on the Atherton Tableland not far from where she grew up.

'How did you find out where I live?' Brifman asked him.

'I have ways and means,' Regan said.

She was shocked that her secret address had been compromised, and by someone as violent and unpredictable as Regan. Considering her safe house had been arranged for her by police, the leak could only have come from within the force.

Meanwhile, Brifman's fantastic stories of corrupt police – of pay-offs for protection, of detectives in both Queensland and New South Wales actually organising armed robberies and splitting the cash, of relentless verballing of defendants, of 'presents' or false evidence being planted on suspects, of violence, murder, torture, sex and mayhem – took a back seat to a looming political event.

The Springboks, the South African rugby union team, were coming to Brisbane, and it would be a moment that would define the premiership of Joh Bjelke-Petersen.

The Eyes of a Killer

In March 1971 the Federal Narcotics Bureau put out its first shingle in Brisbane. It had a small office in Eagle Street in the CBD.

One of the junior recruits was Brian Bennett, a Customs officer who'd transferred from Newcastle to Brisbane the year before.

As a young investigator, Bennett was looking for action. The importation of cannabis, cannabis resin or hashish, and LSD was on the rise. But in those initial months, there was little to get excited about in the Queensland capital.

'In those early days we were scratching around for work,' Bennett recalls. 'Because we were federal, the local state drug squad was a little bit in awe of us. I think they thought we were bigger and better than we actually were.'

Then Bennett got a call from Detective Sergeant Lou Rowan, chief of the Queensland Drug Squad and famous Australian test cricket match umpire.

'I've got a well-known southern criminal as an informant,' said Rowan. 'He's talking big-time drug importations. It's too big for us. Do you want to talk to him?'

Bennett and the head of the small bureau, Vince Dainer, jumped at the opportunity.

'Lou set up a meeting for us,' says Bennett. 'The rendezvous was set – a laneway on the northern side of [Cathie Street, off Petrie Terrace]. It did a dogleg to the right – that's where we had to meet this fellow.

'We pulled up and it was John Regan.'

There, alone in the lane, was one of Australia's most feared gangsters. He wore, as always, a bulletproof vest beneath his civilian clothing.

'He just jumped out of his mugshots: he had the coldest eyes, he had chillingly blue eyes, the coldest eyes on a human being I've ever seen,' remembers Bennett.

Regan, while terrorising Shirley Brifman, was also conducting a little business in Brisbane. He had a sideline renovating properties with his associate and 'legal adviser', John Edward Milligan.

But the two had had a falling-out.

'Regan was very fit,' Bennett said. 'When he got into the car you could almost see the muscles in his legs bulge. He told us he was a businessman from Sydney.

'He said that he'd met this fellow, John Edward Milligan, and . . . he discovered that Milligan was heavily involved in the importation of drugs on a large scale. He said he was against drugs. It was very strange.'

Regan confided that Milligan had secreted evidence from Regan's solicitor's office that would be revealed, and would 'destroy' Regan, if Milligan was harmed. Regan felt he'd been doublecrossed. He described Milligan as 'slippery and dangerous'.

'He produced these photographs, big blow-up black and white photos of Milligan taken from the front and side. Obviously he or someone else had a gun on Milligan when the pictures were taken. Milligan was posing, not looking happy.

'He gave us these and other documents that belonged to Milligan. He handed over file boxes containing cardboard [index] cards.'

Regan claimed that Milligan opened one of these 'files' on anyone he ever met. One card contained details of a young film director in Sydney by the name of Peter Weir. 'It was a crude intelligence database,' remembers Bennett. 'This was a criminal well ahead of his time.'

Regan told Bennett and Dainer: 'I'm going back to Sydney shortly. Go for this bloke, he's big-time and it'll pay off.'

Milligan subsequently became the Federal Narcotic Bureau's first major target.

It learned from Regan that Milligan ran a nightclub called Willie's Bizarre, not far from the National Hotel in the city. It was, according to police, a 'leading drug hangout'.

Bennett commenced some surveillance. Not that it was hard to miss Milligan.

'He was well-dressed, always wore business attire, usually a waist-coat,' recalls Bennett. 'He was very dapper. He was only a smallish man, with a small frame. He had a receding chin, and sort of wavy hair but receding from the front. And he was always clean-shaven.

'A few years later, I was up in Kings Cross in Macleay Street and lo and behold Milligan walks down the street. He was wearing pinstripe trousers, spats, and he was twirling a gold-topped cane. Talk about theatrical.'

Soon after, Dainer was transferred back to Sydney and replaced.

Interest in Milligan dropped off under the new regime. But the dandy drug dealer would soon cross paths in a major way with Brian Bennett.

A State of Emergency

Despite his friendship with Terry Lewis, criminologist and academic Paul Wilson had also grown fond of happy and bubbly Ray Whitrod.

They lived in the same suburb and often dined at each other's houses. In summer, the pair did laps at a local swimming pool in Toowong.

Wilson happened to be in Whitrod's house in July 1971 when Bjelke-Petersen phoned. The premier informed Whitrod that a state of emergency had been declared for the Springboks' upcoming match in Brisbane. The South African rugby union team's six-week tour of Australia was finally bringing them to Queensland.

The state of emergency – under the *State Transport Acts* – gave the government and police infinitely wider powers of civic control and arrest.

The decision naturally disturbed Whitrod. He saw the police not as an arm of government, but an agent for social harmony. He wanted a force that respected civil liberties.

As with his naive discussion over lunch with reporters Ken Blanch and Ron Richards when he first arrived in Brisbane, the confluence of police and politics was anathema to Whitrod. To his detriment, he simply could not grasp the concept.

Unfortunately for Whitrod, too, the powerful Police Union under Edington had its greatest ally in Bjelke-Petersen. The police commissioner, whichever way he turned, was snookered.

Bjelke-Petersen publicly announced the state of emergency on Tuesday 13 July 1971, ahead of the Springboks' arrival eight days later.

Lewis recorded in his police diary on 13 July: 'Office at 8.25am. Asst. Comm. Duncan phoned re instruction from Comm. that staff must be made available during Springbok Visit . . . Asst. Comm. Hughes phoned to say that Mr Whitrod has instructed that every male member of the J.A. Bureau is to be available for the 22nd, 24th, 27th and 31st . . . Saw Duncan and Barlow re: Chain of Command.'

Abe Duncan, who was in the middle of his Brifman interviews, wrote in his own diary for that day: 'With Supt. McMahon left 9.10am and went to Ballymore oval for observations with other police officers re Springbok visit. Saw Det. S. Sgt Lewis re; problems in J.A. Bureau and discussed same with Mr Barlow . . .'

The Springboks' match against Australia would ultimately be held at the Brisbane Exhibition grounds in Bowen Hills, and not the neighbouring home of Queensland rugby union – Ballymore – for security reasons. In expectation of violence, police erected a chain fence around the oval and its wooden stands.

They were correct in anticipating trouble. The Springboks' tour through Perth, Adelaide, Melbourne and Sydney had witnessed scores of anti-apartheid protests and dozens of arrests.

Whitrod himself attended the Sydney match between the Springboks and New South Wales on 10 July and saw demonstrators hurling smoke bombs, fireworks, fruit, beer cans and balloons onto the playing field. About one hundred people were arrested.

In anticipation, hundreds of rural Queensland police descended on

Brisbane to help bolster the ranks in the capital. Country police were housed at the Enoggera army barracks, six kilometres north-west of the CBD.

Whitrod addressed the country troops billeted at the barracks. The Police Union would later claim that he insulted the young men, saying to them: 'If you want to go home to Mummy, put your hand up.' The union told the press that Whitrod's attitude was 'degrading' and 'demoralising'. Their attack was further evidence of the 'sustained bitterness' from the union that Whitrod had been experiencing from his first day.

On Tuesday 20 July, Lewis, having now toiled for almost a decade behind his desk at the JAB, travelled to the Enoggera army barracks – the temporary headquarters of the Police Department's anticipated anti-apartheid offensive – for some specialised training in 'arrest techniques'.

The next day, Lewis was back at the exhibition grounds, as his police diary reads: 'Addressed briefly by Messrs Whitrod and Hodges. Remained there until 1pm.'

Meanwhile, Premier Bjelke-Petersen secretly called on Ron Edington and made an astonishing proposal to him and the Police Union.

According to Edington, the premier promised that police would 'not be penalised for any action they take to suppress' the demonstrators.

'You stay with me and I'll stay with you,' he told Edington. 'At the present moment you've got a claim before the [industrial] court?'

'Yeah, that's right,' Edington answered.

'What are you going for?' Bjelke-Petersen went on. 'I'll make sure that you get it.'

Edington was dumbfounded.

'But how can you interfere with the decision made by the Industrial Court?'

The premier told him not to worry about it.

The Springboks were due to arrive late on the afternoon of Thursday

22 July at Archerfield airport, twelve kilometres south-west of the CBD, and not the major interstate airfield at Eagle Farm. Archerfield was primarily reserved for civil aviation.

That morning, the police fully mobilised. In the theatrette at police headquarters, Duncan attended a briefing on the looming confrontation. The Archerfield arrival strategy was discussed.

Duncan checked on the team's estimated time of arrival. Their plane had been delayed due to fog in Canberra.

At 3.30 p.m. he then repaired to Wickham Terrace and the Tower Mill Motel – one of the few hotels in the city that would agree to accommodate the Springboks. There he joined almost six hundred uniformed and senior police officers.

Lewis reported to the motel earlier in the day. He wrote: 'Then took charge of . . . 50 detectives and plain-clothes personnel there, until Commissioned officers arrived later in afternoon.'

By the time the team bus arrived at the hotel at 5.26 p.m., the peaceful and orderly mood was deteriorating.

Duncan recorded in his police diary that at 5.50 p.m. 'Supt. Barnett, after discussion, directed crowd to move on. After no response, police on duty were directed to move them on . . .'

Whitrod, on the scene, had been contacted by the matron of nearby Holy Spirit hospital, requesting that the noise level be reduced in consideration of the patients.

Many of the police in attendance wore riot helmets and were armed with batons. Undercover police in jeans and leather jackets threaded through the crowd of about two hundred, which had gathered at dusk on the footpath opposite the motel entrance. Among them were Indigenous rights leader Sam Watson and student lawyer and future Queensland premier Peter Beattie.

Whitrod had been installed on a first-floor balcony of the Tower Mill Motel. He was brandishing a loudhailer.

Then the police charged, and the demonstrators scattered. Police at the scene that night recall hearing Whitrod shout 'hold your ranks' through the loudhailer, but hundreds of police ploughed forward, herding the protesters down the steep slope of Wickham Park and off a low stone wall with a drop down to Roma Street.

Several protesters were injured, and a handful arrested.

Clifford Crawford, a young police officer at the time of the incident, says in hindsight 'the commander lost control of the troops'.

Lewis says he was consigned to the side of the motel to ensure that no demonstrators damaged the building. 'I actually wasn't out the front of it,' he recalls. 'There was this charge, for want of a better word, and Mr Whitrod wasn't happy about that.'

Later that night after the riot, the Springboks attended a special cocktail and dinner party for 150 guests, hosted by none other than one of Shirley Brifman's good friends, the Brisbane stockbroker Robin Corrie, at his luxury home at 36 Armagh Street, Clayfield.

Two bus loads of police stood guard outside the house and plainclothes officers were posted in the garden. Ten of the twenty-five-strong rugby squad attended the soiree.

The press reported: 'Lineout expert Frik Dupreez, who towered over the beautiful young girls who flocked around him, and hooker Robbie Barnard said they were at ease socially for one of the few times on the tour.'

The footballers said the demonstrators weren't a problem, just a 'pain in the neck'. Certainly not enough to cause a headache.

At the party, Corrie was showing off his wife of less than a year – the former Andree Roberts. After an acrimonious split with ex-wife Barbara, Corrie won over the glamorous and vivacious Andree, who knew Corrie well.

She had lived locally and often dropped by the Corrie place, where she met friends, including local journalists, and drank at the opulent poolside bar. Crowds of people often partied at the house when Corrie wasn't even there.

At least once a fortnight, a small group of detectives gathered at Corrie's house for spirits and beer.

'They were always in suits and ties and I thought they were just businessmen,' a family member recalls. 'Robin was very good friends with Joh Bjelke-Petersen and often described him as "my most important client". He also gave stockbroking advice to prostitutes.'

On the night of the party, the slender Andree, staunchly anti–Country Party, tried to get a *Courier-Mail* photographer to take a picture of the captain of the Springboks with her Indigenous maid and good friend, Lesley. It caused a minor scandal and embarrassed Corrie, who expected Lesley to wait on the footballers. 'She is not the maid, she is a guest at this party,' Andree was heard to remark.

Demonstrations continued through the Springboks' twelve-day Queensland tour.

Elements of the local press praised Whitrod's leadership during the crisis. The Police Union did not. Predictably, it once again passed a vote of no confidence in the police commissioner. Their assessment? He'd been too soft with the agitators.

Sydney's *Daily Telegraph* said criticism of Whitrod's handling of the situation smacked of the 'Judas Iscariot'. It argued that the state of emergency was enacted to minimise violence and damage to property, and that Whitrod had 'tried and successfully achieved this by peaceful means'.

The report added: 'Certain police factions incensed by the fact they were not allowed to show their prowess at curbing public demonstrations by strong arm tactics, then censure Mr Whitrod for his comparatively peaceful handling of a situation they wanted to turn into a warlike confrontation.'

The *Daily Telegraph* had hit upon the irony of the situation. Here, Whitrod had faced one of his toughest tests: overweight, a bookworm and an office-bound man dedicated to the rigour of administration, he was on show, in a scenario of actual street policing involving physical force, to hundreds of tough Queensland police officers. To his men. They were always going to find him wanting.

The riot, however, was an epiphany for Bjelke-Petersen. He had shown his leadership by invoking the state of emergency. He had seen at first hand how the force of the police, on behalf of the government, and despite Whitrod's unease, could be utilised efficiently to quash public unrest. And he understood that, like a good old-fashioned father, if he threatened to punish conservative Queensland's naughty children, it met with huge voter approval.

On that cold night outside the Tower Mill Motel in Brisbane, the separation of government and police blurred, and Bjelke-Petersen fully recognised its importance as a political weapon.

On the day of the Springboks' match in Brisbane – Saturday 24 July – a local by-election for the inner-city seat of Merthyr took place amid all the anti-apartheid hoopla.

It was won by former Special Branch officer Don Lane.

The Most Hated Man in the Force

The Brifman investigation gave Police Commissioner Whitrod the perfect excuse to implement what he considered to be a vital component of a reformed police force – a smart and sharp internal investigating unit that would root out corruption within its own ranks.

In addition, Police Minister Hodges had announced a separate investigation into allegations of police graft and corruption on the Gold Coast, centring on massage parlours.

As Abe Duncan continued his painstaking interviews with Brifman, Hodges and Whitrod established the Criminal Intelligence Unit (CIU). It was stationed well away from the maelstrom of police headquarters in the city, in a clutch of rooms at the police college in Laurel Avenue, Chelmer.

The CIU opened its doors for business on 21 September 1971. Both the Brifman and Gold Coast investigations were tasked to the unit.

Detective Inspector Norm Gulbransen was named head of the CIU. Other recruits to the so-called untouchables were Detective Sergeant Basil 'the Hound' Hicks, Don Becker, Detective Senior Sergeant Jim Voigt, and Senior Constable Greg Early.

On commencing duties, the staff were handed a document that laid out the aims of the special unit. They were to obtain information regarding all possible systems of graft and corruption to prevent the setting up of 'crime rings' or control of crime by 'crime bosses' through standover men and other methods, and to protect honest members of the force from the pressure coming from crime bosses and their syndicates.

Days before he even learned about his new job, Hicks was phoned by Tony Murphy and summoned to a meeting. Murphy asked him to come to the first floor of CIB headquarters via the back lift, where he met Hicks, and proceeded to the building's roof.

According to Hicks, Murphy said, 'There's no need for us to be always fighting. Why don't you join us? There's nine of us – Terry, Glen, and I are the main three and there's the other six. If you join us, you will be one of the main ones – there will be me, you, Terry, and Glen.'

'What about Whitrod?' Hicks asked.

'We'll surround him.'

As to be expected, the Police Union muscled up against the CIU.

Whitrod declared that his Crime Intelligence Unit would concentrate on a few 'target' criminals. In reality, it would predominantly monitor the financial status of bent Queensland police – how much were they taking in? How much were they spending above and beyond a regular salary? Whitrod wanted to secure some prostitutes as informants to gauge the level of police corruption.

Greg Early was responsible for clerical duties within the unit and he scraped together equipment and established a records section. They were given three rooms at the college and two unmarked squad cars. Each member was issued a bus pass.

The Department of Works fitted new Yale locks to all doors accessing the CIU's three rooms.

Early remembers: 'We got a large combination safe, a safe so big that the floor under the old wooden building had to be reinforced and a crane had to be hired to put the safe in through the front door.'

Early can't remember Whitrod ever visiting the CIU offices. Little was committed to paper by way of memos or instructions. As far as Early observed, all communication with Whitrod regarding the unit's activities was largely private and face to face through Gulbransen.

From the outset, the CIU discussed the use of listening devices and other ways to trap the Rat Pack.

Early quickly began to feel the heat.

'The CIU was despised over its activities and was wrongly credited with being all over the state in a variety of vehicles,' he says. 'I soon realised that I was involved in a political minefield and that my popularity as a police officer had gone downhill even further from having worked closely with Mr Whitrod.'

The Police Union instantly branded the CIU a bunch of spies. Murphy, meanwhile, employed the same modus operandi on Gulbransen as he did with witnesses at the National Hotel inquiry. He travelled to Ayr in north Queensland – Gulbransen's old beat – and sniffed about for dirt.

Whitrod warned the amiable Gulbransen, saying the CIU chief would become 'one of the most unpopular police officers in Queensland'.

It was a gross understatement.

The Magician Comes Calling Again

Just five kilometres south-west of Robin Corrie's mansion in Clayfield, Brifman was falling apart in the Wilston safe house, taking tablets to get to sleep.

Within days of the anti-apartheid protests, New South Wales detectives Williams and Paull were due to arrive from Sydney to grill Brifman yet again about her allegations against Police Commissioner Norm Allan, Fred Krahe, and the rest of her criminal milieu.

And to add to her problems, her husband, Sonny, had been charged with false pretences and was due to face a magistrates court in Brisbane.

In late July and early August, Williams and Paull flew to Brisbane to interrogate Brifman. Later that month Brifman herself went to Sydney on a short trip and was back by 30 August.

Whitrod, meanwhile, didn't want to wait for the Brifman interviews to be concluded before he started pre-emptive strikes against the Queensland officers mentioned in the records of interview to date.

On Tuesday 31 August, he took the unprecedented move of transferring Detective Murphy from the Licensing Branch to the Juvenile Aid Bureau.

It was a massive humiliation for the famous detective. And it was a message to Lewis. Whitrod had put a detective suspected of corruption, courtesy of the Brifman allegations, in the same little basket as the head of the JAB.

Murphy was understandably livid, cooped up with the 'bum smackers' in the office not far from Whitrod's. He took on no official duties under Lewis.

'It infuriated Murphy more towards Whitrod,' Lewis says. '[He] hated it. I don't think he did a day of bloody work.'

Just a few days later, Duncan received an urgent phone call at 10.25 a.m. from a hysterical Shirley Brifman. She was at the Wilston safe house at about 8.30 a.m. when she received another death threat from

Sydney gunman John Regan. Sonny, supposedly unaware of the threat, drove Brifman to her sister Marge Chapple's house in Paddington.

Shirley asked for sedative tablets and her husband gave her two Tuinals, the highly addictive barbiturate depressant, also used in the 1960s and 1970s as a recreational drug called 'rainbows', 'beans', or 'jeebs'. She rested while Sonny and Marge left the house. Minutes later, Brifman called Duncan.

In that call she confided that she'd 'taken some sleeping pills'.

Duncan, Assistant Police Commissioner Val Barlow, and a police-woman headed straight over to the safe house, where they'd agreed to meet. There they found Brifman unconscious under the house. It was yet another overdose.

'I was one of the few who knew where she lived,' Duncan recalls. 'We found her unconscious . . . Val Barlow was a big, strong fellow and she was a small thing. Val lifted her up and we took her to hospital.'

Her stomach pumped, Brifman was housed in the Brisbane general hospital's notorious Ward 16 – a locked psychiatric facility. She was discharged two days later and recuperated with her sister in Paddington.

Duncan had an urgent private discussion with Whitrod about Brifman, then later attempted to interview her about the Regan threat at police headquarters, but she became ill and the interview was abandoned. A police guard was placed on the Wilston safe house.

Then, almost a week later, Glendon Patrick Hallahan, estranged lover of Shirley Brifman and, along with Tony Murphy, one of the star culprits in her damning narrative, did something extraordinary.

He brought his informant John Edward Milligan, drug dealer and former Regan sidekick, into the heart of police headquarters.

Duncan recorded in his police diary: 'Saw Det. Sgt. G.P. Hallahan 9.25am and he introduced John Edward Milligan, who was interviewed by me 9.30am to 11.45am re: Stewart John Regan, Sydney criminal.'

It underlined the arrogance and cunning of Hallahan. Under threat, he went straight into the lion's den. He was showing Whitrod and Duncan that he was cooperating with the Brifman investigation, yet it also put him in a position to find out, first hand, the direction in which the investigation was heading. He showed no fear bringing Milligan into the centre of it all.

Just short of a week later, Duncan received another urgent call, this time from Brifman's sister Marge Chapple. An anonymous female had phoned her house in Paddington, threatening the lives of the Brifman children.

Detective Paull flew back into Brisbane again soon after, and with him was a young detective called Clive Small.

Small – who would later become famous for solving the Ivan Milat backpacker serial killings during the 1990s – was a junior on the Brifman investigation, seconded as an interview transcript typist and a self-described 'get me a cup of coffee sort of guy'.

He says of the Brifman interviews: 'She looked quite a bit older than she was . . . like she'd had a hard life.

'I thought she was a bit shaky . . . She didn't come in as a "Here I am and I'll tell you all I've got". She appeared like a person under pressure.

'The pressure from all sides – the good guys, the bad guys and the crooks – the pressure . . . would have been enormous.'

And it wasn't just Shirley Brifman on the brink.

This Town's Getting Too Hot

Assistant Police Commissioner Duncan was deeply worried about Brifman, and at 8 a.m. on Monday 6 September he telephoned Colin Bennett to discuss her health and the future of her police interviews. Would she be able to continue?

Duncan had a quick talk to Whitrod about the situation, then later that morning a squad car picked up Brifman and brought her into police headquarters.

Police needed to know more about the threat from John Regan and the identity of his blond associate, Milligan.

Meanwhile, the New South Wales head of the double-headed Brifman inquiry – Assistant Police Commissioner Brian Doyle – was, behind closed doors, starting to get tense. Not only had the Brifman revelations begun to internally polarise some elements of the New South Wales force, but information leaks were beginning to hamper the investigation, and many officers south of the border suspected they were coming out of Queensland.

In addition, Brifman continued to be a troublesome interviewee.

In his written assessment, Doyle described Brifman: 'She is an extremely difficult woman to interview on account of her hysterical character, flight of ideas, rapid and dissociated talk and her insistence on saying whatever comes into her mind, even if it is not remotely connected with the subject being discussed.

'She . . . goes into tantrum after tantrum, endeavouring to hold it over you that she won't talk to you anymore unless she does everything her way.

'She will make an appointment and immediately cancel it.'

Brifman again fell ill that day – 6 September – in the interview room with Abe Duncan, and returned to her sister's house to recover.

What she didn't know was that on the Gold Coast that same afternoon, two police officers were breaking into an exclusive multi-level beach house in Hedges Avenue, Mermaid Beach, in search of a missing person.

Once inside, they found their man dead in the main bedroom. It was stockbroker Robin Corrie.

The day before, Corrie and his wife, Andree, and the children had been to a lunchtime engagement party. Conspicuously, Corrie was not eating. He said he had no appetite.

Later, he saw off his daughter at Brisbane airport. She was returning to school in New South Wales. He told Andree that he was going into his CBD office to do some work, but he never returned to the Corrie home in Clayfield.

The next morning, Andree arose at 5 a.m. and found her husband still missing. Perhaps he was on his boat, or had slept overnight in the office. She knew he had a business meeting at 8 a.m. and around that time she phoned his office. The meeting was in progress, but Corrie was not present.

Andree then reported Corrie missing to police.

At 12.15 p.m., two officers from Broadbeach police station on the Gold Coast arrived at the Mermaid Beach holiday house and jemmied a hopper window to gain entry to the property. Corrie was found on the bed. Two tablets and a headache powder in an envelope were found on the dressing table, and nearby a glass containing a small amount of liquid.

Also, police discovered several letters addressed to his family. A post-mortem revealed Corrie, who had just turned fifty-one, had died of a drug overdose (methaqualone or Quaaludes, a nervous system depressant, and pentobarbitone, a barbiturate taken for insomnia).

His son John Corrie, almost eighteen, had driven to the Gold Coast looking for his father. When he arrived at the beach house in Hedges Avenue, he was confronted by two large policemen. They had only arrived five minutes earlier.

They told him: 'There's no use going in there, son, your old man's dead.'

When she learned the news, Brifman was shattered: 'It is so hard to believe it is not funny. He wasn't the type to kill himself but the type if he was hooked to protect his family.'

Brifman found Corrie's suicide incomprehensible, knowing him as intimately as she did. He loved life, and to her knowledge had no financial difficulties, though he had confided in her that his second marriage was not running smoothly.

Then Brifman remembered Detective Hallahan boasting years earlier that he had struck a financially lucrative vein in blackmailing homosexual businessmen.

She wondered if Hallahan wasn't at it again, with men like Corrie.

'I thought . . . maybe Glen was blackmailing Robin because he knew that I used to fly up here for Robin,' she reflected.

It echoed back a decade to the death by supposed overdose of prostitute Leigh Hamilton, having had a run-in with Hallahan.

John Corrie believes there was nothing to suggest that his father died by anything other than his own hand.

'There were pressures from banks and overdrafts, personal pressures, and the business,' he says. 'He'd been through the mining boom of the late 60s, and 1970 and 1971 were terrible years, they were difficult years.'

In reality, his marriage to Andree was already faltering after just fourteen months. According to a family member, she never wanted to marry Corrie in the first place 'but he threatened to kill himself with tablets if she didn't'. He was also losing money and had a pathological 'fear of poverty'. 'He was broke but he actually lived like he had a lot of money,' the family member recalls.

In letters left on the dressing table to his wife, children, sister and company secretary, Corrie indicated that he was heading for financial disaster. He expressed regret for his actions, outlined his share values and asked that his children be well looked after.

The party in Armagh Street was over.

A Nice Man Dies in the Suburbs

John Regan was still haunting Brisbane in spring 1971 when on 18 and 19 September, Abe Duncan, acting on a tip from an informant, cruised O'Connell Terrace, which runs along the edge of the

Brisbane Exhibition grounds in Bowen Hills, looking for any trace of the Sydney gunman.

With Regan and his former sidekick Milligan trying to frame each other with both the Queensland police and the Federal Narcotics Bureau, and with Brifman in hiding and Hallahan thrown into the mix, Brisbane for a moment must have suddenly appeared like a branch office of the Sydney underworld.

The next week, Jack Cooper, the physically imposing manager of the notorious National Hotel, was finishing his shift at around 2.40 a.m. on the morning of Sunday 26 September. Cooper was well liked by hotel patrons and had a reputation for being fair but firm.

Cooper was well acquainted, too, with the likes of Murphy, Hallahan, and the other police friends of hotel proprietor Max Roberts.

That morning, the Adelaide-born former caterer, instead of heading home to his family in Stafford, nine kilometres north of the CBD, drove a few blocks from the hotel to 203 Elizabeth Street, where he had a meal in the kitchen of the Lotus Room restaurant and nightclub. He was joined by good friend and club owner Ray Sue-Tin.

'He came straight through to the kitchen and sat at the kitchen table while I prepared a meal,' said Sue-Tin. 'He came in about three times a week after finishing work and always sat in the kitchen while we talked and had a meal.'

Cooper, Sue-Tin asserted, always enjoyed Chinese food.

Sue-Tin had operated the Lotus Room since 1969 and had a rare 3 a.m. licence. It was one of Brisbane's few late-night clubs, along with the Playboy down at Petrie Bight. Diners were entertained by the Billy Blackmore Trio, a piano, bass and drum ensemble that played everything from jazz to the latest popular songs.

Sue-Tin's wife, Quorling, remembers Cooper coming to the Lotus Room virtually every night for a meal after the National closed.

'He was a very, very nice man,' she says. 'I remember Terry Lewis and Tony Murphy coming in all the time, almost every night during the week. I remember Glen Hallahan coming not as often.'

After his meal, Cooper regularly drove Sue-Tin and Quorling to their home at the corner of Jean Street and Days Road, Grange, on his way back to Stafford.

On that morning, Cooper arrived at Sue-Tin's modest red-brick house, with its poinsettias and a Hills hoist exposed to Jean Street out the back, at around 4.25 a.m.

'He didn't say anything in particular when I got out of his car . . . just "goodnight" or "see you later" or something like that,' remembered Sue-Tin.

Cooper then headed towards his home in Brennan Street, just over five minutes' drive away. When he approached his regular left turn off Shand Street, he noticed in the headlights a barricade of wooden fruit boxes.

He stopped the car and stepped out to remove the boxes when he was cut down by gunfire. The ninety-five kilogram Cooper, forty-eight, was struck by five bullets from a .22 calibre weapon fixed with a silencer. Fifteen bullets had been fired at him. A security dog at an industrial plant opposite the murder scene raised no alarm.

The killer or killers then dragged Cooper's body off the road and dumped it under a nearby tree. The car was left with the keys still in the ignition. Cooper's spectacles had dropped into a pool of his own blood.

Who would want to kill Jack Cooper? He carried no money from the National Hotel's nightly takings, and had no keys to the hotel's safe.

If robbery was the motive, the perpetrators were pitifully informed.

Or had he, as the hotel's eyes and ears since 1966, been accidentally privy to some confidential information? Robin Corrie's death had recently been front-page news. And Shirley Brifman was in town being investigated by police in two states. Had some old police friends of the National, agitated over the current state of affairs, maybe a little drunk in the early hours of that Sunday, or in recent days, let something slip in front of Cooper?

One of the detectives assigned to the murder case was Glen Hallahan.

In a breakthrough in the investigation a month later, the crates were traced to a fruit and vegetable store in inner-city New Farm. Police then identified the murder weapon as a .22 calibre collapsible Armalite survival rifle, and traced its sale to a Fortitude Valley disposals store.

At dawn on 5 November, New Farm businessman Donald John Maher, thirty-one, was arrested and charged with Cooper's murder.

Maher, represented at his trial by Des Sturgess, later admitted in his statement to police that he was present at the shooting of Cooper – the culmination of a robbery attempt gone 'haywire' – but didn't shoot the hotel manager. Maher, who had previous convictions for car theft but was trying to get his life back on track, refused to identify the killer.

His trial, though, revealed a convoluted plot leading up to the slaying. A criminal, Perry Vincent, gave evidence that Maher had offered him money to concoct a story implicating Hallahan in the murder.

Vincent alleged Maher told him that Hallahan, with someone named 'Murphy', had control of brothels on the Gold Coast, and that Hallahan was 'in it, up to his neck'.

Vincent said he was to tell the police that Hallahan had been standing over Cooper's body, and that Maher had exclaimed: 'What have you done?' And that Hallahan replied: 'It's done now.'

Maher claimed that he was physically assaulted while being questioned at CIB headquarters. He also said that Hallahan remarked to him: 'There is a lot of heat on and somebody has to go for it.'

He later protested that his statement was signed under extreme duress, and that his admission that he was present at the shooting of Cooper was 'pure perjury' by police.

Maher was found guilty and jailed for life.

Years later, Whitrod wrote in his memoir: 'I was told confidentially that a second person, who could have been a police officer, was involved in the murder. I was told Donald Maher, who was convicted of the murder, admitted a second person was involved but was too scared to name him to police.'

Under the Microscope

According to Lewis's police diaries, his work at the JAB remained untroubled by the Brifman revelations and the Corrie and Cooper deaths in the latter half of 1971.

He was forging ahead with his university diploma, delivering lectures at the police college, giving interviews to the local press, checking duty rosters and drafting responses to questions asked of his minister, Max Hodges, in Parliament House.

On the day that Corrie's body was discovered, he briefed Tony Murphy on the functions of the JAB.

Still, Whitrod, via Ken Hoggett and others, would not leave Lewis alone.

In late September, Lewis had an actual audience with Whitrod regarding a new police station in Upper Mount Gravatt. The police commissioner wanted Lewis to train officers appointed to the station in how to deal with juveniles.

Was Whitrod trying to marginalise Lewis by sticking him in the suburbs? Lewis soon expressed to Whitrod his 'disinterest' in the idea.

'He wanted to get rid of me,' says Lewis. 'I had passed the exams to qualify for inspector and I was likely to become a commissioned officer. Whitrod thought I should get some uniform experience. He wanted me to go [to Upper Mount Gravatt] as a uniformed senior sergeant.'

In addition, the police commissioner continued to foist staff on Lewis and the JAB. Then came a curious request later in the year.

'Insp. M. Hopgood called at the office re: Diaries completed by me whilst in C.I. Branch.' A few days later he handed to Hopgood his three diaries for '1959–1962, inclusive'.

Why had this period in Lewis's career – the Bahnemann conviction, the closing of the brothels by Bischof, the exposure of the sensational affair surrounding Mary Margaret Fels – suddenly demanded scrutiny from higher powers?

Was it related to Brifman and her time soliciting out of the National Hotel? Or was it just a play by Whitrod to unsettle Lewis?

Two Bulls Lock Horns

New South Wales Assistant Police Commissioner Brian Doyle – described by an officer who worked with him in Sydney in the early 1970s as 'the paradigm honest cop, the no-nonsense tough guy who succumbed to no pressure and took no money', and in charge of sifting through Brifman's allegations against dozens of Sydney police – was about to put on a show that would never be forgotten by those who witnessed it.

He was set to conduct a series of one-on-one interviews with his doppelganger in the force – Fred 'Froggy' Krahe. It was Doyle's job to get to the bottom of Krahe's association with Brifman and the graft he'd been allegedly collecting for years.

But senior New South Wales police were not going to risk another major scandal over the squealing of a drug-addicted prostitute. In late 1971 it was still suffering the reverberations of the Detective Sergeant Phillip Arantz revelations.

Arantz, head of the newly formed Computer Bureau, began feeding in police crime statistics and immediately discovered a discrepancy between the computer tabulations and the figures published in the Police Department's annual reports. He learned that the crime rate in 1971 was in fact seventy-five per cent higher than that publicly presented by Police Commissioner Norm Allan and Premier Robert Askin.

When Allan and other superiors showed no interest in his findings, Arantz leaked the data to the *Sydney Morning Herald*. The response was explosive.

Arantz was deemed insane and was sent to be tested for mental illness at a psychiatric unit. He refused to answer questions when a departmental investigation was launched; he was then suspended without pay.

In the middle of this, Brifman was throwing in her two cents' worth.

The pressure on the Brifman investigation, under Doyle, was immense.

'I found there was a fair deal of paranoia within the team . . .' remembers Clive Small, a junior on the Brifman investigation. 'There were people more senior in the police who were very interested beyond what was reasonable or normal in the investigation.'

He said the management and coordination of the investigation at higher levels was being done from Queensland and leaks were starting to emerge.

Colin Bennett was also mentioning Brifman at length in state parliament and clearly had an inside knowledge of the police investigation. Where was he getting his material from? Who could be trusted?

Brian Doyle's interrogation of Fred Krahe was so intense that paint was coming off the walls.

'Doyle and Krahe,' says Small. 'You didn't want to be there and you knew it'd never happen again. Doyle and Krahe were two people who saw themselves as the best two detectives in the state. When they confronted each other it was sheer tension.

'Clearly there was a hell of a lot of ego between the two men as well. A person like Brian Doyle, his ego would say, "I want to see them arrested and that'll make me the next commissioner." Krahe's would have been saying, "I've done a lot for police, I've probably been paying people off, but what's this bloke Doyle ever done?"'

Krahe was also close to Assistant Commissioner Fred 'Slippery' Hanson – who was being groomed by Allan as the next police commissioner – and there was a feeling within the investigation that they were both hiding things from Doyle and his men.

Small recalls: 'There were a lot of people who didn't like Krahe, but there were a lot of people who respected him. It caused a very severe split in senior police ranks.'

Letters from the Past

The indefatigable Colin Bennett had caused mayhem in state parliament many times since his election in 1960, notwithstanding his sparking the National Hotel inquiry in 1963.

But with a brittle Brifman in the middle of her police interviews in Brisbane, Sydney gunman John Regan on the loose, and National Hotel manager Jack Cooper on the slab in the city morgue, there was never a better time for another Bennett strike.

On Monday 12 October 1971, Bennett asked Police Minister Max Hodges a question without notice. If Bennett tabled Shirley Brifman's record of interview thus far, would the minister correlate their contents dealing with the alleged corruption of Murphy and Hallahan with two letters written by Murphy to Brifman in 1963, prior to the National Hotel inquiry? And having done this, would Hodges then tell parliament what Police Commissioner Whitrod might do about it?

Bennett had two aces up his sleeve – the Murphy letters, given to him by Brifman. The letters proved that Murphy knew at all times the whereabouts of Brifman prior to and during the National Hotel inquiry, and that he knew she was a working prostitute.

On both counts, the letters contradicted Murphy's evidence to the inquiry and on the surface amounted to multiple counts of perjury.

Murphy and Hallahan hit back through their solicitors the next day, and it made front-page news in the *Courier-Mail*: DETECTIVES' DENIALS OF CLAIMS IN PARLT.

Their statement read: 'That a member of the Legislative Assembly would see fit to use the privilege of parliament in this way must surely astound all thinking people.

'Mr Bennett, while airing in parliament unfounded allegations that malign our reputation as police officers, has not seen fit to inform parliament of the background of this woman making these allegations.'

In other words, who could trust a self-confessed perjurer and a prostitute like Shirley Brifman over the words and deeds of two of the state's most famous and revered detectives?

On the same day, Bennett landed some more uppercuts in Parliament House.

At 12.06 p.m. he rose and stated: 'I think it is of great interest that two detectives of the Queensland Police Force should see at this late stage, through the columns of the *Courier-Mail*, to denigrate a woman named Shirley Brifman, whom they both befriended for many years, whom they organised into becoming, from their point of view, the "darling" of the 1963 National Hotel Royal Commission.'

Bennett went on to read passages from Murphy's letters to Brifman in Sydney about gathering evidence against inquiry witness David Young, in which he claimed that no police from Queensland or New South Wales would 'land on her doorstep at any tick of the clock and cause her trouble'.

Bennett went to town: 'Here is one detective in Queensland saying that he has such perfect control of the Queensland and New South Wales Police Forces that he can guarantee to this girl whose record he well knew, that no police would visit her premises.'

Big Russ Hinze attempted to quell the slaughter of Murphy. 'A self-confessed perjurer – and you are reading that rubbish in the House!'

Bennett was unperturbed, reciting Brifman's recent evidence against Hallahan into *Hansard* until his time expired.

Hinze fired back at 12.35 p.m., criticising Bennett's 'diatribe' against 'highly respected police officers'. According to Hinze, Bennett was conducting a long-running vendetta, using his private practice as a lawyer to secure scuttlebutt to air in parliament.

'What ethics has he when a person goes to him as a lawyer and later finds that whatever he told his lawyer is mentioned on the floor of Parliament?' Hinze said.

How could Bennett continue to throw mud at the state's most famous detectives? Murphy was a good family man with several children. Hallahan was also a family man, having recently married Heather, a former barmaid at the Belfast Hotel. He had moved from his bachelor flat to a larger place at Kangaroo Point, just across the Story Bridge.

Erring on the side of caution, Abe Duncan met with Crown Law that same morning to query the tabling in parliament of portions of the Brifman transcripts.

It would be one of Duncan's last duties regarding the Brifman investigation. Whitrod wanted matters ramped up.

'He told me to hand over all those statements to the CIU and Norm Gulbransen and Jim Voigt,' says Duncan. 'I gladly handed it all over.'

Another Overdose, Another Suspicious Death

In the escalating heat of that 1971 spring in Brisbane, another petite prostitute stepped forward to seek both protection from police and to offer some confidential information.

Cheryl Ann Mitchell, twenty-one, had been on the game for more than two years, working out of Sydney's Kings Cross. For a time she had lived with gunman John Regan at his Sydney home in Kensington. He had occasionally 'managed' her as a prostitute.

Falling out with Regan in late 1970, she fled to Kalgoorlie in Western Australia, then worked the streets of Perth before settling on the Gold Coast in time for Christmas that year and moving into a flat supposedly owned by a Sydney friend. He was Leslie Gigler, a former motorcycle racer who went under the name of John Trophy. Gigler was one of Regan's mates and a former business partner. He, too, had fallen out with the gunman and had sought refuge in Queensland.

Gigler was known to police as a bludger, despite his claims he had once operated a garage in Sydney and had other legitimate business investments.

Mitchell settled with Gigler into Flat 2, Sorrento Flats, 24 Old Burleigh Road in Surfers Paradise, a brisk walk to the beach, and romance quickly blossomed.

But Mitchell spent that Christmas in Sydney with her mother and took up again with Regan. They split soon after, this time over a car they had bought together. Regan had used her money to close the deal but demanded the vehicle for himself.

When she took the car, Regan sent a tow truck to her mother's Sydney home to fetch 'his' property. The car wasn't there.

Mitchell sold the car to get Regan off her trail, and returned to Gigler on the Gold Coast. A trained comptometrist, or billing clerk, she secured work at the Temple of Isis health studio in the Sundial Arcade building, Cavill Avenue, Surfers Paradise. It had six rooms and was known to be operating as a massage parlour.

Brifman would later say: 'I saw Regan in Lennons once . . . He was up here to kill Gigler. Regan said, "Nobody doublecrosses me . . . He's got a girl with him that he should not have. Nobody takes something which belongs to me. I'm going to shoot him . . ."'

With the CIU investigating bribery and corruption on the Gold

Coast in September, it appeared that both Mitchell and her lover, Gigler, under threat of Regan, sought a measure of police protection by offering information in exchange for safety. Mitchell helped police, while Gigler agreed to an interview with Colin Bennett.

It was Brifman who told police about Regan's threat to kill Gigler, and it's possible that she facilitated Gigler's meeting with Bennett, her own lawyer.

Mitchell, who had often talked of wanting to 'work square' – or leave her illicit activities for a conventional job – was working as a comptometrist in Brisbane's Spring Hill in the first week of October 1971. Workmates viewed her as a calm and quiet young woman.

Then at 11 p.m. on Tuesday 5 October, firefighters and police rushed to the Sundial Arcade building in Cavill Avenue. The Temple of Isis, sold just weeks earlier, had been torched and razed. Police Minister Max Hodges addressed parliament after the fire, saying the Temple of Isis was 'the subject of a police investigation' into bribery and corruption on the Gold Coast.

Later that week, Bennett tabled a document that received little to no attention from the press. It was his seventeen-page record of interview with Gigler, concerning graft, police corruption, and the massage industry on the Gold Coast.

Did Bennett speak with Mitchell and Gigler about exposing the document? Did he argue that this public knowledge would somehow act as a form of security barrier for the couple?

If he did, he may not have appreciated the full dimension of Regan's violence and madness. This man thought nothing of killing his friends, no matter how close, if he felt it gave him an advantage.

Mitchell and Gigler may also have been given a measure of comfort from a pronouncement by Hodges, again in parliament. The police minister assured Queensland that the Police Department was aware Regan was in the area, and that the Sydney criminal was 'under surveillance'.

Still, Mitchell continued to have nightmares about being beheaded by Regan, and she also heard whispers that a private investigator was hunting for her in the streets of Surfers Paradise.

On Sunday 31 October, Mitchell and Gigler took his speckle-headed Great Dane down to the beach for a gallop. Gigler's brother, passing through the Gold Coast, met up with the couple and it was suggested they hit the town. Mitchell declined, retiring to the Old Burleigh Road flat.

It was hot – the end of spring – and Mitchell dressed for bed in a pair of shortie pyjamas. She had her crossword puzzles and a bottle of Pernod for company.

When Gigler finally returned home, he found her dead in the bedroom. The dog was still lying with her across the bed. Gigler immediately reported the death to Southport police.

They subsequently discovered a bottle of pills near her body. Once again, an overdose of barbiturates was suspected. She died less than a couple of kilometres from Robin Corrie's beach house in Mermaid Beach, where he had expired facing the same ocean just eight weeks earlier.

Whitrod quickly assigned CIU chief, Norm Gulbransen to the case.

Back in Brisbane, Abe Duncan was knee-deep in the Jack Cooper murder investigation. On Tuesday 2 November, the day after Mitchell's body was discovered, suspect Donald Maher was brought into CIB headquarters for questioning. Duncan recorded in his police diary that Maher was under 'strong suspicion'.

On the same day, Duncan's work was interrupted by a curious phone call. Hallahan informant, and former Regan sidekick, John Edward Milligan wanted to talk about a 'note allegedly written by deceased Cheryl Mitchell some time ago'.

Duncan wrote in his police diary: 'Contacted Det. Sgt. G. Hallahan, who later handed in copies of the note which he had obtained from an original shown to him by an informant. Saw Hallahan re: letter

1.45pm. Saw C.O.P [Whitrod] re: same . . . Later saw John Edward Milligan 3.40pm to 4.10pm. Spoke to Supt. Gulbransen and handed copies of documents obtained from Hallahan . . . to P.C. Const. Early.'

Hallahan claimed that a month before Mitchell's death, an informant had shown him the letter. Hallahan had had the foresight to make a copy of the original before handing it back.

The letter, written in Mitchell's distinctive longhand, was addressed 'To Whom It May Concern'.

It read: 'This is to say that it is my belief that a man by the name of John Regan, of 56 Duke Street, Kensington, will make an attempt on my life. Up until several months ago I was living with him and he was taking the money that I earnt as a prostitute in Kings Cross. Cheryl Mitchell.'

It contained a postscript: '. . . I'm sorry that I can't write this letter in more detail, but at the moment I am finding it hard to write even this much.'

If the letter was genuine, how did it fortuitously come into the hands of Hallahan, to be tucked away for a month prior to Mitchell's overdose? And why was Milligan angling to ensure the Sydney gunman became a prime suspect for the death? Was this payback for Regan's attempt to set up Milligan with the Federal Narcotics Bureau a few months earlier?

Or was Gigler somehow involved? By the time of Mitchell's inquest, Gigler and several other potential key witnesses had simply vanished.

A week after Mitchell's death, Gigler happily gave an interview to a local newspaper and posed for a photograph with his dog.

'These girls might see themselves getting married, but to who?' he asked philosophically. 'They've got no respect for the ordinary bloke. He's a mug. They're taking his money all the time.

'All that's left is the shyster.'

The Caravan and the Bug

In late 1971 Detective Glen Hallahan was spreading himself a little thin.

As Brifman continued to sing like a canary to Detective Inspector Norm Gulbransen of the CIU, Hallahan was attempting to pin the murder of National Hotel manager Jack Cooper on Donald Maher, and appeared to be at least peripherally involved in the suspicious death of Cheryl Mitchell.

Still, there was the day-to-day business of his graft collections to consider, and in the last week of December Hallahan planned to make a pick-up from one of his regulars, New Farm prostitute Dorothy Edith Knight.

Knight had been working the riverside suburb as a prostitute since early 1968, and from day one had paid Hallahan twenty dollars a week for immunity from prosecution.

Hallahan had been under surveillance for several weeks, and the CIU had evidence that he first met Knight years earlier in a Brisbane hotel lounge, and had directed her to work with a group of prostitutes out of a city premises. The call girls were often warned of impending police raids.

The CIU's investigations opened a small window into Hallahan's complicated life. They uncovered that criminals had been paying Queensland officers to commit crimes in the state, and that forged ten-dollar notes had been brought north of the border by police. Shirley Brifman's crazy claims were starting to firm into fact.

On that day in December, Hallahan arranged to meet Knight at their usual bench seat overlooking the Brisbane River in New Farm Park.

What Hallahan didn't know was that Whitrod's CIU had had him in its crosshair for some time. With Murphy shelved in the JAB, Whitrod's corruption busters now went directly after Hallahan with an elaborate sting.

The idea was to affix an electronic bug to Knight – the first use of a concealed recording device in Queensland police history – and tape their conversation prior to the money handover. Then police would immediately arrest Hallahan.

There was a whiff of the Keystone Cops about the operation from the outset.

Inspector Tom Noonan – head of the Radio and Electronics Section – was given the job of making the device. He eventually produced a microphone that could be concealed in a Bryant and May matchbox. Wires from the box were then attached to a tape recorder.

The CIU didn't have a recorder on their inventory, so they used one personally owned by Jim Voigt.

Next, they had to set up a discreet observation post.

Senior Constable Greg Early, who was in on the sting, recalls: 'It was resolved to use [Jim's] father's caravan, which had to be towed by Jim's vehicle because the CIU vehicles didn't have a tow bar and would have been easily recognised anyway.'

Detective Inspector Gulbransen, who headed up the trap, took no chances. He even asked Early to get his fitness up to speed: 'I'd played football and he urged me to get back into training . . . When we nicked Hallahan and he ran or swam I had to apprehend him. I started running again in Grinstead Park near my home.'

Early was almost taken off the case when word got back to Whitrod that he was friends with Hallahan. Both had recently attended one of the new arts and science courses at the Kangaroo Point Technical College. Whitrod wanted Early taken out of the unit, but Gulbransen stood by him.

On the morning of the bust, the caravan was positioned on a driveway within the park, not far from the bench seat. Gulbransen, Noonan and two others huddled in the caravan. They were later joined by Voigt and Early.

The bug itself was taped to Knight's torso by Detective Sergeant Basil Hicks.

Hallahan arrived as expected, parking his car not far from the caravan, and joined Knight on the bench seat.

Then disaster struck.

A council tractor towing several mowers started up nearby and the racket could be clearly heard inside the van.

Also unknown to the CIU was the state of the batteries inside the recorder. They were running low on power – nobody had checked them.

When Hallahan stood and returned to his vehicle, Gulbransen and Early struck. Gulbransen retrieved sixty dollars from Hallahan, and Early recorded in shorthand their subsequent conversation.

Early says Hallahan was firstly surprised and then appeared resigned that he'd been caught red-handed. 'He was caught fair and square,' remembers Early. 'When Gulbransen got the money back Hallahan knew Knight had put him in. He realised he was a done duck.'

Hallahan was driven back to police headquarters. When he requested to use the lavatory, Early accompanied him: 'I said to him, "It's strange we get to meet up again like this." He said bugger all.'

The CIU searched Hallahan's police locker and discovered two concealable firearms.

In another first for Queensland, Hallahan was charged with two counts of official corruption and brought before a magistrates court that afternoon. He was granted bail of three hundred dollars on the condition he have no contact with Knight, who was 'afraid of Hallahan'.

That day, Hallahan, thirty-nine, was suspended from duty.

How had he walked into such an obvious trap? Or had he reached a point where he considered himself untouchable?

Ron Edington, former president of the Police Union, says: 'He was a peculiar type of a bloke, old bloody Glen . . . bloody unscrupulous bastard, he'd do anything, you know . . . Fancy a stupid detective like

[that] walking down through a park . . . You'd get a bit suspicious, wouldn't you?'

Early adds: 'He must have known we'd been asking around for months. He must have thought he was immune.'

After everything Hallahan had been involved in over the previous two decades, it took a makeshift listening device with dicky batteries, an old caravan, and sixty dollars to bring Hallahan before a court for corruption.

Now for Murphy

Over at the Licensing Branch, Jack Herbert was quietly running the Joke and still delivering payouts to his mates, as regular as clockwork, at the beginning of each month.

Murphy was still taking in eight hundred dollars a month – an annual total of double his police wage. Herbert alleged that Lewis received a nominal amount.

While money wasn't a problem, Whitrod was. His wet behind the ears Criminal Investigation Unit had ensnared Hallahan. Now they were coming after Murphy.

Herbert and the Rat Pack had survived previous scrutiny through sheer cunning and the very thing they were trained to do as detectives. They may have shown creativity in exercising the verbal, but their ability to collate hard facts was just as formidable.

As Whitrod tightened the noose, they had to apply equal pressure.

So when Papua New Guinea–based barrister Eric Pratt – a friend of Lewis from the 1958 police interchange program – was in town on business, Lewis and Murphy arranged a meeting. Jack Herbert was asked along. Herbert had once worked as a police officer in Victoria, as had Pratt.

They met during the day at a motel on Coronation Drive overlooking the Brisbane River, not far from police headquarters.

'I recall a discussion there about Whitrod,' Herbert said. 'I took it that [Pratt] knew him quite well, actually, from the conversation which followed along the lines that the boys – that is, the police in New Guinea – were willing to put a keg on for the Queensland boys for having Whitrod.

'I also recall him stating that the only way to beat Whitty was to inundate him with paperwork . . . that he couldn't handle it.'

Lewis was fully aware of Whitrod's attempts to destabilise him. The police commissioner had planted new recruits in the Juvenile Aid Bureau (another was installed in late 1971), he was trawling through Lewis's old police diaries from his days in the Consorting Squad, and was conducting a ceaseless audit of the JAB's working patterns. Whitrod harassed Lewis for statistics and was clearly mounting a case against him and the JAB. But for what purpose?

Lewis again sought a personal audience with the police commissioner, but to no avail.

With Hallahan awaiting his corruption charges to be heard in court, Detective Tony Murphy, wearing a dark suit, arrived at the Queen Street chambers of his lawyer, J.P. Elliott, just prior to 1 p.m. on Friday 4 February 1972.

They were soon met by Gulbransen, Becker, Voigt and Early of the CIU.

Murphy was interviewed by the team for two hours and fifteen minutes over four charges of perjury stemming from false evidence he allegedly gave over Shirley Brifman at the National Hotel inquiry in late 1963.

Becker had earlier advised Early, the shorthand expert and interview stenographer, that he wanted every 'um', 'er' and 'ah' included in the transcript, right down to the last letter and punctuation mark.

Murphy answered all the questions put to him and told the investigators: 'I find myself charged because of the untrue, malicious statements of Shirley Brifman, a drug addict, a self-confessed perjurer, prostitute and police informer, who has so obviously fabricated certain statements about me, hoping somehow to evade the consequences of the law with respect to her in New South Wales introducing her thirteen-year-old daughter to the sordid life of a prostitute.'

Murphy went on to suggest that Brifman had colluded with the member for South Brisbane, her lawyer, Colin Bennett, who had held a 'grudge' against him and other police since the National Hotel inquiry had failed to find any evidence of police wrongdoing.

'I am not guilty of this charge,' Murphy added in his usual confident way.

Becker then arrested Murphy by virtue of a warrant, and he was escorted to the Brisbane city watchhouse, where he was formally charged. He was briefly held in a watchhouse cell before he appeared in the courtyard at 4.08 p.m. The prisoner was called to appear before the magistrate at 4.21 p.m.

Becker requested that Murphy be remanded until 18 February. The detective was granted bail of four hundred dollars.

The hearing was over by 4.40 p.m.

It was front-page news in the *Courier-Mail* the next day: DETECTIVE IN COURT ON PERJURY COUNT: 1963 NATIONAL HOTEL INQUIRY SEQUEL.

Murphy, forty-four, was suspended from duty. Within a couple of months he would be going to trial over the perjury charges. And the chief witness against him would be his old lover, informant and patron, Shirley Margaret Brifman.

The arrest and charges shocked Murphy's friends in the force and his family. Wife Maureen Murphy says the charges were 'something small, pitiful', and that 'Whitrod was just determined to get him one way or the other'.

A Sudden Death in Bonney Avenue

It wasn't a happy Christmas for the Brifman family at the end of 1971.

Shirley had had a huge falling out with her sister Marge Chapple in November, and had taken the children and vanished. With threats of death from a Sydney gunman, mysterious phone calls, drug overdoses, and the constant attention of police, it is little wonder that Marge, with her own family to take care of, had run out of patience.

Brifman also started telling family and friends that she had been diagnosed with cancer.

By the New Year the Brifmans reappeared, settling into a new safe house – a first-floor, three-bedroom flat at 75 Bonney Avenue, Clayfield. The flat was part of a large, subdivided Queenslander that contained the Brifmans' spacious upstairs apartment and two smaller downstairs flats.

The property was just six blocks away from the Armagh Street mansion of stockbroker Robin Corrie, Brifman's deceased friend.

While Queensland and New South Wales investigators had largely finished their formal interviews with her, and with Hallahan charged with corruption and Murphy charged with perjury, Brifman was on her own and vulnerable.

In a panic, she hit the phone, constantly calling her lawyer, Colin Bennett, and his wife, sharing her fears and anxiety over the safety of herself and her children.

Bennett's daughter Mary recalls a curious incident that occurred six months earlier following Brifman's blowing the whistle on corrupt police.

Colin Bennett was phoned in the early hours of the morning at his home in Highgate Hill, by police at the Upper Mount Gravatt station. They said his presence was required at the station as his client, Shirley Brifman, had been found dead of a drug overdose.

'Dad got dressed and was just backing the car out when he stopped and came back inside,' Mary says. 'It didn't sound right. He made some phone calls and discovered that Brifman wasn't dead but very much alive. He always wondered if the police had tried to lure him out on that night, and why.'

Brifman rang old girlfriends, particularly Lily Ryan, whom she'd known since well before the National Hotel inquiry days in Brisbane. She also kept in touch with journalist Brian 'the Eagle' Bolton, an alcoholic newshound who worked out of the *Sunday Sun* offices in the heart of Fortitude Valley. Another journalist at the end of interminable phone calls from a nervous Brifman was the *Sunday Mail*'s Ric Allen.

In early January 1972, she summoned Allen to the Bonney Avenue flat. They sat and talked in the lounge room, which had its own wooden bar and shelving separating it from the dining room. 'I want to tell you my story before I die,' she supposedly told Allen. 'I've got cancer and the doctors have given me twelve to eighteen months to live.'

She made a similar cry a few months earlier to Norm Gulbransen of the CIU, who concluded: 'This is very likely a move to gain sympathy.'

Ellen Russell, Brifman's niece and daughter of Marge Chapple, says: 'Shirley never had cancer. If she had cancer she would have told her sister.' Did she ever suggest to any member of the family that doctors had diagnosed her with cancer? 'No.'

In mid-February, around the time of Murphy's next appearance in court over the perjury charges, Brifman told Allen that a woman had phoned the flat – Brifman had a silent line with permission from the Postmaster-General – and threatened the life of her youngest child, son Sid, then eight years old. It was eerily similar to a threat from a female received by phone at the Chapple household, across town in Paddington, the year before.

'I've got things to do before I can die,' she told Allen. It was a curious use of language, if the quote is accurate. Before I *can* die. As if the decision was out of her hands.

Brifman's eldest daughter, Mary Anne, had rejoined the family from Moree by the time they moved to Bonney Avenue. She also had a new beau, 'Graham', a local boy who worked at a petrol station in nearby Kalinga and was very quickly drawn into the drama of the Brifman household.

Graham remembers seeing Tony Murphy in the last weeks of February 1972.

'He actually came around to the flat a couple of times and spoke to Brifman outside . . .' Graham says. 'She was having an affair with Murphy.

'She said to me: "They're out to get me, I want to get them before they get me." I thought, This is a lot deeper than I ever thought.

'Shirley did a lot of screaming all the time. I'd say she was having a breakdown. She was going off her head a little bit.'

On top of the Murphy case, Brifman was finally facing her own court appearance in Sydney on 17 March. The pressure had become intolerable.

In late February, Brifman once again phoned journalist Allen. She supposedly told him, 'I know I have cancer. The thought of dying is with me all the time.'

To add to Brifman's depression, she learned a few days later that her good friend Lily Ryan had actually succumbed to the disease. It was a devastating blow, and it further fed Brifman's own paranoia that she might suffer a similar fate.

The next day, Brifman phoned Colin Bennett at his offices at North Quay, looking for a sympathetic ear. She got Bennett's wife, Eileen, on the line.

'She said she had to go into hospital for an operation and asked me if I had seen where Lily Ryan had died,' Eileen recalled.

Brifman wanted to attend Ryan's funeral, but was feeling too tired and ill.

Earlier that week, former Regan sidekick John Edward Milligan was chatting to his mate Glen Hallahan about the impending perjury case against Tony Murphy. With the case due to be heard in a couple of months, time was running out.

According to Milligan, Hallahan let him know that the problem of Shirley Brifman would soon be no more: 'I was told by Glen four days before . . . she was going to be murdered. I was told . . . that Shirley Brifman's problems had finally been solved, that she'd be no more worries shortly.'

On that Friday evening, 3 March 1972, Brifman stayed in with husband Sonny, daughters Sonya and Helen, and son Sid. Early in the evening, Mary Anne had gone out with Graham.

Over in Garfield Drive, Lewis was presumably home with his family, having knocked off for the weekend at 5.10 p.m. He had a long weekend to look forward to, with Monday off duty.

Meanwhile, Detective Murphy, suspended, was supposedly in Sydney, conducting inquiries relating to his forthcoming court appearance in April.

At around 9.30 p.m. in Bonney Avenue, Brifman occupied her time by polishing an antique phone.

Soon after, Mary Anne and Graham returned to the flat. Sonny, Sonya and Sid were in the back rooms. Helen was asleep in the narrow room off the foyer.

As for Shirley, by now she was restlessly pacing the apartment, dressed in her nightgown. She was agitated. Occasionally she burst into tears and whimpered.

Graham, who had not known Mary Anne for long and 'had morals', decided to sleep alone on the couch in the large foyer. He says he was a light sleeper.

Towards 11.30 p.m., he noticed Brifman moving through the flat in the dark. She went into the rear room, where her husband slept. She checked Mary Anne and Sonya in the main bedroom. She stood briefly over Helen in the side room and then quietly came into the foyer area, where Graham was resting.

He sensed Shirley standing near the couch.

'That night was quite eerie – I'll never forget that night,' Graham recalls. 'You know when you get a feeling that someone is watching you?'

Graham opened his eyes. He saw Brifman standing over him in the dark. She was wearing a floral nightie with side pockets.

'It's all right,' she said to him. 'It's only me.'

She seemed frightened.

'What's wrong?' he asked her.

'Nothing,' she said.

He sensed that Brifman was waiting for someone to come to the front door, that she had a prearranged meeting with somebody.

He says, 'Why would she come and stand near me in that room? She was uneasy, she was scared.'

For whatever reason, Mary Anne was roused from her sleep.

At about 11.50 p.m., just as Graham had predicted, a car pulled up outside the Bonney Avenue flat and the engine was cut. Then faint footsteps were heard coming up the brick front steps.

Shirley Brifman went to the door. She may have seen a blurred face through the oval leadlight inset in the door, with its four small red roses. She opened the door halfway.

'I heard a muffled voice,' Graham remembers. 'I was pretending to be asleep with my eyes closed. It was Shirley's voice and a man's voice, that's all I heard.

'It could have been a woman with a deep voice, it was muffled. It was midnight, probably a little later.'

Brifman and the stranger talked for about ten minutes inside the foyer. Mary Anne came out of the main bedroom and joined her mother halfway through the conversation. She remembers her mother putting her arm around her. Mary Anne says the visitor was a middle-aged woman wearing spectacles. Near the end of their talk, the woman, heading out the door, handed Brifman an amber vial.

'I was fifteen,' Mary Anne recalls. 'Not a lot of things were that interesting to me about my mother's life at that time. But I always remembered that night.

'When the visitor left, I asked my mother who it was. She said it was [someone associated with] Tony Murphy. Tony and this visitor delivered the stuff, the vial, to my mother that evening. My mother said Murphy was downstairs. That's what she said. I never sighted him.'

Mary Anne says her mother received a quantity of drugs that night that were guaranteed to kill her. The options were to take an overdose and die, or face being tortured again and having her children's lives terminated.

Mary Anne says: 'She'd had many overdoses. They delivered her something that was going to work.

'She knew. My mother knew. She couldn't take any more, really. If she didn't do it, they'd do it for her in a bad way. When she put her arm around me it was an odd thing for her to do. It was like she was saying goodbye.'

At around 6.30 a.m. the following day, Graham got dressed and went to work at the petrol station.

At 8.15 a.m. Mary Anne and her young brother, Sid, went into the small room off the foyer. Little Helen was still asleep in a narrow cot in the room.

Sid fled at what he saw. Mary Anne wasn't far behind.

Shirley Margaret Brifman, thirty-five, was dead, propped up on a number of pillows.

'She was like frozen – the rigor mortis had set in,' Mary Anne remembers. 'She was lying back . . . half sitting up. Her hand was frozen up in the air.'

Mary Anne immediately dashed to the phone table in the hallway off the kitchen, and called the ambulance.

'My sisters and brother had a look and that was that,' Mary Anne says. 'They didn't go back in. That was too scary for them because of how she looked.'

Police eventually arrived in Bonney Avenue, followed by the press.

Mary Anne says: 'I remember a few years later, a detective acquaintance of mine told me that on the day of my mother's death, when it came over on the [police] radio, nobody wanted to respond because they were all scared. Their reputations could be tainted. No normal, straight detective wanted to go to the house.'

In addition, a teenage Mary Anne noticed how 'loose' the investigation seemed from the outset. The death scene wasn't sealed. Detectives tramped in and out of the house.

'They allowed me to go back in the room and sit next to my mother,' she says. 'I was in there for thirty or forty minutes, sitting in there by myself. I tried to tell them what had happened the night before, about the visitor, but nobody wanted to talk to me. The police were trying to avoid me.'

Sonny Brifman lingered in the background, trying to look after his young children.

Basil Hicks of the CIU was on the scene. He claimed to have found, wedged beneath the two mattresses under Brifman's body, an empty Mogadon bottle.

With the Clayfield flat in chaos, Graham was working at the petrol station when an unmarked squad car pulled up. He was not even aware Brifman was dead. He'd left for work before the body was discovered. He didn't know that he was one of the last people to talk to Brifman and see her alive, except for Mary Anne and the stranger at the door.

'Four cops pulled up in a car,' he says. 'They kept asking me, "Did you see anybody? Did you see anybody there?" I knew they were involved in it. It was a very dangerous situation. They could put you behind bars or dump you in the river, no problem.

'I said to the cops straightaway – after what Shirley had told me – I said, "I didn't see anybody." I thought they'd do me in. "No mate, I didn't hear anything." They left me alone after that.

'I have no doubt they did her in.'

Graham returned to the flat and 'couldn't believe' the number of police and media. 'I'm ninety-nine per cent sure [Murphy] was there that day,' he says. 'He was the only one I recognised. I'd recognise him now if I saw him. I did see him a few times. I knew who it was.'

Brifman's body was taken to the city morgue. An autopsy would conclude that she died of barbiturate intoxication.

Later that day, Sonny went to break the news to Shirley's sister Marge. Niece Ellen Russell and her husband, Robin, were there when he came into the house.

'It was on the Saturday,' says Robin. 'He said, "Oh, Shirley's dead." He was not excited about it. It didn't seem as if it meant anything to him. He wasn't broken up when she died.

'Sonny didn't care. It was just the money she brought in.'

The coroner recommended no inquest into Brifman's death, given the police report concluded there were no suspicious circumstances. Her file was classified IDU – inquest deemed unnecessary.

The official police files – interview notes, photographs, evidence, fingerprinting results – disappeared into the Queensland Police Department archives.

As for Brifman, her body was flown home to Atherton, the place of her youthful promise.

On Thursday 9 March, a small service was held in the low-set, corrugated iron–roofed Presbyterian church at the corner of Jack and Alice streets. The service was presided over by the Reverend Roy Wright, then in his early thirties.

He recalls one of the most unusual country funerals of his career: 'The casket wasn't an ordinary coffin . . . This would have been brought up from Brisbane. I know it was quite an expensive casket she was buried in.'

He says the burial ceremony at the town cemetery was equally conspicuous.

'There were lots of people around with sunglasses on,' Wright says. 'I'm not sure whether they were checking who was at the funeral . . . There were people there that were kind of taking note, I thought. I don't know from which angle . . .'

The reverend also noticed an expensive bouquet of flowers that graced the casket lid before burial. It was from a prominent QC, most probably her lawyer, Colin Bennett.

Shirley Margaret Brifman was laid to rest in Section K, Plot 12, of the Atherton lawn and general cemetery. There was no headstone.

Fracture

Hallahan may have been arrested over a paltry sixty dollars received from prostitute Knight, but the situation was making his police and criminal associates in both Queensland and New South Wales extremely nervous.

Not only was he the first ever Queensland public servant to be charged with official corruption, but his connections with the underworld were now vast and intricate. One slip and the entire murky infrastructure in two states could be exposed.

Informant John Edward Milligan offered his support and assistance to Hallahan before the matter got to court.

'I went over to see him, to see if there was anything I could do . . .' Milligan said in an interview with federal narcotics agents years later.

For the weeks leading up to the committal hearing, it was too dangerous for Hallahan to make direct contact with any of his informants, criminal friends or police colleagues.

Milligan, and others, became Hallahan's conduits.

'Glen's wife was meeting Billy Phillips at the bottom of the garden to try and collect information about a dozen different things . . . The immediate plan was to try and get the girl, the prostitute who'd set up Glen, and get her out of the way, to assassinate her,' Milligan alleged.

Somehow Phillips located Knight. She was being guarded by police, and a caravan – possibly the same one used in the Hallahan sting in New Farm Park – was stationed out the front.

Knight naturally feared for her life. She, too, made the assumption that Hallahan would have her killed.

Milligan, it turned out, knew a member of the family that was harbouring Knight, 'a criminal in Queensland, a knockabout guy', and was asked to 'get in touch with him and pump him for information'.

According to Milligan, associates of Hallahan sent the word out in Melbourne that 'gangsters were needed' to help 'abduct the girl'. In 'the crisis of Glen's arrest', Milligan met some of the heavy hitters of the underworld, including Lennie McPherson, one of the most powerful men in Australia's crime scene.

'Lennie came up personally to offer his services . . .' Milligan said.

According to Milligan, a member of the Queensland Drug Squad secretly met Hallahan at his Kangaroo Point home and passed messages back to McPherson.

Milligan claimed that he saw McPherson – who needed to converse with Murphy but couldn't be seen with him – in the vicinity of Hallahan's house.

Milligan said Murphy was tipped off that Whitrod and his CIU went to extraordinary lengths with their surveillance: 'He couldn't take the risk of going to Glen's house, and so intermediaries were used . . .'

Whitrod was gunning for Hallahan and Murphy, and shortly after Brifman's death he went up another gear. Hallahan was charged with counselling a criminal, Donald Ross Kelly, to hold up a bank at Kedron in Brisbane's north. The CIU said it had evidence that Hallahan had received part of the proceeds of the robbery.

Whatever the motivation, one thing was patently clear: Hallahan was attracting too much heat.

He'd have to go.

A Round of Beers at the Belfast

Five weeks after Brifman was found dead by her daughter and son in the flat in Bonney Avenue, Detective Murphy was formally acquitted on four counts of perjury.

During the trial, Murphy's counsel, Des Sturgess, claimed that the charges against Murphy were a 'malicious prosecution of a political nature', and that Murphy had been targeted by Whitrod and his minister, Max Hodges, for his strong affiliation with the Police Union.

On Friday 7 April 1972, the magistrate concluded after a four-day hearing: 'I don't believe any properly instructed jury would convict Murphy on the evidence.'

The forty-four-year-old detective, of Rosewall Street, Upper Mount Gravatt, was discharged from the Brisbane magistrates court.

That afternoon, Terry Lewis recorded in his police diary: 'Insp. Steele phoned re suspension of Det Sgt 1/c Murphy lifted immediately'.

And that night, according to bagman Jack Herbert, one of Murphy's favourite watering holes – Barry Maxwell's Belfast Hotel in Queen Street – was packed to the gills with wellwishers. He recalled that it was so crowded it was difficult to get to the bar.

'I have been fingerprinted, photographed and placed on file,' an annoyed Murphy told the *Sunday Sun* on his acquittal. 'It stinks; I'm as dirty as hell.'

The headline for the page-four story on Murphy read: THE END OF ALL THOSE GHOSTS FROM THE NATIONAL. The chief witness against Murphy had conveniently overdosed, but Shirley Brifman's name was only mentioned once in relation to one of the four perjury charges. Her death was not mentioned at all.

Sturgess would later say the death of Brifman was in fact a 'calamity' for Murphy 'because it allowed vicious rumours to circulate that in some way he was responsible for her death'.

'This Brifman allegation . . . had been retailed to the authorities by the reckless Col Bennett,' recalls Sturgess. 'Bennett was a very passionate sort of fellow. He exercised no care over what he said. He was not a bad person. He was an emotional fellow. He never looked before he leapt.

'Murphy, of course, protested his innocence very vehemently, but that'd be Murphy, he was always very vehement in these things.

'The prosecution proceeded. At the end of the case the magistrate threw it out, and that was that. And so he should. There was no bloody case at all.'

A barman at the Belfast certainly heard the rumours surrounding Brifman's sudden death: 'Maxwell said he had either heard or suspected that Murphy gave her some "Minties". That, you know, she died of poison.'

Jack Herbert said he would have discussed the death of Brifman with Murphy and others but couldn't recall any details of these conversations. He insisted that he had no knowledge of Murphy being connected in any way with Brifman's death.

One officer who knew Brifman from the late 1950s said: 'Shirley was a tough old bird. She didn't kill herself. I knew they'd do her in. I knew they would.'

Meanwhile, Murphy's exoneration was a huge victory for anti-Whitrod forces.

The Police Union went to town, accusing Police Minister Hodges and his department of trying to deplete the union's defence fund with its rash of charges against officers. And, in turn, break the union's power.

'There was no evidence against me in the first place,' Murphy said. 'The charges were brought simply because of my union activities.'

Police Union President Ron Edington said that Murphy's case exemplified a new low under Whitrod's administration. In the past, tolerating one criminal informant often led to the apprehension of twenty or thirty other criminals. Now, by exposing informants like the late Shirley Brifman to the public gaze, a precedent had been set that jeopardised the informant–police relationship.

Murphy went on sick leave after his court victory. He felt the case had prejudiced his future, and that his children had suffered over the slander on his name.

On 23 May 1972, it was reported that Murphy was back on duty at the JAB.

Lewis duly recorded the moment in his police diary.

Mister Milligan, I Presume

Down at the Federal Narcotics Bureau in Eagle Street, agent Brian Bennett got a compelling tip-off.

An excellent informant who ran the Trans Australian Airlines bonds store out at the airport had phoned to report some suspicious rolls of fabric.

The bureau had begun to log increasing illegal imports of cannabis and LSD. A new fad was also LSD in capsule form, known on the street as California Sunshine or California Traffic Lights for their distinctive red and green colours.

Bennett headed out to the airport.

Bennett's informant claimed that two rolls of fabric had arrived from Nepal via Bangkok. Both were about three feet long and were 'exceptionally heavy' for what they were purported to be.

Bennett says: 'One in fact contained fifteen kilos of hashish from

Nepal – black hash – and the other, fifteen kilos of Thai cannabis in the form of Buddha sticks, which were just starting to emerge on the Australian drug market, a new phenomenon.'

'I examined this stuff and teed it up with my source to delay anyone picking it up, to get word to me and we'd be out there as quick as we could.'

Soon after, the airline source phoned again and Bennett made a dash to the airport. There, walking out of the bonds store with a roll of fabric over each shoulder, was John Edward Milligan, habitué of Willie's Bizarre, Hallahan's informant and John Regan's sidekick.

'John Milligan,' Bennett said, 'I'm a senior narcotics agent. What have you got there?'

'Nothing,' Milligan said, unflustered. 'I'm picking these up for a friend.'

'You're under arrest,' Bennett said.

Milligan was handcuffed.

'Mr Bennett,' Milligan said, 'there's no need for those handcuffs. You know I'm not a violent person.'

Bennett never forgot that exchange of dialogue. Bennett had not identified himself by name to Milligan, yet the drug dealer knew who he was.

'He was a smart cookie,' says Bennett. 'He had obviously carried out some counter-surveillance on me.'

Bennett's new boss – Max Rogers, a former Victorian Homicide Squad officer who'd only recently joined the bureau – arrived and took charge. They conveyed Milligan back to the bureau office, where he was charged with two counts of possessing prohibited imports.

'I caught him with the dope over his shoulder, clearly in possession,' remembers Bennett, 'and I gave my evidence at the committal, but he wasn't convicted, it just sort of died away. Milligan then went on to work solely for Rogers as his personal informant.

'Informant number 138 – that was Milligan.'

White-anting Lewis

Meanwhile, Ray Whitrod's campaign against Terry Lewis – the final member of the so-called Rat Pack triumvirate yet to feel serious pressure from the police commissioner – was quiet, coordinated and relentless.

As Lewis approached his tenth anniversary in charge of the JAB, Whitrod was steely in his determination not only to paint the bureau as a relic of the Bischof days, but to catch out Lewis as incompetent.

Whereas other officers had their official police diaries checked by superiors once a month, for example, Lewis's were looked over and ticked off once a week like clockwork.

In mid-April 1972, Whitrod sent in a senior officer to run a fine-tooth comb over the JAB operations. Lewis was repeatedly interviewed and ordered to gather innumerable statistics.

Lewis was given the onerous task of checking each file held by the bureau for instances of child recidivist behaviour. These, in turn, were cross-checked with adult fingerprint records.

Further, Lewis was instructed to go through his own police diaries for 1971 and 1972 and itemise every visit to a juvenile offender's home, each office interview, and how much actual time was spent on every case.

If Whitrod thought he'd break Lewis with the sheer physical weight of the work, he was mistaken. Diarising and the collation of data were Lewis's bread and butter. His focus and attention to detail were second to none. These precise qualities were the bedrock of Lewis's entire working life. He had developed and perfected these skills, which he knew would elevate him through the force; it was an act of sheer personal will.

For months Lewis did as he was asked. He had little time for family or friends, though his police diary does record that on a morning in June he was a spectator at the 'Full Court re admission of E. Pratt to the Bar'.

As the white-anting continued, Lewis must have twigged that Whitrod was planning to dismantle the JAB.

On Wednesday 26 July, he wrote in his police diary that 'Mrs

M. Patrick, 45 Stanley Ter., I'pilly called re speaking with Mr Whitrod and hearing that J.A. Bureau being closed. Miss R. Power, Channel 7 news later phoned re Mrs Patrick contacting them. Mr D. Lane M.L.A. and Brigadier Geddes phoned re same matter.'

Lewis was naturally dismayed. For years he'd run what he thought was an efficient bureau based on warning troubled juveniles, rather than charging them and putting them through the court system. He favoured prevention over cure.

Whitrod begged to differ.

'He wanted to charge all youngsters to boost his statistical returns, and I opposed that,' Lewis says.

In a move that ensured Lewis's complete alienation, Whitrod encouraged the establishment of a parallel unit to deal with juvenile offenders – the Police Education Liaison Unit – which operated under the umbrella of not the police force, but the State Children's Services Department.

An anecdote about the methods of the unit got back to Lewis and he used it as an example of a statistics-obsessed police commissioner gone mad – 'One of the unit officers was recorded as interviewing one young boy who, on twelve occasions, had gone and stolen a pencil from a store, and he was charged with twelve charges of stealing.'

Then from 1 January 1973, the inevitable occurred – the JAB came under the control of the Children's Services Department.

Lewis couldn't stem the tide. Whitrod was slowly levering him out of the JAB, and he knew it.

A Big Scalp

Awaiting trial for nine months, the suspended Glen Hallahan was muzzled by his corruption charges, at least on the surface, and out of direct contact with his mates in the force.

His implication in the bank robbery at Kedron had already fallen over in court; now he faced the matter of receiving payments from prostitute Dorothy Knight.

Finally, on Friday 6 October 1972, the Crown announced in the Brisbane magistrates court that it would offer no evidence against the charge. The case was dismissed.

Lawyer Kevin Townsley had earlier defended Hallahan against the Knight charge in the lower court and called on Des Sturgess to assist as it came to trial proper.

Having studied the brief, and facing evidence that included secretly taped recorded conversations between Knight and Hallahan, Sturgess concluded: 'We haven't got a feather to fly with here.'

Townsley was more confident. 'I think we might be able to argue that the tape recording is inadmissible. I think it's possible.'

'You've got more confidence than I have,' Sturgess said. 'You handle that side of the argument and I'll just listen.'

On the Friday before the trial went to court, Sturgess had a meeting with Townsley and Hallahan at his own chambers at the Inns of Court.

Sturgess remembers the meeting: 'Hallahan evinced a great deal of interest in what judge would be taking the matter. So much so that the solicitor went over a couple of times to the registry at District Court to find out.

'Finally, he came back and said it's going to be Eddie Broad. That was a bit surprising. Eddie Broad didn't do much of this work. He was involved in Licensing.

'Immediately . . . relief flooded over Hallahan. Five minutes later he said, "I've had enough, you'll have to excuse me." Another police officer was there waiting for him; they were going for a drink.'

Hallahan was not in court when the case was dismissed. His informant John Edward Milligan would later reveal that Hallahan had visited Broad's chambers before the trial commenced and offered what he knew about the judge's sexual history. In short, he threatened to blackmail Broad. Townsley says: 'I find it hard to believe [that Broad was compromised by Hallahan]. Our legal argument was an absolute clincher. The listening device was a clear contravention of the federal *Telephonic Communication (Interception) Act*. It was a dishonest prosecution from the word go.'

After the trial was over, and despite the victory, Sturgess offered Hallahan an observation: 'I don't think your future is very bright in the police force.'

'No,' replied Hallahan.

Sturgess suggested he strike a deal with Police Commissioner Whitrod – resign, walk out, and 'that'd be the end of it'. Hallahan agreed. The suspended detective hadn't been able to get to his police locker and its contents. He wasn't sure what else might be in store for him by way of charges.

'I approached Whitrod. He was relieved, too. He was glad to get rid of him,' says Sturgess.

On the following Monday at 9 a.m., Detective Hallahan was formally reinstated into the force. Within minutes, he tendered his resignation.

His solicitors issued a statement: 'All matters of complaint against him have now been resolved and he was this morning reinstated. However, he feels his interest in his future and that of his family will be best served in other spheres.'

Hallahan offered a single comment to the press: 'In some ways I am sorry to be leaving.'

Whitrod's crack team – the CIU – had put both Murphy and Hallahan in the dock in a single calendar year. But its strike rate in terms of convictions was nil.

Still, it had exerted enough pressure to get rid of one of the most famous and lauded – and one of the most corrupt – detectives in the history of modern Queensland policing, while still in his absolute prime.

Sturgess reflects: 'You've got to imagine a young fellow intensely enthusiastic about the business of the police. He enjoyed the hunt.

'He found a lot of the legal rules to be silly and would have developed contempt for the legal process. He would have been prepared to break rules and cut corners.

Sturgess didn't believe Hallahan profited hugely from his misdemeanours.

But was Hallahan corrupt?

'Oh yes.'

Warnings Ignored

In the early hours of Wednesday 17 January 1973, a popular café in Brunswick Street, Fortitude Valley, inexplicably went up in flames.

Firemen arrived at Alice's Café and Coffee Lounge at 3 a.m. but could not save the business. The café was closed at the time and the damage was estimated at twenty thousand dollars.

Alice's – a miniature nightclub that was popular with local gays – was owned by John Hannay, the former manager of music group The Planets.

Then, just over a month later, the Torino nightclub – also in Fortitude Valley – was destroyed by what police presumed to be a bomb. The Ann Street nightclub, renowned for its food, was owned by Italian brothers Frank and Tony Ponticello, and was completely gutted by the blast. Both the front and rear doors were blown out.

Again, the venue was closed at the time and no injuries were reported.

Former bouncer John Ryan claims to have received information prior to the Torino blast that Tony Murphy was showing interest in taking over the club as a 'retirement investment'. He says that two women he knew overheard Murphy discussing the takeover with other police in a restaurant.

The *Courier-Mail* reported two days after the bombing that CIU chief Norm Gulbransen was working on the case.

Then, on the morning of Tuesday 27 February 1973, Sergeant Bill Humphris of the Commonwealth police force paid a visit to Whitrod's CIU out at the police college in Chelmer. Humphris had received some extraordinary intelligence that needed to be relayed immediately to Queensland police.

Humphris sat with Jim Voigt and told him that on the day after the Torino bombing he was contacted by one of his informants. The informant said that in early January he was approached by a criminal called John Andrew Stuart. Late in 1972 Stuart had been arrested on a break and enter charge in Sydney but had been bailed out by two brothers unknown to the informant.

In exchange for bailing him out, the brothers wanted Stuart to go to Brisbane (Stuart's home town) and tell local nightclub owners that a Sydney syndicate was about to make a push on their turf and they 'better go along with their wishes'.

Stuart explained to the informant that he did as he was told, and the brothers indicated that a couple of nightclubs might have to be 'bombed' to let owners know that the syndicate meant business. He was claiming extortion.

Stuart said he had paid the bail money back to the brothers and wanted nothing to do with any bombings. He added that he planned to contact the member for South Brisbane, Colin Bennett, Basil Hicks of the CIU, and journalist Brian Bolton, and ask them to accompany him on a tour of Brisbane nightclubs, where Stuart would state before witnesses that he would not be connected with any bombing campaign or future trouble.

Humphris's informant did not hear from Stuart again until two nights before the Torino bombing. He left a phone message.

According to a report compiled by Humphris on the matter: 'I asked my informant why he was disclosing this information to me and also why Stuart would have told him. He said that Stuart told him that the Sydney brothers told him that they intended to bomb the Whiskey Au Go Go nightclub, St Pauls Terrace, Brisbane, by placing a bomb on the ground floor of the building while patrons were being entertained on the floor above. My informant claims that Stuart wanted no part of maiming or possibly killing innocent persons.'

Torino's bombing had been big news. But what was this about the Whiskey?

Voigt was not the only Queensland police officer warned about the strike on the popular nightclub.

John Ryan had heard since late December the year before that a club was 'going to go off'. He was working as a bouncer at the Whiskey but was told in early March by co-proprietor Brian Little that his services were no longer required. Ryan was anxious over the intelligence he was receiving from the streets about the Whiskey.

'I spoke to Voigt I don't know how many times,' says Ryan. 'I spoke with Basil Hicks at the CIU. I rang the boys in Licensing and a police officer mate at the Fortitude Valley station. I know for a fact that the information I gave made it all the way up to the commissioner, Ray Whitrod.

'They were all warned and they did nothing.'

In the early hours of Thursday 8 March, the Whiskey Au Go Go was torched. A band had been playing inside and late-night patrons were enjoying the music. The firestorm killed fifteen people.

It became, in an instant, the scene of Australia's biggest mass murder.

Whiskey

With the burning of Alice's and the bombing of Torino, Brisbane could have been forgiven for thinking it was suddenly at the heart of some vicious gangland turf war.

And by extension, it made sense that such deadly force, previously unseen in the city, had to be the handiwork of more sinister forces out of Sydney or Melbourne. Perhaps the warnings from former local boy John Andrew Stuart, a violent, unpredictable criminal, about a Sydney underworld takeover of Brisbane's nightclubs weren't far from the truth.

Stuart was close to journalist Brian Bolton, often feeding him gossip and innuendo that became fodder for Bolton's news stories in the popular *Sunday Sun*. But when Stuart began talking of a Sydney criminal push into Brisbane, and the imminent attack on the Whiskey, Bolton was alarmed and passed on the information to authorities. Bolton was Bill Humphris's confidential informant.

The reality was that Brisbane's nightclub scene had been seething with its own internal discontent since late in the previous year, and it had to do with long-standing rivalry and accusations of theft between nightclub managers and their owners. In a small town, competition was fierce, and retribution swift and personal.

The Little brothers – Brian and Ken – owned the Whiskey Au Go Go and the more salubrious Chequers in Elizabeth Street, Fortitude Valley. Both clubs went into liquidation in late 1972 after allegations emerged of staffers skimming from the tills and mismanagement.

Entrepreneur John Hannay had control of Alice's, and was managing the Whiskey. Hannay and the Littles went way back to the early 1960s, and often supported each other with various business ventures.

At the end of 1972, Hannay allegedly suggested that doorman and security guard John Bell be sacked, as he no longer suited the style of the two clubs. Bell, according to friend and fellow bouncer John Ryan, went hunting for Hannay to teach him a lesson.

'Bell was going to smash him,' says Ryan.

The Littles were terrified of an enraged Bell. They continued to pay his weekly wage, though he didn't appear on the doors of the clubs.

Bell ultimately caught up with Hannay, according to Ryan, and hospitalised him. Hannay was later removed as manager of the Whiskey. This, then, set off a small local feud that would grow out of control.

In the New Year a known petty criminal with a speciality in arson attempted to torch Chequers. He only managed minor damage to the stage. A second attempt caused more destruction but did not destroy the club.

Then Alice's was torched, followed by Torino.

Meanwhile, John Andrew Stuart had arrived in town, big-noting himself and mixing with some of his old criminal associates and mates from his youth. Stuart had a reputation from his early teens, having stabbed a boy in a brawl in Fortitude Valley in 1955. Stuart had always wanted to be a gangster, and he was on his way.

'He had a big rep,' says John Ryan. 'That was a big deal in the 1950s, carrying a knife. Then he went to Westbrook.'

The Westbrook Farm Home for Boys, near Toowoomba, had a brutal reputation. Reformatory inmates would later report wholesale sexual abuse, torture and cruelty perpetrated by staff. On his release, aged eighteen, the highly intelligent Stuart was primed for a life of violence and crime.

'He started out as a burglar in Sandgate and around Chermside,' says Ryan. 'When he got out of Westbrook he was the swaggerer, the big, bad gangster. I'd see him down at the Hub, a milk bar opposite the Dawn picture theatre on Gympie Road.

'He liked to create fear. He wanted to be the Stewart John Regan of Brisbane. He was violent but he wasn't very good at it. It didn't matter. You always suspected he might be carrying a knife or a gun, and that was enough.'

Stuart went to Sydney, home to genuine gangsters, and was incarcerated for numerous offences, including assault. In prison he met another product of several boys' homes – James Finch. Finch himself was jailed for attempting to murder Regan and was ultimately deported back to his native United Kingdom.

Stuart had returned to Brisbane in late 1972 not on a mission to take over the city with his muscle and badness, but by order of a New South Wales court.

Sydney detective Roger Rogerson was familiar with Stuart, having arrested him once for stealing a car.

'He was insane – I'd say he'd be a psychopath,' says Rogerson of Stuart. 'I'll tell you how mad he was. He was locked up at Long Bay gaol. He made an allegation he'd been bashed or flogged by arresting detectives.

'Two guys from headquarters went out to investigate his complaint – Karl Arkins and his sidekick from Internal Affairs.

'They met in this room and Stuart jumped up, king hit Arkins and smashed his jaw. Then Stuart went to court charged with grievous bodily harm.'

Stuart managed to secure bail with a condition – go back to Queensland.

Rogerson says, 'I'll never forget, Lennie McPherson once said to me, "Roger, you can control a bad man, but you can't control a mad man."'

Just prior to the Whiskey bombing, Stuart sent for Finch and paid his fare back to Australia. The ticket was booked under the name 'Mr Trauts' – Stuart spelled backwards. Finch had been close to Stuart's mother, Edna, who had fallen seriously ill, and was ostensibly coming back to see her.

In early 1973, Stuart was conspicuous in Fortitude Valley, acquainting himself with the nightclub scene. The word was out that the Little brothers wanted to take back control of Chequers – they believed they could turn it around and into profit.

According to Ryan, Stuart was used by the Littles to talk up the so-called extortion threat against the Whiskey and other nightclubs, hoping to scare off the liquidators. The Littles' plan was to burn the Whiskey, take the insurance payout, and use it to reinvest in the classier Chequers.

At about 2.10 a.m. on Thursday 8 March 1973, two twenty-three-litre drums of diesel were emptied in the foyer of the club and lit. Plumes of smoke were sucked up the stairwell and into the club. Patrons scrambled to escape through windows and a locked fire escape. The fifteen deaths were caused by asphyxiation.

While Stuart and Finch were in the vicinity of the Whiskey when it went up, there has always been conjecture about the perpetrators and their motive. Was it an insurance job gone wrong, involving a small team of criminals associated with Brisbane's so-called Clockwork Orange Gang? Or did Stuart, a lunatic who was trying to make a name for himself in the underworld, commit the crime? Was all his bluff and bluster in the previous months about a Sydney takeover an attempt to establish a pre-emptive alibi? If that were his intention, it had the opposite effect – Stuart was firmly in the eye of police even before the mass killing.

Police were under enormous pressure to apprehend the murderer or murderers.

Roger Rogerson, then in his early thirties, and other members of the New South Wales Special Crimes Squad were flown to Brisbane on the morning of the bombing to assist in the investigation and to clarify Stuart's claims.

'Stuart kept saying it was Sydney criminals, the Mr Bigs – Lennie McPherson, George Freeman. He was dropping a lot of names,' says Rogerson.

'And there was a journalist [Brian Bolton] up there writing up stories about Sydney crims taking over the Valley. It was all bullshit he was getting from Stuart . . .

'We knew that Stuart hadn't lit the fire because he had an alibi. We then came across Jimmy Finch, a Dr Bernado's boy. He was the key to it.

'I don't think they believed they were going to kill anyone.'

Detective Pat Glancy was on duty that Thursday and remembers taking a curious phone call down at police headquarters. It was from Sydney gunman John Regan.

'He asked me if he was wanted [for the fire],' Glancy recalls. 'He wanted to know if he was to be interviewed . . . He told me he'd come up from Sydney . . . He said if I interviewed him one on one in a neutral location he would do it without a solicitor. But if we wanted to talk to him in police headquarters he'd bring a legal representative.'

Regan flew to Brisbane and Glancy met him by arrangement at a Chinese restaurant in Fortitude Valley. They had a meal.

'He was one of the coldest people I've ever met,' says Glancy. 'He didn't drink. He had orange juice. He didn't smoke. He was quiet. Whereas John Andrew Stuart was a loudmouth. He was a bloody idiot.'

Glancy told Regan that police had been looking all over Brisbane for Stuart and the Sydney gunman offered to help out. 'He was either trying to help us, or get us off his back,' Glancy recalls. 'I mentioned Billy Phillips and how he might know where Stuart was.'

Regan said, 'I'll go and see him if you like.'

After the meal, Glancy drove Regan over to Phillips's home and tattoo parlour in Stanley Street, South Brisbane.

Regan got out of the car and went around to the back of the premises. He knocked on the door and Phillips emerged. The two had never met. When Regan mentioned Stuart, Phillips went berserk, saying he had nothing to do with the Whiskey fire and killings.

Then the visitor said: 'I'm John Regan.'

Phillips went 'white as a ghost'. He immediately offered some locations where Stuart might be found.

'Remember this,' Regan added as he was about leave. 'If you mention to the police that I'm up here, it'll get to me and I'll come back and see you.'

Later, in Glancy's old Vauxhall, Regan offered a unique public service regarding John Andrew Stuart.

'I'll kill him if you like,' Regan said to Glancy. 'Do you want him dead?'

Glancy met Regan for breakfast on the Saturday morning, and the gunman flew back to Sydney.

Stuart was arrested later that evening, following a tip-off from Stuart's brother Dan.

'We got a call from Danny saying Stuart and Finch were at his house at Jindalee,' says Glancy. 'There was a barbecue on at the house. A couple of car loads of us went out there.

'As we arrived, a woman came out of the house. She said, "I'm getting out of here, it's going to be a blood bath."

'I was the first one in and I saw that Stuart had something behind his back.'

Glancy asked him what he was holding and raised his gun. Stuart produced a hunting knife. Glancy struck the knife and Stuart's hand with the gun but then pulled back and cocked his weapon.

'If you don't drop it, I'll shoot,' Glancy ordered. Stuart threw the knife across the room.

Stuart was cuffed and taken out to one of the police cars. James Finch, who was in the backyard of the property, bolted when he heard the fracas inside. He was picked up the next morning at a nearby shopping centre.

'When we drove into headquarters, Stuart, who was in the back seat, wouldn't shut up,' says Glancy. 'He had his head down and he was shouting that everyone was trying to kill him, that the police were trying to kill him.'

Stuart and Finch were interviewed extensively by police. Present, among others, was Roger Rogerson. Unsigned statements were produced and both men were charged with murder.

'I remember the day we had Stuart in the CIB,' says Rogerson. 'Whitrod came in . . . a little dumpy bloke. He came in with shorts on and white sandshoes and he was all confused and didn't know what to say. [The other detectives] pissed him off as quick as they could so they could get back to work.

'I don't think Whitrod had ever seen a murderer before. He came in to have a look at one.'

From the outset, Stuart volubly and violently protested his innocence, claiming he was verballed.

On the Sunday after the tragedy, Police Commissioner Whitrod issued a public statement denying that he and Queensland police had been warned of the attack on the Whiskey:

> Mr Whitrod completely refuted suggestions and allegations that either Mr Brian Bolton, a journalist employed by the *Sunday Sun* newspaper, or Mr John Ryan, a private detective, had given police such a warning. The Commissioner stressed that at no time did any other individual or organisation give such a warning concerning the incident . . . It has been established that no such warning was ever given to the CIU.

On the day of the fire, Lewis recorded in his police diary that he had been internally queried about whether the JAB 'had been warned on the 7th inst that crime would be committed on Whisky Au Go Go that night'.

Someone was telling lies.

Meanwhile, Glancy took another call from John Regan.

'He was extremely pleased that Stuart and Finch had been arrested.'

Lewis on the Carousel

Whitrod's Education Liaison Unit – in competition with Lewis's Juvenile Aid Bureau – was causing friction within the community and also inside government.

High school principals complained through 1973 that the new unit's direct, proactive approach of apprehending and charging all young offenders, as opposed to the JAB's warning and counselling in the spirit of the *Children's Services Act*, was a source of concern.

In June 1973, Lewis was further given instruction that the Prosecution Section of the Queensland police would no longer handle any more Children's Court cases on behalf of the JAB. In short, it could carry the burden itself.

Incredibly to Lewis, one of the leading police officers heading up the rival Education Liaison Unit was none other than Lorelle Saunders, the young teenager he had repeatedly counselled for disruptive behaviour in the early days of the JAB.

Despite everything, Police Minister Max Hodges made sure that Whitrod's reform of the handling of juveniles went through.

According to Lewis's police diary, in August 1973 he was informed that he would be appointed inspector from 4 September. He had finally received his promotion. He was also told, in the same phone conversation with a Police Department secretary, that he was being transferred to 'Communications'.

Lewis was presented his new badge of rank by the police commissioner at a formal ceremony on Saturday 25 August. It was his day off, but Whitrod had requested his attendance.

The following Wednesday, Lewis requested a new cap and pair of shoes. He was instructed, by orders of Hodges and Whitrod, to report for duty in Communications on Monday 3 September. It would be the start of a period when Lewis would be bumped around departments and police stations both in Brisbane and within the south-east corner of the state.

Whitrod was clearly testing Lewis. Unlike Murphy and Hallahan, he had no opportunity to pursue charges of corruption and the like against Lewis. But could he tip Lewis out of the force by making his working life impossible?

Despite his promotion he had already suffered: the new appointment included an unwritten insult to all officers who served in plain clothes. Lewis was going back to uniform.

To the end, Lewis was still receiving calls about recalcitrant children and offering his advice.

But it was all over.

On the Saturday before he began his new job, Inspector Terry Lewis went into the JAB office one last time 'and packed books and other material and moved it all' home.

The Missing Defendant

A week after Lewis started his new job in Communications, the trial of Stuart and Finch commenced in Brisbane.

At their committal hearing in the Holland Park magistrates court in June, Stuart's brother Dan said Stuart had told him he planned to get into the Brisbane nightclub scene by extorting one hundred dollars a week from each venue.

Stuart exploded: 'You are lying! You are lying! You are lying for a reward, Dan.' The government had issued fifty thousand dollars for information leading to a conviction.

The court heard that when the actual fire was lit, Stuart was at the nearby Flamingo nightclub. It also heard that Finch had confessed the crime to police in an unsigned statement.

The committal hearing was interrupted when Finch swallowed metal fragments and was admitted to hospital.

Their trial was scheduled to begin in the Criminal Court on 28 August but Stuart had swallowed twisted paper clips prior to the opening day and was hospitalised.

A week after the trial finally opened on 10 September, Stuart was once again in hospital having metal pieces removed from his stomach. It was a pattern that had repeated itself over weeks.

Justice Lucas, tired of Stuart's antics, instructed that the trial would go ahead in the defendant's absence. He said Stuart would be provided transcripts of each day's proceedings. Finch sat handcuffed in the dock.

With no scientific evidence to tie Stuart and Finch to the scene of the mass murder, the prosecution went about dismantling Stuart's crazed alibi about a Sydney takeover of Brisbane nightclubs.

Called to the stand to dispute Stuart's assertions were some of the most celebrated gangsters in Australian criminal history.

Lennie McPherson, denying his nickname, 'Mr Big', said he had once met Stuart in a pub in Sydney but had had no contact with him since. He denied Stuart's assertion that he and Stuart had arranged to meet on the Gold Coast in September 1972, where McPherson had a holiday house. McPherson admitted that he knew a man named Regan.

Next, Graham 'Mad Dog' Miller, a self-employed salesman 'of toys and blankets', told the court that he never said to Stuart that he, McPherson, and Regan had been interested in a new Brisbane night-club called Blinkers.

He admitted that he had bailed Stuart out of prison in December 1972 following the assault on senior police officer Karl Arkins. Miller recalled that Stuart was thinking of getting involved in the Brisbane nightclub scene; Stuart apparently said that soon he would be 'Mr Big' and McPherson would be 'Mr Little'.

Underworld figures James 'Paddles' Anderson and John Regan were also called. Regan was described as a 'company manager'. He told the court he had no interest in Brisbane nightclubs, but was in town three weeks before and a day after the bombing (when he agreed to meet Glancy).

On 11 October, the trial had to be convened at the Royal Brisbane hospital so Stuart could answer evidence brought against him.

The special 'hospital court' was actually a seminar room in the hos-pital's pathology building. Stuart, covered in a blue blanket, lay on his side on a gurney.

'John Andrew Stuart, can you hear me?' Justice Lucas asked.

Stuart reportedly raised his head slightly then closed his eyes and 'settled deeper into the blankets'. He ignored the entire proceedings, which lasted for just half an hour.

As for Finch, he denied ever lighting the fire. He said that on the morning of the deadly blaze he was home in bed.

On the evening of 22 October, both Finch and Stuart were found guilty on a joint charge of having murdered Jennifer Denise Davie, one of the Whiskey victims. It took the jury just two hours to return the guilty verdicts.

Stuart was well enough to attend court on 23 October for sentencing. He was brought manacled from the hospital and under heavy police guard. He spat in the face of Chief Crown Prosecutor L.G. Martin, QC, saying: 'You'll never wash that off – you'll have it on your face until the day you die.'

The judge sentenced the pair to life imprisonment. Stuart's final court appearance lasted three minutes.

In the Shadows of the Blackall Range

Just as he had done as a young man when his career in the RAAF evaporated, Glen Hallahan repaired to the Sunshine Coast hinterland after resigning from the Queensland police force.

As a teenager he'd cut timber in Cooran. Now he left the city behind and settled on acreage in the tiny district of nearby Obi Obi, with its school of arts and community hall and a smattering of farms flush on Obi Obi Creek.

Overnight, Hallahan had gone from consorting with some of the most significant police and felons on the east coast of Australia, to being a fledgling farmer in the shadows of the Blackall Range.

At some point he secured the local post office sub-branch. He also toyed with growing fruit and vegetables.

It couldn't have been a greater contrast to his prior life.

Then, late in 1973, he was back in the newspaper headlines. The tabloid *Sunday Sun*, now under Ron Richards, had hired him as a special investigative reporter. Hallahan's tenure was short-lived and he produced no memorable stories on crime and corruption.

Clearly, Hallahan was trying to make ends meet the best way he could.

Yet despite his apparent tree change, he still kept in close contact with John Edward Milligan.

The Whiskey's Other Victims

On a warm Friday in January 1974, Barbara McCulkin, housewife and mother, was desperately trying to find private investigator John Ryan, former bouncer at the ill-fated Whiskey Au Go Go nightclub and owner of a business that used dogs and muscle to protect Brisbane's car yards at night.

McCulkin was the estranged wife of Billy 'the Mouse' McCulkin, an alleged member of the Clockwork Orange Gang that also included the boxer Tommy Hamilton and criminals Vince O'Dempsey and Gary Dubois.

Despite Stuart and Finch being imprisoned for life for the Whiskey bombing, there were persistent rumours around town that the Clockwork Orange Gang was involved in the mass murder and possibly the Torino bombing as well.

Billy McCulkin, a former hotel yardie, was a one-time dog to the former detective Glen Hallahan.

Just two months before Barbara's frantic phone calls, Billy had moved out of the family home in Highgate Hill with a new girlfriend. Barbara, left with two daughters, Vicky Maree, soon to turn thirteen, and Barbara Leanne, eleven, was feeling the pinch over the Christmas and New Year period without Billy's support. Though he still came around often to see her and the children, Barbara was getting angry.

In fact, in the lead up to January, she had started intimating in public – at bars and clubs – that she knew the real story of the Whiskey bombing, and that it wasn't just the handiwork of Stuart and Finch.

The word on the street, too, was that Barbara McCulkin was going to be 'knocked'. She was talking too much.

Barbara eventually did get Ryan on the phone that Friday, and what she told him was extraordinary.

'She said she was going to blow her guts on the Whiskey, she'd had enough, and she wanted to get into a safe house, she wanted to be hidden away,' Ryan remembers. 'John Andrew Stuart had been to her home a few times in the lead up to the bombing. And she said she was present when Billy McCulkin was on the phone making arrangements about the fires, plural.

'She had information on the Clockwork Orange Gang and its links to some Queensland police.'

Ryan's instinct was to go around to the Highgate Hill house immediately and make an assessment of the risk she was under. He suggested it, but Barbara put him off.

'It was her daughter Vicky's birthday on the Sunday and they were going to have a party . . . Also, on the Monday, Billy was due to come around and see the children.'

In the meantime, Ryan made a few calls and provisionally arranged a safe house for Barbara and her daughters in northern New South Wales. It made sense that Barbara would want her daughters to see their father for the last time before they went into hiding.

Early that week Ryan heard nothing from Barbara, so on the Tuesday he and his business associate went to the Highgate Hill house to investigate. They saw uncollected mail in the letterbox. Nobody answered the door.

Ryan made some casual inquiries with neighbours and learned

that there'd been a huge 'domestic' at the McCulkin house the night before. Nobody reported it to police because it was a regular event at Barbara's place.

Another neighbour reported seeing Barbara being forced into a waiting car, and possibly one of the children being shoved into the boot.

'I couldn't believe it,' Ryan says. 'I couldn't believe nobody called the coppers.'

Billy McCulkin later alleged that he went around to the house the next day, on Wednesday 16 January, and similarly found it deserted. The lights were still on and a blouse was beneath the needle of a sewing machine.

The McCulkin girls had vanished without a trace.

Billy Sets His Own Fire

It was hardly a publication that raced off the newsstand.

The *Port News* – the journal of the Waterside Workers' Federation (Brisbane Branch) – was published every two months. In 1974 it was edited by William (Billy) Stokes.

Stokes was no angel. He'd had numerous run-ins with the law since he was a teenager and graduated to theft and other petty crime. As a boy, his mother had actually taken him into CIB headquarters one Saturday morning, where he was given a good talking-to by every child's friend, Frank Bischof. The 'go straight' chat was like water off a duck's back to Stokes.

Fleeing charges in New South Wales, Stokes bolted to New Zealand in the early 1970s, where he worked selling advertisements into small magazines. It gave him enough experience to take up the editorship of the *Port News* when he eventually returned home.

In Brisbane, Stokes was acquainted with Tom Hamilton, an aggressive petty criminal and boxer (under the pseudonym Ian Thomas).

Hamilton and his droogs caused mayhem in Brisbane as the Clockwork Orange Gang, named after the novel about youth and violence by Anthony Burgess and the subsequent film, directed by Stanley Kubrick in 1971.

Stokes knew that Hamilton and his gang were paid by Vince O'Dempsey and Gary Dubois to bomb Torino nightclub in Fortitude Valley, prior to the Whiskey fire. He had witnessed them bragging about it.

So after the Whiskey bombing, and as editor of a local journal, albeit small and not particularly influential, Stokes decided to slowly but steadily publish what he knew and learned about the mass killing.

Was it an attack of conscience from the boy who refused to take Bischof's path to righteousness? Or was the *Port News* a form of public insurance for Stokes? Whatever the explanation, he began his Whiskey campaign in the April 1974 issue, a year after the bombing.

The cover featured an uninspiring photograph of a damaged ship container being hoisted in the air by a crane. But inside was a three-page feature on the Whiskey bombing, bearing the headline: THE WHISKEY – A WHITEWASH?

Stokes's article concentrated on the numerous warnings given to police prior to the fatal bombing, in particular from Bill Humphris of the Commonwealth police. He also reproduced the letter sent from Commonwealth Police Commissioner Davis to Queensland Police Commissioner Whitrod after the bombing, reiterating that Humphris had visited Whitrod's CIU on 27 February – the week before the Whiskey blew – and had passed on information to Jim Voigt.

Stokes also published an extract of Humphris's confidential data gleaned from an informant. In it, Humphris detailed the informant's extensive contact with criminal John Andrew Stuart in the lead up to the bombing. Elsewhere in the account, Stokes questioned the validity of Stuart's and James Finch's so-called confessions and other aspects of the trial.

Reading between the lines, Stokes believed at the time that Stuart was innocent.

Stokes, who was clearly intelligent and could write, had begun a rolling *J'accuse*-style series of feature articles that would ultimately culminate in an explosive exposé on the real figures behind Brisbane's series of nightclub firebombings, and in particular the tragedy at Whiskey Au Go Go.

Stokes had lit his own fuse. And the little *Port News* was about to punch way above its weight of influence.

The Elderly, Bewildered Orphan

At around 2 p.m. on Friday 12 July 1974, pensioner Frank Bischof was shopping in the Barry and Roberts department store in Queen Street, the city.

Bischof was a regular customer of the iconic Brisbane store, not far from where he served the glory days of his working life as a leading detective in the old CIB headquarters on the corner of George and Elizabeth streets.

On this day, Bischof, seventy, was browsing nonchalantly when he took a Barry and Roberts grocery bag from beneath one of the checkouts and placed inside several packets of cigarettes and a pouch of tobacco.

Shortly after, he popped into the same bag a dog toy, nineteen fertiliser discs, a packet of plant nutrients and a tube of woodwork glue.

Meanwhile, Bischof had attracted the attention of store security officer Yvonne Beckett. She kept a close eye on the former Queensland police commissioner as he proceeded to the checkout and paid for a single pack of cigarettes before leaving the store via its Elizabeth Street exit.

Beckett followed Bischof and approached him. Would Mr Bischof be happy to accompany her back to the store security office? The old man agreed.

Walking to the office, Bischof held up the bag and asked: 'Can I pay for these here?'

The police were called.

'Does it have to go this far?' he pleaded with Beckett. 'Is Mr Barry in? I'm a personal friend of his.'

Inspector W.L. Bennett of the city police arrived soon after, immediately recognising Bischof as the former police commissioner. Bischof engaged in some patter with the senior officer, telling him that his health and memory were good despite his occasional bouts of hypertension.

Bennett levelled the allegation of shoplifting against him; Bischof said he'd see Mr Paul Barry and Police Commissioner Ray Whitrod on Monday and the matter would be cleared up.

It wouldn't. He was charged on a summons complaint with stealing goods to the value of $6.12.

Bischof, officially listed as a 'police pensioner' of Barkala Street, The Gap, sought the assistance of legal legend Dan Casey, his old mate.

Just prior to the committal hearing at the end of the year, Casey approached Des Sturgess.

'One morning Casey came tapping on the door of my room looking glum,' Sturgess recalled in his book *The Tangled Web*. '"I've got Bischof below," he told me. "He insists on pleading guilty. Can you come and talk to him?"

'I went to Casey's chambers where I saw Bischof hunched in a corner.'

Sturgess observed that all of Bischof's 'formidableness' had disappeared over the years: 'He now just looked like an elderly, bewildered orphan.'

Sturgess attempted to slap some sense into the pitiable Bischof.

'Good God, Frank,' he said, 'have you stopped to think about your friends who once admired you? You're now going to reveal yourself to them as nothing but a cheap crook and let them know the people who ran you down were right all along.'

It seemed to work. Bischof agreed to defend the charge.

He was committed for trial after a psychiatrist concluded that Bischof was an 'old and very sick man', suffering a severe form of clinical depression. The psychiatrist detailed how, when Bischof was commissioner, police had to disarm him on one occasion to prevent him from taking his own life.

In the end, the Crown filed a no true bill – a decision by the Queensland attorney-general that no indictment would be presented and that to continue against Bischof would not serve the community interest.

The Big Fella went back to his cactus garden in Barkala Street and waited to die.

The Relieving Inspector

With Hallahan gone and Murphy posted to Toowoomba, up on the Darling Downs and a couple of hours' drive out of Brisbane, Whitrod continued his war of attrition against Terry Lewis.

After several months relieving in Communications and on mobile patrols, Lewis sought and was granted a meeting with the police commissioner. On Tuesday 22 January 1974, he noted in his police diary: 'Saw Mr Whitrod, C.O.P., re positions of Compt-Gen of Prisons and C.O.P. Tasmania and my career possibilities in the Q.P. Force.'

Lewis was having serious doubts about his future, and even contemplated changing careers.

Having pitched in during the great Brisbane floods of 1974, Lewis was at Roma Street railway station at 7 a.m. on Tuesday 25 April, and soon on a train heading to Mackay, about 970 kilometres north of

Brisbane. It pulled into town at 4 p.m. and he was on duty at the local police station at 8 a.m. the next day.

By August he was back working the Brisbane Exhibition at Bowen Hills, then in mobile patrols followed by relieving duties in the South Brisbane police district.

On Monday 14 October, Lewis took temporary command of Redcliffe police station, then in November, Norm Gulbransen, now assistant police commissioner, told him to return to South Brisbane.

On Boxing Day 1974, Lewis was offered what he might have interpreted as a glimmer of hope. His police diary recorded: 'A/Comm Gulbransen phoned me at home re leading contingent to Darwin. He later phoned re departing TAA 3am on 27.12.74 with 11 other men.'

His Cyclone Tracy tour of duty to Darwin must have indicated to Lewis that he was at some level a respected senior officer, and that the police commissioner had faith in his abilities. Lewis went on to perform admirably during the aftermath of Tracy.

Had Whitrod punished him enough?

It didn't appear so. While his relieving duties were about to end, Whitrod had another surprise for Inspector Lewis.

He would soon be on his way to the sheep and cattle town of Charleville, 740 kilometres west of Brisbane. Murphy would similarly be posted to Longreach, 1177 kilometres north-west of the capital.

If Whitrod couldn't get them to resign, then he'd stick both men way out west.

It was to prove a colossal mistake.

A Meeting at the Majestic

At the height of the Rat Pack's animosity towards Police Commissioner Ray Whitrod, private investigator John Ryan claims he got a curious phone call from Terry Lewis.

Ryan was set to fly out to Papua New Guinea on a company fraud case.

Lewis, Ryan alleges, asked him to a confidential meeting in the bar of the Majestic Hotel on the corner of George and Turbot streets in the CBD, not far from police headquarters in Makerston Street.

Lewis was waiting. Sitting at a table not far from the bar was Detective Tony Murphy and some other officers.

'I hear you're off to New Guinea,' Lewis said. Ryan was flabbergasted. Had Lewis found out about the trip through Ryan's visa application?

Lewis also knew that Ryan was seeing a friend of a friend who worked in government administration in Port Moresby.

Lewis was interested in a dirt file on Whitrod, former Papua New Guinea police commissioner.

'Here's the offer, John,' Lewis apparently said. 'You and I know there's a file. If a copy of that file was to be given to me, I guarantee that your security company will have every single government security contract for the next twenty years. You would be made for life.'

Ryan had heard of the Whitrod file. It contained some damning material about an Australian prime minister and his illicit affair with a visiting national leader during a state visit to Papua New Guinea. It also may have contained information about Whitrod and the use of a government aircraft for personal purposes involving Whitrod's wife. But Ryan didn't concede that to Lewis.

'It's going to take a while, John,' Lewis supposedly said, 'but I am going to be the next police commissioner. This is the opportunity of your lifetime. Whitrod would be embarrassed out of the post.'

Ryan said he'd do what he could.

Ryan remembers: 'The one thing I noticed was that Murphy, although seated some distance away, never let his eyes waver from us . . . I knew then that what I had suspected was true. Tony Murphy was the power.'

If accurate, the attempt to gather incriminating evidence on Whitrod from a prior life had an uncanny resemblance to the Rat Pack's digging into the lives of witnesses to the National Hotel inquiry – David Young and John Komlosy.

Lewis denies the meeting ever took place.

Get Herbert

By 1974, Jack 'the Bagman' Herbert, running the Joke out of the Licensing Branch, was beginning to receive intelligence that Whitrod and his CIU were about to train a spotlight on him.

Bill Osborne, who supported Young and Komlosy's claims at the National Hotel inquiry, was sent back to run the Licensing Branch. There was talk that Whitrod had given him instructions to clean the place up and end the Joke. Osborne flatly told Herbert: 'There's to be no Jokes in the office, Jack.'

Herbert was snookered.

'I could feel the storm clouds gathering over my head,' Herbert said. 'I was a detective sergeant but the powers that be wanted me out of the Licensing Branch. I'd received the gypsy's warning from a friend that the CIU was investigating me.'

On 7 June, Herbert – due to be transferred on promotion to the CIB – met with Norm Gulbransen. 'He informed me that he was under specialist treatment for a malignant growth,' Gulbransen recalled, 'and made a very emotional appeal to be allowed to remain at the Licensing Branch on the grounds that the stress and worry of taking up a new position . . . could adversely affect his chances of recovery . . .'

The CIU's Basil Hicks told Gulbransen not long after the interview that he had confidential information 'from a very reliable source' that off-racecourse phone betting was thoroughly organised and that Herbert oversaw police protection for SP bookmakers.

After a number of abortive raids on SP bookmakers, both Herbert and Osborne were transferred to the Public Relations Section.

With friends Lewis and Murphy being hammered by Whitrod, and the Joke having temporarily evaporated, Herbert retired medically unfit – he had recently had an operation on a melanoma. Bill Osborne retired the same day, his assignment from Whitrod seemingly a success.

The new inspector in charge of Licensing was the imposing Arthur Pitts, fifty-six, a no-nonsense policeman who had been given orders to crack down on illegal SP bookmaking.

Pitts laid seventeen charges in his first three months. The branch's arrest statistics for SP bookmaking prior to Pitts had been three prosecutions in four years. Bookmakers caught in the rash of arrests included Herbert's Gold Coast friends Stan Saunders and Brian Sieber. According to Herbert, both men saw him after their arrests and asked what he could do for them.

In the early weeks of his retirement, and following Pitts's blitz, Herbert heard that SP bookmakers wanted to start up a new Joke, and wanted him to act as an intermediary with Pitts.

Could Herbert have a word with Arthur and get something going?

Thinking he was set to play the game, Herbert and Detective Neal Freier introduced a bookmaker named Paddy McIntyre to Pitts at the new Licensing chief's home in Newmarket on 11 December 1974. McIntyre handed twelve hundred dollars to Pitts. It appeared the new Joke was born.

However, with Pitts's cooperation his house had been wired, and Basil Hicks was present, hiding in another room when the money was handed over.

'By gee, you've got a good spot here, Arthur,' said Herbert, complimenting Pitts on his home.

'Yes, yes,' Pitts said.

'Bloody beautiful,' Herbert added. 'I bet you've had many a glass of beer and swallowed it out there?'

'I've had some enjoyable evenings out there with my wife. You care for a drink?'

'Not for me, Arthur.'

Herbert told Pitts that word had spread around that Herbert had 'got a quid': 'I'm not as bad as I've been painted,' Herbert said, 'but then again I'm bad enough.' He said if Pitts came on board, he could expect fifteen hundred a month.

Herbert, Freier and McIntyre were arrested on the orders of Whitrod just two days later and charged with having attempted to corrupt Pitts.

So began the so-called Southport Betting Case, an epic trial that would end up embarrassing Whitrod and his entire crack CIU team, and exemplify the supreme cunning of Jack Herbert.

In over three years Whitrod and the CIU hadn't laid a glove on the Rat Pack and Herbert. And Premier Bjelke-Petersen and his Cabinet colleagues were beginning to notice.

The Southport Betting Fiasco

In the lead up to the trial of SP bookmakers Sieber and Saunders at the Southport magistrates court in mid-1975, then the corruption charges against Herbert, Freier and MacIntyre later in the year, the anti-Whitrod forces had had enough.

It was time to fight fire with fire.

Upon Herbert's arrest early that December morning, his solicitor contacted Des Sturgess. Could Sturgess appear in court and apply for Herbert's bail? He did.

A couple of days later Sturgess attended the Queensland Police Union's Christmas party.

'The party was nearly over . . .' Sturgess recalled. 'Among the people still remaining were Lewis and a police officer named Murphy who immediately joined us and began to talk about Herbert . . .'

Murphy was furious about Herbert's arrest.

At Sturgess's suggestion the three left the union office and had a beer in a nearby hotel.

'Once more Herbert's prosecution became the topic,' said Sturgess. 'I suggested Murphy and Lewis had enough troubles of their own and should keep their noses out of it.'

'I always stick to my mates,' Murphy yelled in the crowded and noisy bar. He then repeatedly said of Whitrod: 'If only I knew how to fix him.'

On the footpath outside the bar as they were leaving, Sturgess dropped a valuable insight into Murphy's lap.

'He's got an Achilles heel, you know,' Sturgess said of Whitrod.

'What?' asked Murphy.

'The verbal,' the lawyer answered.

At some point this intelligence was passed on to Herbert, who concocted a brilliant scheme. He secured a small tape recorder and instructed a constable working in the Licensing Branch to secretly tape Pitts and the other officers involved in the case. It would prove to be a masterstroke.

The constable captured hours of discussions as Pitts and his men built their prosecution cases against the bookmakers and Herbert and his crew. The transcripts, later produced in court, revealed that Pitts had failed to get a proper warrant to search in the case of Sieber and Saunders. Months later, and just days before the case was to go to court, Pitts and other members of the branch drew up a number of false warrants. The conversations between Pitts and his men concerning the issue of the warrants were all recorded in crystal clarity by Herbert's battery-powered recorder.

The magistrate found the police evidence tainted, and Sieber and Saunders were discharged.

The result ignited a furore in parliament. This had been a highly publicised case and here were Whitrod's lily-white crime busters conspiring to fabricate evidence in a court of law.

The public clamour prompted Bjelke-Petersen to call for an official inquiry into police corruption. In effect, the premier, beginning to tire of Whitrod's theatrics and faced with a police force on the brink of mutiny, wanted to detonate the Criminal Intelligence Unit.

It was time to call in Scotland Yard.

O'Connell and Fothergill

In response to Bjelke-Petersen's promise of an inquiry, Police Minister Max Hodges asked the agent-general of the Queensland government in London to find two senior independent officers to prosecute the task.

On Friday 22 August 1975, Scotland Yard investigators Commander Terence O'Connell and Detective Superintendent Bruce Fothergill flew to Brisbane to commence inquiries. They had eight to twelve weeks to get the job done. Police Commissioner Whitrod outlined the inquiry's terms of reference.

Their brief was to 'investigate allegations of corruption and mal-practice by members of the Queensland Police Force', made during Sieber and Saunders's hearing in the Southport magistrates court.

The Queensland police gave the investigators assurances they would have 'unrestricted access to all documentary information in its posses-sion, and to serving members of the Force'.

O'Connell and Fothergill faced immediate hurdles. The public prosecutor was appealing the Southport decision, and Herbert and his co-defendants were still waiting to be committed for trial. Any evi-dence from material witnesses would be sub judice.

Nevertheless, they set about interviewing as many officers as they could – particularly Licensing Branch members going back a decade – under the restrictions.

They were welcomed by the police force as warmly as Whitrod had been in 1970. Even worse, they were Poms.

Lewis remembers the two Englishmen.

'I was at the Gabba then and they asked me to come over to headquarters and be interviewed,' he says. 'Neither of them were dynamic detectives. I mean it's ridiculous. You would know better than most people to bring two outsiders into your bloody joint and get them to start questioning the boys about whatever. You know, where do you go?'

By mid-October, O'Connell and Fothergill had interviewed 298 police officers and civilians.

Ron Lewis, who was working in Whitrod's CIU, was seconded to assist the two Scotland Yard detectives. He took numerous statements from police officers and provided these to O'Connell and Fothergill.

'We worked on a need-to-know basis in that office,' Ron Lewis says. 'If I didn't need to know something I wasn't told.

'In those days it was difficult without a computer. They'd take a statement, underline any relevant points, put them on a card and cross-index them. They stored the cards in a shire hall. The floor collapsed with the weight of the cards they gathered. They were good workers.'

In a memo to Whitrod dated 30 September, O'Connell indicated his final report would cover corruption and the possibility of a judicial inquiry. It was enough to satisfy Whitrod that Scotland Yard's men were on the scent of what he had suspected for years.

They flew back to London on 17 October. Their investigation was temporarily hamstrung by the drawn-out Herbert court case.

As the memo to Whitrod hinted at, their brief but intense inquiries in Brisbane did seem to yield fruit. They were told that SP bookmaking and corruption was rife; the corruption was most concentrated in the Licensing Branch.

Lawyers, police, and members of the public continually referenced the existence of a so-called Rat Pack, even two packs – one consisting of Lewis, Murphy, and Hallahan, and the other of Herbert and his cronies in Licensing.

O'Connell and Fothergill wrote their report.

'Their report went to Joh,' says Ron Lewis. 'I understood there was an order for its destruction from the Premier's Department. That was my understanding. I never saw the report.'

As for Terry Lewis, he didn't think much of the inquiry. He says: 'It was a waste of time and money. And I don't think anyone took them down to the pub to have grogs with them.'

Out West

In late 1975, the news of Lewis's transfer to Charleville caused enormous disruption up at 12 Garfield Drive.

Lewis now had five children – the eldest daughter, Lanna, was in high school, and the youngest, John, was just six years old. How would they cope in the bush? Should the older children be pulled out of school at such a crucial time?

Through contacts he made as head of the JAB, he managed in principle to secure his children's schooling in the event his career never brought him back to Brisbane.

Lewis headed out to Charleville alone, leaving wife Hazel at home to manage the transition: 'I went into the empty [police] house,' Lewis says. 'We bought a second-hand bed and a duchess. I got some bits of wood and some bricks for a bookshelf. I thought I'd be out there for a while.'

By chance, Lewis arrived to a flooded country town. With his experience in Darwin still fresh in his mind, he swung into action.

'Having worked in an operations centre, I knew what should or perhaps could be done . . . and I got two helicopters up from the RAAF in New South Wales and got them into Charleville,' Lewis recalls. 'We didn't lose a life and we got people in who were having heart attacks and all sorts of things, so that went over pretty well.'

Lewis also made a point of travelling to every police station in his district. It took him a week to get from Tambo to Thargomindah to Hungerford, Cunnamulla and Morgan. His district encompassed 336,000 square kilometres.

Even way out west, Whitrod continued to drive Lewis to distraction.

'Every morning we'd go and inspect the district and in those days Mr Whitrod was mad about statistics,' he says. 'We used to have to ring the regional superintendent in Toowoomba and tell him . . . how many traffic tickets you've got in Charleville. The streets were half a mile wide with two men and a dog in them half the time. And you'd ring up: "Oh, not many tickets."'

Lewis, too, was a different style of officer to some of his Charleville predecessors. He had yet to learn the unwritten rules of rural hospitality.

'Terry wasn't the sort of bloke who'd walk out on the street and say hello and how ya going,' says one local.

But he quickly adapted, and set about impressing the community. His epic, tireless work stint during the floods had shown a commitment to the people of Charleville. It was, on the other hand, Lewis manifesting the belief that had kept him in good stead since he was a child – without the ability to express emotion, even to his own family, he earned affection and respect from others through sheer hard work.

Over time he became a popular member of the community.

More importantly, his stint out west gave him a crucial crash course in the ways of National Party politics and how it related to the men and women on the land.

Vital to that education, too, was his friendship with Neil Turner, the young National Party member for Warrego. He'd only been a member for less than two years when Lewis arrived in Charleville. Undoubtedly, through Turner, Lewis began to appreciate on a whole new level what appealed to someone like Premier Joh Bjelke-Petersen.

The biggest problem for Police Commissioner Ray Whitrod in banishing Lewis and Murphy to the west was logical yet unforeseen – in the country, both men had time to think.

And to plot.

Surprise Visitors

For a remote Queensland country town, Charleville in the early months of 1976 was attracting its fair share of VIPs.

As Inspector Lewis worked away at the police station downtown, beside a solid and stolid brick bank, fielding calls from local mothers about an upcoming teenage dance to be held by the Warrego Pony Club, and meeting and greeting the locals, he received the unexpected news that Premier Joh Bjelke-Petersen was planning to visit.

In late February, prior to the big event, Lewis discussed the premier's security with a superintendent in Toowoomba.

Lewis noted in his police diary for 3 March: 'To Airport and met Hon. J. Bjelke-Petersen and party. To State School, High School and Convent. Then to Warrego Club for lunch and meeting.'

Lewis returned to the police station before rejoining the premier later in the afternoon, accompanying him to the local School of the Air. Then: 'To Airport and farewelled Premier.'

By the end of that month he would also meet the National Party member for Gregory, Bill Glasson, at the airport and dine twice with Queensland Health Minister Dr Llew Edwards. He would also have the opportunity to make the acquaintance of the premier's personal pilot, Beryl Young.

On Monday 12 April, Lewis was suddenly phoned by Whitrod's right-hand man, Norm Gulbransen, about the plan to build new watchhouse cells attached to the Charleville police station – they had been damaged by fire some time before.

Then on 28 April, Lewis was back out at the airport to pick up some surprise visitors – this time Police Commissioner Ray Whitrod and his minister, Max Hodges. Lewis took them back to the police station, where they inspected the watchhouse and discussed sites for the new cell blocks.

Lewis was perplexed by the two most powerful men in the Queensland police suddenly gracing his district with their presence.

'It was just a flying visit,' says Lewis. 'Hazel made some biscuits. They had that at the police station with a cup of tea and they left.

'Nothing was discussed about me or my future. It was just bullshit, I think. It was just so that Hodges could come out and look down on me.

'Why fly a minister and a commissioner out to have a look at a little country watchhouse?'

There are numerous possible explanations for their turning up unexpectedly on Lewis's rural doorstep. Hodges may indeed have wished to flex his muscle at Lewis, sending the inspector a message that he could expect to be in rural Queensland for the long haul.

It was likely, too, that both men had learned of Lewis's meeting with Bjelke-Petersen and his recent flurry of political guests. Arriving in Charleville showed that they were keeping a close eye on him.

Also, Jack 'the Bagman' Herbert's corruption trial was soon to commence in Brisbane. If Whitrod failed to score a conviction, the reputation of his Crime Investigation Unit would not only be in ruins, but a laughing stock that began and ended with Whitrod.

Throughout the force, Whitrod was being comically referred to by his new moniker – Koko the Clown.

Over biscuits and tea in that old wooden Queenslander in downtown Charleville, the tension must have been palpable.

Nobody around that kitchen table knew that a sequence of events was about to occur that would incinerate Whitrod's grand reformation.

One Night in Cooktown

On the wall of Premier Joh Bjelke-Petersen's relatively new office in the Executive building in George Street was a huge map of Queensland.

Fixed to it was a stubble of pins – green pins indicated that the premier had made a single visit to that city, town or hamlet, blue for two visits, and red for three.

Bjelke-Petersen was obsessive about getting out of the south-east corner of the state and into rural Queensland or up and down the coast. He felt people in remote areas had a right to see their premier in person, so at first he used his own single-engine aircraft to travel intrastate; then the government leased a larger plane for this peripatetic leader.

As for the dozens and dozens of pins on the map, they had a specific purpose. 'They were to tell you where you hadn't been,' says Allen Callaghan, Bjelke-Petersen's former government news and information officer.

'We did a lot of these tours. [Later] we bought an unpressurised Piper Navajo. You could hop in and out and come home again fairly quickly.'

By mid-1976 Bjelke-Petersen was hearing and sensing a lot of discontent within the police force. He didn't like it. As he dropped in and out of little rural air strips right across the state, his first contact on these trips was the local police.

When the premier started getting direct complaints over and over about the performance of Police Commissioner Whitrod, from even lowly constables, a pattern began to form in his mind.

Callaghan says: 'Whitrod was a breath of fresh air [when he first arrived], but . . . he was an academic cop. He really was an armchair general. There was a feeling within the government that the force needed reform, overhauling or modernising. The feeling later on was: now we know why the other forces got rid of him.

'[The pattern of complaints] came from the country force,' says Callaghan. 'For them to speak out directly to the premier was almost unprecedented.

Callaghan clearly remembers one trip to Cooktown in either late 1975 or early 1976. The premier and Callaghan had tea in the police residence attached to the local station. The sergeant in charge was Ray Marchant.

Callaghan recalls Marchant's key complaint: 'Whitrod had set a quota of arrests and prosecutions per month. They were recorded on what was called "kill sheets".'

When Bjelke-Petersen seemed incredulous, Marchant produced an actual kill sheet to prove his point.

Back in Brisbane, Bjelke-Petersen asked Police Minister Hodges whether this was correct – that all stations across Queensland were required to meet quotas. Whitrod apparently denied it.

'I saw Joh's Danish jaw come out,' says Callaghan. 'It's something you wouldn't want to trip over.

'Whitrod had lied about something so important. This is what did Whitrod in as far as Joh was concerned. He had lied . . .'

Waiting for a Plane in Cunnamulla

During 1976 the premier travelled incessantly throughout Queensland, and he began putting a specific question to the array of constables, sergeants and inspectors he met straight off the plane: if you're unhappy with the current police commissioner, who would you replace him with? Give me five names.

'It was an unofficial poll in a sense,' says Callaghan. 'The name that kept coming up out of the rank and file was Terry Lewis.

'We didn't know him from a bar of soap. We were aware that he had been awarded the George Medal. But it was consistent across the ranks. Their answer [to Joh's question] was Terry Lewis. No one came within a cooee of Lewis.'

Callaghan confirms that Joh began making some inquiries about Lewis. He discovered that Whitrod had exiled Lewis to Charleville.

'Lewis wasn't aware of this,' says Callaghan, 'but [he] was under scrutiny. The next time Joh went to Charleville he made a point of meeting Lewis.'

That historic moment occurred in Cunnamulla, in Inspector Lewis's police district, on Sunday 16 May. In town for the 36th Country Cabinet Meeting, Bjelke-Petersen and his entourage arrived at the airfield in dribs and drabs throughout the day. The premier, along with his private secretary, Stan Wilcox, and ministers like Tom Newbery, flew in on the government aircraft at 5.30 p.m.

And as was custom, there at the airfield waiting to greet the plane was a dutiful Inspector Lewis.

'He was there to meet me when the plane arrived,' Bjelke-Petersen said. 'It was the first time I had set eyes on him, and I found him a very pleasant and obliging man, who seemed anxious to do anything he could to help me and generally make my visit enjoyable.'

Callaghan also recalls the day the premier and the inspector first met: 'I remember walking from the aircraft and there he was. He would have spoken to Joh about police matters affecting his district.'

Had Callaghan been travelling with the premier during that earlier visit to Charleville on 3 March? If so, why would he say they didn't know Lewis 'from a bar of soap'? And why would Bjelke-Petersen assert that he first 'set eyes on' Lewis on 16 May, when Lewis's police diary clearly reveals a fly-in, fly-out meeting between the two more than two months before this?

The premier and the bulk of his Cabinet stayed at the New Cunnamulla Hotel in Jane Street – a classic two-storey brick and wood Queensland pub with long verandahs.

On Monday 17 May, Cabinet convened in the Paroo Shire Council chambers for their meeting. During that day, one item of business was the approval of a number of senior police promotions. All went through, with Police Minister Max Hodges present at the meeting.

A Cabinet dinner was held at their hotel, followed at 8.30 p.m. by an informal 'open' function, ostensibly for members of the public to meet their government representatives.

Inspector Terry Lewis was also invited.

'I certainly will never forget meeting [Bjelke-Petersen] at Cunnamulla . . .' says Lewis, who had drinks that night with various ministers, including Norm Lee and Tom Newbery.

At some point early in the evening, Lewis says either Stan Wilcox or Allen Callaghan showed him the approved list of promotions and asked for his opinion. Callaghan denies he produced the list to Lewis: 'Stan might have but why would he do that if it was the first time he had met Lewis?'

Nevertheless, Inspector Lewis thought some of the promotions were 'ridiculous' – awarding young officers portfolios they simply didn't have the experience to handle, gifting others ranks two or three beyond the expected progression. Lewis, outcast in Charleville, was incensed.

As with that ill-fated luncheon at Paul Wilson's house by the Brisbane River six years earlier, Lewis decided to give Hodges the benefit of his uncensored opinion.

'The promotions and transfers came up,' recalls Lewis. 'I told Hodges what I thought. I said some of them were terrible. So we ended up exchanging words and I can still hear Norm Lee saying, "Give it to him, go on, don't back down, give it to him!"'

Lewis believed he had nothing to lose.

The next morning, the ministers began making their way back to Brisbane. It was up to Lewis and other local officers to ferry ministers and their staff from the hotel and out to the airfield.

Lewis unluckily scored Police Minister Hodges, who was due to fly out at 8 a.m. aboard a King Air charter.

'Hodges sat in the front seat of my car and never spoke to me,' says Lewis. 'We only had two cars so I took them out then went back and took others.'

The government aircraft had already left at 7.30 a.m. It was scheduled to arrive at Eagle Farm at 9.30 a.m., and head straight back out to Cunnamulla to pick up the premier.

Why was Joh Bjelke-Petersen one of the last to leave Cunnamulla that day? Only he and his private secretary, Wilcox, remained for the late flight.

It was Inspector Lewis who drove the premier and Wilcox to the airfield.

'There was quite a considerable wait for the aircraft and during that time he just talked to me and I talked to him,' says Lewis. 'It was just a pure fluke that I was the one that took him to the airport. I can't say why he wasn't the first person on the plane earlier that morning. Whether he deliberately didn't get on an earlier aircraft I will never know.'

Up until that meeting, Bjelke-Petersen claimed Lewis was only known to him as 'a name', principally, as the officer whose 'fine work' had founded and built up the Juvenile Aid Bureau, and as the recipient of the prestigious George Medal for Bravery.

According to Lewis they talked 'for what seemed like a couple of hours at least'.

'We were standing at the fence,' recalls Lewis. 'It was hot. I was in my full uniform.'

Lewis says they discussed Police Commissioner Ray Whitrod, Police Minister Max Hodges and Lewis's own ideas for restructuring the force. Callaghan thinks the discussion at the airfield would have been at most 'exploratory', with the premier getting the measure of the man who seemed so popular with rank and file officers across Queensland.

'The premier did ask . . . "What would you like to do . . . ?" And I said what I'd really like one day was to be the superintendent in charge of the academy to teach young people to be police officers.'

It was extraordinarily ambitious of Lewis. Here was a private audience with the premier of Queensland. And if word got back about his disloyalty to the police commissioner, what did it matter? Lewis was convinced he would be exiled in the bush for years, if not the rest of his career. He had already informed Hazel to pack her bags and bring youngest son John out to the sticks. The Lewises weren't going anywhere for a long time.

Just as he had given Hodges a piece of his mind, so, too, was he forthright with Joh.

Understandably, they instantly clicked. Lewis had come from the school of hard knocks, and though self-educated – he would use his downtime in Charleville to complete his degree in public administration – he had a simultaneous suspicion of and an attraction to society's various stratums. He could mix with political leaders, academics, the wealthy and the railway fettler. It was Lewis's genius to be able to quickly read a person's political and social leanings, empathically tune in to that and not only connect with it but use it to his advantage.

Behind everything, though, was Lewis's fascination with power.

'He didn't bung on any airs,' he says of Bjelke-Petersen and their first real conversation in Cunnamulla. 'We talked quite easily . . .'

Had Lewis, in Bjelke-Petersen, found another father to impress, just as he had with Frank Bischof?

Within days of that meeting, Lewis sent the premier a dossier. It bore the hallmark of Lewis's now familiar habit of disseminating not only lists and check sheets that bolstered his own reputation, but snippets of gossip and observation designed to charm the recipient of his meticulous paperwork.

Included in the dossier were his constantly updated police and academic achievements, especially his bravery award and his Churchill Fellowship, a list of officers who had bypassed Lewis on promotion, and some tittle-tattle about Whitrod possibly being affiliated with the Australian Labor Party. This, he knew, would register with the National Party premier.

The dossier was subsequently received by Wilcox and filed.

Driving back to Charleville on that autumn afternoon after the

Cabinet visit, with the premier flying back to Brisbane, what went through the mind of Inspector Lewis?

During that two and a half hour journey north along the Mitchell Highway, did he hope for any outcome whatsoever, having had the ear of the premier? Would his frankness contribute to the undermining of his enemy, Whitrod? Would he be considered for a promotion that he believed he deserved? Or would it all come to nought?

Conversely, what was Bjelke-Petersen mulling over, flying above St George and Dalby and on to Brisbane at four hundred kilometres an hour with pilot Beryl Young in the cockpit, and private secretary Stan Wilcox in the aircraft cabin tying up the paperwork for the 36th Country Cabinet Meeting?

The premier knew that morale in the state's police force was at an all-time low. He believed Whitrod had made a mess of things after six years, and was aware that even Liberal–National Party members were tired of the police commissioner.

Bjelke-Petersen may not have given the tall, gangly Inspector Lewis another thought. But they had now met twice and had developed at the very least a tentative rapport.

With Whitrod's lie about the 'kill sheets' still fresh in Bjelke-Petersen's mind, and having yarned with Inspector Terry Lewis in the autumn sunshine – the man so highly regarded by rank and file across Queensland – the way to solve the Whitrod problem must have started to form in his mind.

The premier needed a catalyst to set in train the removal of the Queensland police commissioner.

And within months of meeting Lewis, Joh would be gifted not one but two scandals that would see Raymond Wells Whitrod resign and, in fear of his life, flee Queensland forever.

THE STORY CONTINUES IN *ALL FALL DOWN*, COMING IN LATE 2013.

Author's Note and Acknowledgments

Three Crooked Kings and its forthcoming sequel, *All Fall Down*, would not have been possible without the cooperation of former Queensland Police Commissioner Terence Murray Lewis. He decided, at the age of eighty-three, that he wanted his story told.

On 1 February 2010, we began what would become almost three years of interviews at his home in north Brisbane, and he was always convivial, courteous, and helpful. *Three Crooked Kings* and its sequel incorporate some of that interview material. In addition, hundreds of other people were interviewed in an attempt to accurately recreate an important period in Queensland history. On several occasions, Lewis's version of events and my own research took different paths. In these instances, he was always given a right of reply.

Several leading figures in the narrative, since deceased, were not afforded that opportunity. Through my personal interviews and documentary evidence I have made every effort to present a balanced story.

Lewis's collection of documents and memorabilia was also invaluable. His personal archive is an astonishing record of events not just with regard to the Queensland police force going back to the 1940s, but as social history more generally. The Fryer Library at the University of Queensland now holds the bulk of it.

I am greatly indebted, also, to writer and friend Doug Hall for his important role in the early stages of this journey.

I would like to thank the many people I spoke to in an attempt to piece together the narrative of Lewis's career and the careers of his contemporaries. They included many retired police officers, former politicians, lawyers, ordinary citizens, and the relatives of men and women who were directly and indirectly involved in this drama.

Apart from Lewis's own contacts, I offer my appreciation to Mick O'Brien, state president of the Queensland Retired Police Association, for helping me get in touch with numerous former officers, who were generous with their time and memories. They include: the late A.B. 'Abe' Duncan, Ron Edington, Ken Hoggett, Ron Lewis, Ross Beer, John Meskell, Don Braithewaite, Bruce Wilby, Janet Brady, Noel Creavy, Fred Collins, Ian Hatcher, Cliff Crawford, Pat Glancy, Jim Shearer and John Morris. A special thank you to Greg Early for his valuable contribution. Additionally, my thanks go to Queensland Police Minister Jack Dempsey and former Queensland Police Commissioner Bob Atkinson.

Three Crooked Kings was also crucially informed by dozens of former Queensland police who anonymously offered their observations and insights. My thanks to you.

I (and the state of Queensland) owe a great deal to Nigel Powell, former Queensland Licensing Branch officer, whose bravery in speaking out in the late 1980s played a key role in the establishment of the Fitzgerald Inquiry into police corruption, and who persevered with me over a number of years. Thank you, Nigel, for your generosity of spirit and your friendship.

In addition, my thanks to former New South Wales police officers Clive Small and Roger Rogerson for their recollections.

In the federal police arena, I am enormously grateful to former narcotics agent John Shobbrook, another dedicated policeman who suffered for his sense of right, and who gave of his time, recollections and superb memoir to fill in some gaps in this narrative. Thank you, John. Your contribution has been immense. I am also thankful to Brian Bennett, Max Rogers, Bob 'Doc' Gillespie, and Ian Alcorn.

I also offer my thanks to: Terry Lewis's family; Maureen Murphy and her family; Des Sturgess; Allen Callaghan; Mary Bennett and Judith Murphy; Terry White; Sir Llew Edwards; Sir Leo Hielscher; Mike Ahern; Peter Beattie; Judy Spence; Paul Wilson; Malcolm Cummings; Jim Birrell; Richard Bentley; John Corrie; Peter Grose; Andree Look; Ken Lord; the Reverend Roy Wright; Hagen Bahnemann; Carmel Bird; Robin and Ellen Russell, Les Hounslow, William 'Billy' Stokes and John Wayne Ryan.

One of the central narratives of this book is Shirley Margaret Brifman's tragic story. It could not have been told without the help and cooperation of her eldest daughter, Mary Anne Brifman. Thank you, Mary Anne, for your patience with innumerable questions both face to face and on the telephone. And thank you to others who chose to remain anonymous in the telling of Shirley's story.

The bedrock of this book was, of course, put in place by some of the country's most accomplished journalists, and their groundbreaking work not only contributed to the infrastructure of the narrative but is the reason for it existing in the first place.

I am indebted to Phil Dickie, my former colleague at the *Courier-Mail* newspaper, whose work contributed to the establishment of the Fitzgerald Inquiry into police corruption in Queensland in 1987, and whose book, *The Road to Fitzgerald and Beyond*, was for me an ever-present guiding template. In addition, thank you, Phil, for giving me permission to explore your papers held by the State Library of Queensland and the John Oxley Library and for keeping me on the right track as I worked through this labyrinth.

I owe an equal measure of gratitude to that other instigator of the Fitzgerald Inquiry, Chris Masters, whose 'The Moonlight State' report on ABC's *Four Corners* in 1987 changed the state's history. Thank you, Chris, for your generosity.

Many other journalist colleagues have contributed to this book. I offer a sincere thank you, in particular, to two trusted mates, Des Houghton and Hedley Thomas. Thank you, Des, for reading the page proofs and offering your valuable insights. And Hedley, your advice on portions of the manuscript was gratefully received and implemented.

My gratitude also goes to: Ken Blanch; Alex Mitchell, who, along with Phillip 'the Captain' Knightley, has been a mentor for more than twenty-five years; Judith White; David Hickie; Julianne Schultz; Peter Hansen; Evan Whitton; Gerald Stone; Quentin Dempster; Paul Weston; Alan Hall; Michael Praine; the crew, past and present, at *Qweekend* magazine, the *Courier-Mail*, including Susan Johnson, Matthew Fynes-Clinton, Trent Dalton, Francis Whiting, Leisa Scott, Amanda Watt, Alison Walsh, Phil Stafford, Anne-Maree Lyons, Sandra Killen, Genevieve Faulkner, David Kelly, Russell Shakespeare, Bruce McMahon, Kylie Lang, Sandy Bresic and Christine Middap. To Mike Colman, friend and colleague, thanks for listening to the hundreds of uninvited reports on the progress of the book. I would also like to pay tribute to Greg Chamberlin. Additional thanks to colleagues Rose Brennan, Ellen-Maree Elliot, and Kara Billsborough. I also offer my gratitude to my friend Tony Reeves, investigative journalist and author, for his wisdom and generosity. I would like to acknowledge, as well, the late Brian 'the Eagle' Bolton, Ron Richards and Ric Allen.

The writing of *Three Crooked Kings* and its sequel was aided and abetted by the understanding and generosity of my senior colleagues at News Queensland. The book would still be in manuscript stage if it wasn't for the faith and guidance of David Fagan, Queensland editorial director of News Queensland, Michael Crutcher, the editor of the *Courier-Mail*, and Sue McVay, managing editor, News Queensland. And thank you to all the staff of News Queensland for your forbearance.

I owe a great deal to the library staff at News Queensland for being so welcoming and helpful. The same applies to the staff at the John Oxley Library and the State Library of Queensland. Again, I am indebted to the National Library of Australia's online digitisation repository, Trove.

Several important books were repeatedly referenced, or directly quoted, throughout these pages, and I would like to thank the authors and publishers for permission to reproduce extracts in *Three Crooked Kings*:

In Place of Justice by Peter James, The Shield Press, 1974

The Prince and the Premier by David Hickie, Angus & Robertson, 1985

The Road to Fitzgerald and Beyond by Phil Dickie, UQP, 1989

The Hillbilly Dictator by Evan Whitton, ABC Books, 1989

Don't You Worry About That! by Johannes Bjelke-Petersen, Angus & Robertson, 1990

The Sundown Murders by Peter James, Boolarong Publications, 1990

A Life of Crime by Paul Wilson, Scribe, 1990

Honest Cops by Quentin Dempster, ABC Books, 1992

The Long Blue Line by W. Ross Johnston, Boolarong Press, 1992

Trial and Error by Don Lane, Boolarong Press, 1993

Reform in Policing: Lessons from the Whitrod Era by Jill M. Bolen, Hawkins Press, 1997

The Tangled Web by Des Sturgess, Bedside Books, 2001

Before I Sleep by Ray Whitrod, UQP, 2001

It's Only Rock'n'Roll But I Like It by Geoffrey Walden, QUT, 2003

The Bagman by Jack Herbert with Tom Gilling, ABC Books, 2004

Quotes were also taken from an extensive interview conducted with Ray Whitrod by Robin Hughes for the Australian Biography project in 2000. Thanks to the National Film and Sound Archive for permission to reproduce extracts from the interview transcript in *Three Crooked Kings*. I would also like to acknowledge use of quotes from an interview with Sir Thomas Hiley by Andrew Philp in 1987. Additionally, I came late to *The Most Dangerous Detective: The Outrageous Glen Patrick Hallahan* (ebook, 2012) by Steve Bishop, a superlative piece of investigative journalism.

I owe a great deal to all at the University of Queensland Press for coming on this journey with me. As publishers of books by Dickie and Whitrod, it made sense that *Three Crooked Kings* and its sequel should find a natural home at UQP. Thank you to CEO Greg Bain for being such a powerful supporter of both Queensland (and national) writing, and the cultural future of the state. Publisher Madonna Duffy, your courage drove this book to completion and I offer you my professional thanks and an enormous personal admiration. Thank you, Rebecca Roberts, for a superb edit; Teagan Kum Sing, for great work on the permissions; and Meredene Hill for your attention to detail, professional support and the laughs. Thank you, John Hunter, for your early engagement with, and enthusiasm for, the project.

Finally, a heartfelt thank you to my wonderful wife, Katie Kate, and our children, Finnigan and Bridie Rose, for putting up with my long absences and hours locked away in the study. All that I do is for you.

Index